Sport in the G

General Editor: J

SUPERMAN SUPREME

SPORT IN THE GLOBAL SOCIETY

General Editor: J.A. Mangan

The interest in sports studies around the world is growing and will continue to do so. This unique series combines aspects of the expanding study of *sport in the global society*, providing comprehensiveness and comparison under one editorial umbrella. It is particularly timely, with studies in the cultural, economic, ethnographic, geographical, political, social, anthropological, sociological and aesthetic elements of sport proliferating in institutions of higher education.

Eric Hobsbawm once called sport one of the most significant practices of the late nineteenth century. Its significance was even more marked in the late twentieth century and will continue to grow in importance in the new millennium as the world develops into a 'global village' sharing the English language, technology and sport.

Other Titles in the Series

Shaping the Superman
Fascist Body as Political Icon – Aryan Fascism
Edited by J.A. Mangan

Scoring for Britain
International Football and International Politics, 1900–1939
Peter J. Beck

European Heroes
Myth, Identity, Sport
Edited by Richard Holt, J.A. Mangan and Pierre Lanfranchi

Tribal Identities
Nationalism, Europe, Sport
Edited by J.A. Mangan

Sporting Nationalisms
Identity, Ethnicity, Immigration and Assimilation
Edited by Mike Cronin and David Mayall

Footbinding, Feminism and Freedom
The Liberation of Women's Bodies in Modern China
Fan Hong

The Games Ethic and Imperialism
Aspects of the Diffusion of an Ideal
J.A. Mangan

The Race Game
Sport and Politics in South Africa
Douglas Booth

Rugby's Great Split
Class, Culture and the Origins of Rugby League Football
Tony Collins

The First Black Footballer
Arthur Wharton 1865–1930: An Absence of Memory
Phil Vasili

Cricket and England
A Cultural and Social History of the Inter-war Years
Jack Williams

France and the 1998 World Cup
The National Impact of a World Sporting Event
Edited by Hugh Dauncey and Geoff Hare

SUPERMAN SUPREME

Fascist Body as Political Icon – Global Fascism

Editor

J.A. MANGAN

University of Strathclyde

FRANK CASS

LONDON • PORTLAND, OR

First published in 2000 in Great Britain by
FRANK CASS PUBLISHERS
Newbury House, 900 Eastern Avenue
London, IG2 7HH

and in the United States of America by
FRANK CASS PUBLISHERS
c/o ISBS, 5804 N.E. Hassalo Street
Portland, Oregon 97213-3644

Website: www.frankcass.com

British Library Cataloguing in Publication Data

Shaping supreme : fascist body as a political icon – global fascism.
– (Sport in the global society)
1. Fascism and art 2. Symbolism in politics 3. Masculinity in art
4. Body image – Political aspects
I. Mangan, J.A. (James Anthony), 1939–
704.9'423

ISBN 0-7146-4955-4 (cloth)
ISBN 0-7146-8014-1 (paper)
ISSN 1368-9789

Library of Congress Cataloging-in-Publication Data

A catalog record of this book is available from the Library of Congress.

This group of studies first appeared as a special issue of *The International Journal of the History of Sport* (ISSN 0952-3367), Vol.16, No.4, December 1999 published by Frank Cass.

Printed in Great Britain by
Antony Rowe Ltd., Chippenham, Wilts.

Dedication

Publish your message in the open face
Of the sun, and do all the good you can.

JOHN WESLEY

Superman Supreme is a Millennium year publication. It offers an appropriate moment, therefore, to pay affectionate tribute to Frank Cass, Stewart Cass and Jonathan Manley – professional colleagues and, I hope, personal friends of long standing – for their conviction, encouragement and endorsement.

J.A.M.

Contents

List of Illustrations

Myths, Icons, Images

This century is ours
and we shall live
it in the full beauty
of our Manhood

Theo Lang, British Union of Fascists, February 1935

It is not difficult to understand that continual ecstasy can lead men to forget death and seek immortality in pursuit of shared goals. But ecstasy of any sort is essentially periodic and transient, it cannot be long sustained. How then could youths who had hardly yet begun to live endure the prospect of their own probable death? The fact that thousands of them could do it was palpable enough; the how of doing it was something of a mystery … There are soldiers in the Anglo-Saxon world and perhaps many more in Teutonic and Slavic lands, to say nothing of the Orient, for whom death is fulfillment. Unless we try to understand the motivation of this kind of soldier, we can make no claim to grasping the full nature of **Homo Furens**.

J. Glen Gray, *The Warriors: Reflections on Men in Battle* (New York, 1959), pp.110 and 116.

A good soldier is the product of his whole environment, not just a military academy.

J.R. Hale, *Renaissance War Studies* (London, 1983), p.361.

Series Editor's Foreword

J.A. MANGAN

'At most times,' Jonathan Sumption has depressingly observed, 'war has been the principal collective enterprise of mankind. It has given human societies their identities. It has shaped their institutions, and provided the ultimate test of their solidity.'[1] Few comments sum up the essence of the societies of *Superman Supreme* as neatly as Sumption's. To meet the ultimate masculine test of war, influential actors in these societies attempted to shape a supreme superman: heroic, inviolable and dominant. There is, of course, another side to the enterprise caught in these lines of Robert Browning:

> Politics? Spend your life,
> To spare the world's:
> Improve each unit by some particle
> Of joy the more, deteriorate the orb
> Entire, your own: poor profit, dismal loss![2]

The sought supremacy of the Fascist Superman was an overweening ambition that ended in 'dismal loss' for countless millions. Mercifully, it was an ambition not an achievement.

Superman Supreme reviews Fascism and the Fascist body globally. It takes up where *Shaping the Superman* left off and considers the role of the male body in international Fascism as an icon of political and military power. In global Fascism, as in Nazi Germany, as was made abundantly clear in *Shaping the Superman*, sport was central to the creation of the muscular militaristic body of the Fascist superman. It developed power, fitness and aggression – essential elements of the successful warrior. He, in turn, was to ensure security, safety and invulnerability.

In both *Shaping the Superman* and *Superman Supreme*, this martial male body is the common denominator and its purpose and preparation is the common concern. Scott Fitzgerald once wrote: 'show me a hero and I will write you a tragedy'.[3] Both *Shaping the Superman* and *Superman Supreme* record the tragedy of human hubris.

J.A. Mangan

International Research Centre for Sport, Socialisation, Society
University of Strathclyde
March 2000

NOTES

1. Jonathan Sumption, *The Hundred Years War*, Volume Two (London, 1999), p.xi.
2. The poetical works of Robert Browning, Volume XII, 'Red Cotton Night. Cap Country or Turf and Towers', (London, 1889), p.89.
3. F. Scott-Fitzgerald, 'The Note-Books', *The Crack Up* (New York, 1945).

PROLOGUE

Global Fascism and the Male Body: Ambitions, Similarities and Dissimilarities

J.A. MANGAN

The title of this second volume dealing with the male body in the iconography of Fascism reflects, of course, an ambition rather than an achievement. The supremacy of the global Fascist Superman never became a reality but was certainly an intention. *Superman Supreme* explores the use of the image of the male body for this purpose in European, American and Asian Fascism of varying degrees and various interpretations,[1] and the differences and similarities involved. Among the similarities is the fact that sport in all the cases in this volume was at the centre of the induction of the male body (and mind) into martial self-sacrifice. Sport was an important part of Fascist socialization. The reasons are not hard to find. Sport develops muscle and muscle is equated with power – literally and metaphorically. War, the essence of Fascism, demands physical fitness and sport helps promote this fitness. Competitive sport can help develop attitudes of aggression and aggression is essential in war.

While 'Fascism' is a concept extending beyond single systems of rule to 'generic types'[2] thorough comparative analysis has been in short supply, with the result that 'approaches have been top-heavy in their reliance on the case of Nazi Germany'.[3] In consequence 'much comparative work remains to be done on the character of Fascist institutions in power'.[4] It is for both these reasons that *Shaping the Superman*, the companion volume in this series, which dealt with the Aryan Fascist body as a political icon, is followed here by *Superman Supreme*, a volume on global Fascism and the Fascist body as a global political icon. The Fascist body was crucial to Fascism.

There is another reason for *Superman Supreme*. Karl Dietrich Bracher, who has been 'at the pinnacle of scholarship'[5] on Nazism since the 1950s, has asserted that 'the primary question of the totalitarian character of political systems cannot be shirked either in the interest of scholarly clarity and objectivity, or in view of the political and human consequences of such dictatorships and the tendencies towards totalitarianism in present-day society'.[6] His view is the view of the contributors to *Superman Supreme*.

Roger Griffin asks if an investigation into the nature of Fascism can justify 'the intellectual, publishing and paper resources expended on it',[7] in view of the fact that it unleashed horrendously destructive perspectives and wars, and its 'New Order in which nations would be refounded on "healthy" principles and the New Man who would inhabit it', remains a chimera.[8] In reply to his own clearly rhetorical question, he argues that in the late twentieth century with its turbulent ideological, political and social climate ' … the dynamics of Fascism and the place it occupies in the unfolding of modern history can best be understood by the non-Fascist'.[9] For this reason, its raw materials of militarism, racism, charismatic leadership, populist nationalism, fear of the forces of decadence, deep anxiety about the modern age and longings for a new era are all 'active ingredients in contemporary history'.[10]

Indeed, as Griffin suggests, it is especially timely *now* at the dawn of the twentieth-first century to study the nature of Fascism:

> At a time when ethnic nationalisms are displaying increasing virulence, and even the most dispassionate armchair politician or contemporary historian is torn between premonitions of cataclysm and hopes of a new dawn, it makes smaller demands on the 'historical imagination' to understand the perverse mythic logic which underlies the Fascist project of destroying the old order so that the nation can be created anew.[11]

In Europe in the 1920s, comments Juan J. Linz, in response to war and post-war dislocations, there emerged 'similar [Fascist] movements which in their nationalism attempted to emphasize their links with the historical past of their country and with the unique problems faced by their states and societies in a post-Versailles world'.[12] They turned to Italy and more particularly to Germany for guidance. This is equally true of America and Asia. Fascism that was ultra-nationalist became an international movement similar to the internationalism of the movements the Fascists opposed[13] Linz is in no doubt that Fascism made its appearance, not only in Europe, but across the globe.[14] The contributors to *Superman Supreme* bear witness to this.

Fascism in general, Linz also points out, as have many others, 'did not appeal to a particular social constituency defined in terms of socio-economic interest, religious institutional loyalty, or ethnic national identity'.[15] It appealed across constituencies. One important reason, especially where youth was concerned, was its distinctive style: its rhetoric, its symbolism, its chants, ceremonies and uniforms attracted many young people.[16] Its emphasis on the physical, its stress on sport of all kinds and its elevation of muscle over mind, not least in para-military games, eventually translated into real-life action, was also a widespread attraction. Fascism was 'everywhere a para-military political organization ready to use violence against its opponents'.[17]

Its appeal then was its ideology, its ritual, symbolism and liturgy, its athletic activities and its eventual brutal, direct and effective forms of political action. All these ingredients added up to an appeal based on emotion, myth, idealism and action underpinned by 'a vitalistic philosophy'.[18] Thus it is important, observes Linz, 'to pay infinitely more attention to the positive appeal (things it stood for) rather than the negative appeal (things it stood against)'[19] and the needs it satisfied. Here the ritual, the symbolism, the rhetoric, the exciting physical forms of participation[20] – 'the sublimated expressions of criminal impulses',[21] were central to its success. They all receive attention in *Superman Supreme*.

In short, Fascism contained powerful addictive components – 'an appeal to emotion and sentiment, to the love of adventure and heroism, the belief in action rather than words, the exultation of violence, even death'.[22] These components were combined seductively to offer a secure sense of belonging, a reassuring discipline and a belief in worthwhile sacrifice. Fascism satisfied both the desire for the heroic deeds of romantic individualism and the desire for submergence in a glorious collectivity.[23] It also soothed those in the atomized societies of the 1930s desperate for inspirational leaders and fused them with those in earlier generations who had worshipped strong military heroes.[24]

After an erudite discussion of the academic complexity, not to mention confusion, that faces the student of Fascism, Roger Griffin, in his authoritative *The Nature of Fascism*, states that no amount of research will resolve the lack of consensus: 'in fact it can only tend to make it more acute because as new historical perspectives emerge with the unfolding of contemporary events, as new paradigms come to be employed in the social sciences and as researchers make empirical advances and creative leaps in their investigations of Fascism in its concrete manifestations, so the term "Fascism" itself will be turned into any number of new ideal types'.[25] In view of this, among other things, he recommends an investigation of 'a common core of Fascist phenomena which can be treated as its definitional minimum, while allowing for the profound differences which exist between the Fascism which took power in Italy and all other movements subsequently associated with it'.[26] This will be the approach of *Superman Supreme.*

Griffin speaks of the continuing 'conundrum' of Fascism as a concept despite enormous amounts of research time and mental energy spent on its study, and remarks that such is the 'divergent opinion surrounding the term that some such observation is *de rigueur* as an opening statement'.[27] He certainly has a point when he suggests Fascism as a concept has become a conceptual labyrinth and that scores of self-appointed Ariadnes dangle threads temptingly in front of interested students and specialist academics showing them the way out, but with each route leading to a different exit, or often as not, to another turn in the maze.[28] Among the interpretations[29] is one that sees the Fascism of the 1930s as 'an essentially new force and a major factor in contemporary history within Europe *and* [emphasis added] outside it'.[30] This is the interpretation adopted in *Superman Supreme.*

Of course, there were profound differences between German Fascism and the Fascisms of Western Europe, South America and South-East Asia. For one thing German Fascism was pre-eminently racist. German Fascism was unique in its primacy of Volk, nature, race,[31] while Italian Futurism, for example, exalted in action. Nevertheless, in all cases in and beyond Europe, belief was made concrete within the terms of each ideological framework. Implementation of belief was promulgated by means of energetic political appeal, by compelling propaganda and by aggressive militarism.[32] And the martial male body was a common denominator in all this.

As *Superman Supreme* makes clear, and as was stated in the Foreword to *Shaping the Superman*, the vision of *homo fascistus* was similar in many respects throughout the world. Thus, to reiterate once again, while 'Fascism had many faces, "to maintain that Fascism was a purely isolated phenomenon which can be understood only in its national context, country by country, would be to ignore the broader dimensions of this historical phenomenon of the twentieth century, for close and deep similarities undoubtedly existed. There may be no single, all embracing

Fascism, but there are unquestionably patterns which can be analysed with a degree of precision."'[33] The purpose and the preparation for this purpose of the male body was one of them.

It is well to recognize that Ian Kershaw, after a careful consideration of the arguments for and against Nazism as a unique form of Fascism, concluded that while 'the peculiar features which distinguish Nazism from the other leading manifestations of Fascism are only to be fully comprehended within the structures and conditions of German socio-economic and ideological-political developments in the industrial-bourgeois era', nevertheless, he added, the 'similarities with other brands of Fascism are profound, not peripheral'.[34] These similarities, Kershaw argued, include:

> ... extreme chauvinistic nationalism with pronounced imperialistic, expansionist tendencies; an anti-socialist, anti-Marxist thrust aimed at the destruction of working-class organizations and their Marxist political philosophy; the basis in a mass party drawing from all sectors of society, though with pronounced support in the middle class and proving attractive to the peasantry and to various uprooted or highly unstable sectors of the population; fixation on a charismatic, plebiscitarily legitimized leader; extreme intolerance towards all oppositional and presumed oppositional groups, expressed through vicious terror, open violence, and ruthless repression; glorification of militarism and war ... dependence upon an 'alliance' with existing élites – industrial, agrarian, military, and bureaucratic – for their political breakthrough; and at least an initial function – despite a populist-revolutionary, anti-establishment rhetoric – in the stabilization or restoration of social order and capitalist structures.[35]

To this list should be *added* the projection of the martial male body as a symbol of state power: his powerful body personified the powerful state.

This comparative study of the political use of the male body is certainly exploratory, tentative, incomplete. Nevertheless, the hope is that it will stimulate other studies of the male, *and* female, body in twentieth-century society as a tool of political ambition. As we approach the twenty-first century it is often remarked that technology in war will make muscle redundant. However, it should not be forgotten that in Ruanda only recently the machete killed more men, women and children than the laser-guided missile. And this was not an isolated incident.[36]

Furthermore, the muscled Superman, and increasingly in an androgynous global culture, the Superwoman, is found everywhere in the modern myth-making, violence obsessed media. He, and increasingly She, serve a perennial purpose – the pursuit of security, safety and invulnerability. Muscle is made to this end. Beyond myth, muscle, power and aggression are developed on sports fields, in weights rooms and in gymnasia. The strong body as a metaphor for security and supremacy – political, social and sexual – is a contemporary image of international aspiration. It will still be at the disposal of the ideologue who has need of the iconic warrior in the future as it has been in the past.

The bravery, courage and defiance of this warrior, it has been asserted, are too easily misapplied and used for immoral and ignoble purposes. This realization lies at the heart of Milton's early repudiation of the heroic in *Paradise Lost*.[37] Satan may have possessed heroic qualities, his devils may have been braver than any recorded heroes, but their heroism and bravery were destructive. With these two volumes on the Fascist body as political icon now completed, these lines from Book IX of *Paradise Lost* are worth recalling:

> To overcome in Battel, and subdue
> Nations, and bring home spoils with infinite
> Man-slaughter, shall be held the highest pitch
> Of human Glorie, and for Glorie done
> Of triumph, to be styl'd great Conquerors,
> Patrons of Mankind, Gods, and Sons of Gods,
> Destroyers rightlier call'd and Plagues of men.
> Thus Fame shall be achiev'd, renown on Earth,
> And what most merits fame in silence hid.[38]

It should also be recalled, however, that warrior heroes are universal, continual and exalted in the world's cultures. The reason is clear: they symbolize security. They are positive as well as negative representations. They will not go away. State, culture and society will not permit it.

'Fascism is a genus of political ideology,' Griffin suggests, 'whose myths come in its various presentations in a palingenetic form of popular ultra-nationalism.'[39] This idea of a 'palingenetic myth'[40] is of fundamental significance to both *Shaping the Superman* and *Superman Supreme*. It is omnipresent in history: 'it is a central motif of religious, mythical and magical thought encountered literally the world over',[41] it is also a secular motif 'central to the Renaissance vision of the West's cultural history, as the term itself indicates'.[42] It occurs continually in political movements. It is present at moments of perceived political decline and attempted renewal:

> Against this background, the expression 'palingenetic myth' comes to denote the vision of a revolutionary new order which supplies the affective power of an ideology ... When this is a political ideology it will centre on a new society inaugurated through human agency and not a millenarian vision of a new world in a metaphysical and supra-historical sense. At the heart of palingenetic political myth lies the belief that contemporaries are living through or about to live through a 'sea-change', a 'watershed' or 'turning-point' in the historical process. The perceived corruption, anarchy, oppressiveness, iniquities or decadence of the present, rather than being seen as immutable and thus to be endured indefinitely with stoic courage or bleak pessimism, are perceived as having reached their peak and interpreted as the sure sign that one era is nearing its end and a new order is about to emerge.[43]

In other words, it is both the offspring of despair and the child of hope.

Fascism of all shades, as George Mosse remarks, fed on dissatisfaction with the modern world. It attempted to create a 'new sense of belonging' and a 'new meaning in life',[44] and new systems of power. National Socialism, for example, asserts Mosse, was analogous to a religion, and the movement acted as if belief in its beliefs would grant the disillusioned comfort and a sense of belonging which society failed to provide.[45] In fact, everywhere it occurred, Fascism represented a flight from present reality. It became a new 'religion' 'with its own ideals, mysticism and liturgical rites'.[46] It represented a glorification of secular ideology posing as an innovatory religion. It offered a new start. The term 'palingenesis', deriving from *palm* (again) and *genesis* (creation), refers to a new start or regeneration after a period of crisis or decline and is associated just as much with a secular (for example, the New Germany) as a mystical (for example, the Second Coming) reality.[47] Significantly, one 'characteristic sub-myth of such hopes of transformation in the idea that a "new man" is destined to appear, a politicized version of the archetypal "hero myth"'.[48]

In an attempt to explain the attraction of Fascism, at merely one level but one of special importance to this volume – male response, Griffin enlists Theweleit's exploration of the inner compulsions and the motives of a group of German proto-Fascists and future Fascist activists after 1918. Griffin wisely warns that 'we must never lose sight of the fact that only a small percentage of the population, and then only in special historical circumstances, will fall prey to this particular elective affinity'.[49] They cannot stand, states Griffin, for all Fascists, let alone all males. Perhaps not, but what of their influence when they have achieved positions of influence? The answer is to be found in recent twentieth-century history.

Theweleit argued of his sample of proto-Fascist and future Fascist activists obsessed with the conflict with the Communists, that psychologically 'they were not-yet-fully born'.[50] This state of affairs 'induced not only an urge to turn their body into a [military] machine so as to tame the chaotic world of instincts and emotions, but a radical misogyny or flight from the feminine, manifesting itself in a pathological fear of being engulfed by anything in external reality associated with softness'.[51] The outcome of the psychological syndrome afflicting these men, argued Theweleit, was 'the "soldier male" driven by a longing to transcend the hell of his private life in a collective struggle against an inner chaos which had been projected onto society'.[52] In Theweleit's view:

> The texts of the soldier males perpetually revolve around the same axes: the communality of the male society, nonfemale creation, rebirth, the rise upward to hardness and tension ... The man is released from a world that is rotten and sinking (from the morass of femaleness): he finally dissolves in battle.[53]

Of course, the 'psychological dynamics of Fascism are ... destined to remain in the last analysis shrouded in mystery and speculation'.[54] To be realistic, 'they are simply beyond the explanatory powers of the human sciences'.[55] Nevertheless, Theweleit does highlight features of the idealized image of the Aryan Superman that had a wide currency *beyond* Germany as will now be demonstrated.

These studies of the metaphorical and literal use made by Fascism of the male body in Europe, America and Asia in the projection of the Fascist new man of destiny, are not a study of attempts at global cloning. They reveal clear similarities and clear dissimilarities. They point up individualism as well as commonality.

In Italy, the Fascist Superman was personified, as nowhere else, by the Leader. As Gigliola Gori writes, 'The exaltation of the virile body as a metaphor for Fascism was common to all Fascisms, but its manifestation in the body of the Duce was a peculiar Italian phenomenon [and] the Duce, symbol of Fascist virility, became the source of inspiration and his athletic body was celebrated in literature, in the figurative arts and on film.'[56] In consequence, the cult of the Virile Male became embedded in a society that, responding to 'the consolidated instincts of an Italian society ... was deeply sexist and strongly patriarchal'.[57] The image of Mussolini became 'a holy icon and a public allegory'. In Mussolini the Superman of Nietzsche became *forma mentic* – the New Man of the New Italy – strengthened by war, gifted with sublime perversity, triumphant over man and God. The Duce became his own icon. Mussolini was made myth by means of an unrelenting propaganda directed by himself. He mobilized the new technology of radio, photography and cinema to present himself as 'the Envoy of Destiny', symbolizing the perpetual virtues: 'heroism in war, compassion for the humble, sobriety in life, tireless ability in work and athletic dynamism'. With a body, 'always young', these virtues were permanent. Thus the image of the Fascism of the Duce was that of 'the eternally young and powerful male' serving the cause with dedication. Through this imagery Italians, traditionally individualistic and indulgent, were to be transformed into an elect race of Supermen – virile, dynamic, bellicose.

Mussolini, however, did not fail to reinforce iconic imagery with structural innovation – the mass meetings, the uniforms, the schools, the militaristic youth movements, the mass spectaculars produced 'a militarized nation'. To promote his Fascist creed of activism, power and grace

> to the usual ceremony with its rites and symbols were added demonstrations of gymnastics, athletics and sports in the name of activism and of physical power. Among those remembered are the Littoriali, Agonali, Ludi Juveniles, Campi Dux and OND contests where, in the presence of the Duce and other leaders, crowds of spectators followed the braveries of the athletes in uniform. These athletes embodied the uniformity and order of Fascist aesthetics in the geometric perfection of their choreographic executions.[58]

In this, however, he was not unique. European, American and Asian Fascism did the same to create a totalitarian conformity compelling in its images of beauty, strength, order and discipline.

Nevertheless, despite the use of sport as a projected, protected and privileged instrument of political ambition and a massive programme of national expansion in the 1930s, according to Gori, 'the Italian male did not completely change ... into the strong, sculptured and obedient warrior ready to die for the cause'.[59] Italian individualism, the product of secular, geographic, historical and cultural divisions, won out in the end. In the final resort, the Italians were as much spectators of, as participants in, Fascism.

In Austria the Deutscher Turnerbund (DTB) and the Nazionalsozialistische Deutsche Arbeiter Partei (NSDAP), argues Wolfgang Weber and Paula Black, worked together to create a Greater Germany in which the Austrian Fascist New Man had all the qualities of, and was virtually indistinguishable from, the German Nazi Superman. The bodies of both, first and foremost, were instruments of the state.

The common features of both the DTB and the NSDAP included subscription to the same idealized body image, its reliance upon social Darwinism and a belief in its contribution to strong political union. Perceptions of the male body, political ideology and effective action were closely linked. Male association, identification and effort were bound together by a single purpose – to prepare the male body for the highest and most specific form of masculinity: military action in pursuit of a supreme Fascist state. In Austria, as in Germany, the body was far from ideologically neutral. Its portrayal had a political construction. The exercised male body was a political statement. Austrian gymnasts worked 'to strengthen the male body in readiness for struggle'.[60] They were part of a long Teutonic tradition. Gymnastics in both Germany and Austria from the time of Friedrich Ludwig Jahn had been a preparation for war. Jahn's 'gymnastics' were para-military activities and included marching, shooting, riding and fencing. Austria inherited this interpretation. The DTB practised military gymnastics. Its gymnasts were co-founders of various branches of the NSDAP and 'had a prominent role in the building of the Austrian SA (Sturmabteilung, storm troopers). In due course then, the NSDAP and the DTB had common ideological, political and military aims. They worked for unity with Germany through militaristic sports, through the strengthening of physical and mental fitness and through subscription to a belief in the 'tribal' identity of the Germanic people.

> A national uprising and a lasting strengthening of our will to survive through the difficulties of the time and to go on collecting our energies until the one big moment when our leaders will call us to help in the rebuilding of the great and unified fatherland which will include all German tribes.[61]

The body of the Aryan 'tribal' member, according to Nazi propaganda, fully accepted by the DTB, symbolized 'Purity of Race'; 'the hard Aryan body and the disciplined Austrian gymnast's body were placed at a point on the evolutionary scale higher than those inferior bodies that did not match the idealized body image'.[62] The Fascist bodies of the Austrian and German Supermen were indistinguishable – in preparation, in purpose and in purity.

In Bulgaria, as Vassil Girginov and Peter Bankov make plain, despite claims to the contrary, inspection of the country's history provides persuasive evidence of the domination for a time, of Fascist ideological doctrine and an 'aspiration to create an "Aryan" manhood'.[63] Nevertheless, as not uncommon elsewhere, the shaping of the Bulgarian Superman was complex, incomplete and controversial. It was not a self-generated national impulse but was generated, indeed imposed, from outside. It was imported: 'According to the Nazi racial doctrine, Bulgarians as a Slav nation were given the role of culture-bearer nation. Therefore they had to follow … the real Nazi model.'[64] Imposition did not stimulate total support. Although it was referred to as the 'Prussia of the Balkans', Bulgaria came nowhere near to competing with Nazi Germany in fanaticism, conformity and implementation. Imposition produced internal dissonance allowing, among other things, the use of sport as a mass manifestation of pro-Communism and as, at least, a gesture of non-discrimination against Jews.

Nonetheless, there was subscription to Fascism which was chauvinistic, nationalistic and militaristic. Moreover, three fundamental and interrelated elements – ' "athletic" manhood, state political intervention in sport, and the loyal political leadership formed the core of a Fascist body Politicum'.[65] Thus the Bulgarian Superman became a dual metaphor for the athletic body and the body politic. Bulgarian Fascism wholeheartedly supported 'not all, but certainly some of the major ideas of Fascist ideology, including the emergence of the Superman as the epitome of the political athlete and … commitment to power, discipline and virility in the interests of the restoration of national dignity, and for the construction of a new society'.[66] Endorsement was facilitated by long tradition of masculine potency embodied in the Bulgarian myth of Karli Marko – the indigenous Bulgarian Superman of legend. He was part prototype for the New Fascist Bulgarian Man. There was also a direct historical link to the militaristic masculinity of Jahn. Sport, once again, was preparation for war. Indeed, Bulgarian Fascism seems to have improved on the three basic innovations of Jahn.

> Firstly, corporeal education was placed at the heart of the educational system as a 'paramount condition for any education', thus it was the chief contributor to 'the creation of the healthiest and the purest Bulgarian view of life'. What is more, it was given a role in the achievement of a long-term objective – 'the creation of a handsome, healthy and desirable body type'. Secondly, sport was seen as public necessity, and the best guarantee of individual and public health. Thirdly, the military nature of Bulgaria's sport … adopted by the state, [was] incorporated into the school system and national sports movements.[67]

In summary, in the hands of official zealots sport played a full part in the submission of brain to brawn in the creation of a Bulgarian national Superman moulded and controlled by the state.

In Denmark, as Hans Bonde reveals, for Niels Bukh, admirer and advocate of Nazism, the culture of the body was inseparable from the culture of politics. Bukh was captivated by Fascism. He was convinced that his authoritarian masculine gymnastics 'were highly compatible with German National Socialism and its cult of the Führer'.[68] He admired the 'Nazi cult of beauty and homage to the young, racially pure, perfect body'.[69] Through his gymnastics Bukh disseminated the Nazi mythology of the Nordic race by means, among other things, of the selection of blond performers with blue eyes. And like the Nazi, his vision was of youth in sensible revolt:

> Youth is what we need, and the day is perhaps not so far off – at least I don't think so – when the young will take a hand. I won't say here what I would do, I only say that it is what we need. Oh, you should see how satisfied, happy and enthusiastic the Germans are under their new form of government.[70]

Bukh's gymnast represented a Danish 'new man' who repudiated the degenerate and flabby body of modern civilization, and whose own body was demonstrative of a political culture that was certainly masculine if not overtly militaristic. In this regard, and in his admiration of authoritarian control in and beyond the gymnastics arena, Bukh was a proselytizer for the male body as an inter-war political icon.

As Teresa Aja remarks, in Spain Fascism survived longer than anywhere else in the world. This Fascism, despite similarities with Fascism elsewhere, had peculiarly *significant* differences. In Spain, as was true generally, Fascism arose out of a conviction, following the depression of the 1920s, 'that the existing political order could no longer guarantee the economic interests of the middle and upper classes'.[71] Be that as it may, religion represents 'the fundamental difference between German Nazism, Italian Fascism and the Fascism which developed in Spain'.[72] Nationalism and the Church underpinned Franco's Spanish Fascist state. In the Valley of the Fallen, Franco's monument to the Fascist heroic dead, the bodies of the warriors of Fascism *and* Church were enshrined and celebrated.

In other respects, Fascism followed a regular highway. It has several approach lanes. Gimínez Caballero became 'totally captivated' by 'Roman' Fascism[73] and promoted sport and an élite of supermen – 'the Heraklidan Fist' who would guide and control the masses. Onésimo Redondo Ortega founded a political activist group characterized by economic radicalism and religious conservatism and committed to violence in pursuit of political ends. 'Youth … should love violence as a matter of course. National violence is just, is necessary, is convenient.'[74] With Ramon Ledesma Ramos, an admirer of Nazi Germany, Redondo formed the Nationalist Syndicalist Offensive Juntas. José Antonio Primo de Rivera founded the Falange. He looked to Fascist Italy for inspiration and stood for the defence of 'Christian values against the dangers of Marxism'.[75] He fused the various Fascist movements in being during the Republic established in 1937 on the abdication of the monarchy. Then in 1937 Franco ('Caudillo of Spain by the Grace of God') on the death of Rivera, brought all Fascist groups under his control.

His Fascist militaristic, Spartan view of life was set out in 1940, in a speech celebrating the fourth anniversary of the national uprising, 'We do not want life to be easy and comfortable. We want life to be hard, life to be difficult, we want the life of virile peoples … Five hundred thousand dead were offered in the first European battle for the new order, for the salvation and the unity of Spain … Spain … now has regained its strength and virility. It has two million warriors ready to fight to defend its rights.'[76]

Sport was an integral part of Franco's Fascism, albeit not as enthusiastically utilized as in Germany and Italy. It was, nevertheless, centrally controlled and administered, and considered a means of exhibiting Spanish 'virility and fury'.[77] Through sport Hispanic masculine values about which the Falange talked so much and so often – virility, impetuosity and 'fury' – 'would be incarnate'. Francoism projected, as in all the totalitarian regimes, an idealized image of militarized man. 'It was a case of making physical and moral violence not only tolerable, but agreeable, endowing them with a mask which was attractive to the senses.'[78]

First and foremost, there was the myth of the 'soldier-monk', a combination of austerity, spirit of sacrifice and impassiveness when faced with bloodshed. While the Francoist soldiers are represented as valiant athletic heroes, there is an almost religious preoccupation with the slimness of physique: 'the figures are elongated in the style of El Greco and at times even the hero athletes are endowed with a certain feminine halo'.[79] These Spanish Supermen were as much icons from the past as from the present. Some Spanish Fascist images of heroic masculinity, therefore, were imbued with distinctive idiosyncratic characteristics. In the paintings of M. Bertuchi, soldier heroes 'salute the vision of the Crucifixion of Jesus which appears above the clouds'.[80] On the other hand, comics for children depicted more representative Fascist Supermen of giant proportion, of enormous musculature, of cold purpose, of a total courage born of invulnerability accompanied almost invariably by an admiring, handsome, blonde young boy.

Fascist masculine images went hand in hand with fashion and monumentalism – dress was militarized, youth and the sport of youth were militarized, and collective celebrations became mass military style spectaculars. Yet all this occurred within a framework of Catholic tradition. This was the peculiar hallmark of Spanish Fascism which resulted in a singular iconic image of the soldier-monk.

In the words of Tony Collins, 'It is difficult to overestimate the importance which the BUF [British Union of Fascists] attached to the question of masculinity.'[81] For Theo Lang of the British Union of Fascists for one, 'the centrality of manhood to Fascist politics'[82] was clearly understood and appreciated. Indeed the BUF itself was a 'self-defined masculine organization' locked into rhetorical outpouring such as 'Fascism believes in manhood, in courage, in determination, in selflessness, in the essence of life.'[83] For the BUF 'Fascism and masculinity were one and the same'.[84]

The BUF drew on a manliness born of the imperial militaristic masculinity of the late Victorian and Edwardian era.[85] Indeed, in Collins' attractive expression, 'the BUF's politics could be described as the ethos of public school masculinity reinvented as a political programme'.[86] In this respect it was as much British as German in inspiration. An updated Imperial Manliness was integral to its supremacist paramilitary politics. And at the core of this supremacist masculinity was the male body. Indeed, the Fascist state in being was the perfected, disciplined, strong male body transmogrified into a political body 'as in the human body every limb and organ is attuned to serve the whole of the body, so in society every section and interest must be subordinated to the general interest of the State as a whole. This is the corporate conception of society … what is called Fascism of National Socialism.'[87]

'Hardness' was the password of the BUF. It was projected in prose and picture. Sir Oswald Mosley made use of the rhetoric of steel, struggle and sacrifice to promote the perfection of the Fascist man. Others relied on metaphors such as 'iron in our spirits', 'metallic thought', 'concrete hardness'.[88] British Fascist 'warriors of the new age' were depicted in drawing and illustrations as 'idealized with angular sharp figures with exaggerated muscular development, staring determinedly into the distance'.[89] As befitted warriors embarked on violent revolution, the BUF embraced 'an ordered athleticism of life' and 'a morality of the Spartan pattern' and as with Sparta, 'the pervasive sense of violence was at the heart of the BUF intellectualism'.[90]

British Fascism unquestionably mirrored German Fascism – in the belief in the potency of the natural state of manhood – hunter, pioneer and soldier, in the rejection of the degeneration of urban living, in a brutal racism and in a belief in the paramount value of physical education to ensure the physical power to achieve its ends by force.

Thus British Fascism was an amalgamation of British tradition and Nazi invented tradition. It was both national and international. And in one regard, it had strong similarities to Italian Fascism – in the personification of the physical Superman in its leader Sir Oswald Mosley; allegedly of magnificent physique, he was the very embodiment of British Fascist manhood.[91]

In one regard the BUF was highly individualistic – in its opposition to the Second World War – 'its most important, and arguably its only, break from the British public school masculine ideal of the pre-World War One era. For while it embraced the cult of the manly warrior, its

Fascist ideology prevented it from embracing the forthcoming war in the same way as the approach of war in 1914 was welcomed with open arms by those who were educated into what Mangan has described as a "martial, moralistic manhood".'[92]

In the shifting kaleidoscope of Fascist uniformity and uniqueness, the Fascist aesthetics in Brazil of the 1930s and 1940s provide a glittering display. Brazilian Fascism demonstrated 'a less than total devotion to German Fascist models and principles'[93] perhaps surprisingly in this 'traditionally authoritarian society', but then perhaps not, with Brazil's extraordinary evolutionary combination of 'feudalism, Thomism, capitalism, liberalism, hierarchy, favours, corporatism, class domination, bureaucratic insulation and dualistic reason'.[94] One consequence of this rather bizarre ideological combination, as Lamartine Da Costa and Plinio Labriola comment, is that aesthetic experiences rather than moral judgements serve as guidelines for action in contemporary Brazil. The ethics of an aesthetic comprising a strong assertion of the hedonistic politics of the body dominate modern Brazilian culture – the consequence of a unique history of romanticism, supremacism and racism, and for a time, Fascism.

During the Fascist period under the dictator Vargas and known as the Vargas era (1930–45), this combination of uniformity and uniqueness was apparent from the fact that:

> … some features, characteristic of Hitler's regime in Europe, were rejected in favour of a modernist aesthetic, which had remained rooted in Brazilian regional values since the 1920s … under Vargas the country experienced both a Fascist rationale and leadership as a syncretism, involving an acceptance of European Fascist influences but only in association with local and cultural traditions and innovations carefully selected and emphasized by leading intellectuals.[95]

This syncreticism is perhaps best understood, Da Costa and Labriola suggest, by reference to Umberto Eco's concept of 'Ur-Fascism' – eternal Fascism with its essential component of action as beautiful in itself and not requiring reflection. Brazilian Fascism, made up of three elements: the Nazi German, Fascist Italian and the 'Integralista' – the Brazilian version of Fascism and each with its own identity, rituals and actions,[96] was concentrated in the southern parts of Brazil and in São Paulo and Rio de Janeiro. The fundamental ideals and actions of

Brazilian Fascism were simple, it was a 'primordial Fascism, coinciding with a traditional authoritarian mentality',[97] but its origins were diverse and linked to distinctive community aspirations as well as twentieth-century political diffusion. In all this, the Vargas government acted as overall puppet-master 'manipulating each one according to national and international priorities, in what may be called Syncretic Fascism'.[98]

Subscription to the physical was one element common to all the Brazilian Fascist groups. Various celebrations, the 'Race Day', 'Fatherland Week', 'Flag Day', orchestrated by the Vargas propaganda machine, were 'testaments to the body's imperative' rather than subscriptions to ideological mandates[99] in Brazilian Fascist politics.[100] The Brazilian *Turnen*, for example, in which actions were framed in bodies, provided aesthetic meditations reinforcing ethnic commonality and reaffirming unifying traditions, rather than affirming ideological commitment.[101] Zeev Sternhell, who 'postulates a culturally bound Fascism initially committed to an ideology but eventually adjusting to the local requirements of mainstream politics', nicely describes Brazilian Fascism.[102]

In a sentence, a preoccupation with the body in and through sport was the commonplace of Brazilian Fascism.[103] It welded individuals, élites and masses in 'a totalitarian society as a visual entity'.[104] Body, spectacle and politics fused together in Fascism's theatricals.[105] Such functionalism, of course, is hardly sufficient as a complete explanation of Brazilian Fascism. There is also the matter of the celebration of the body in the form of allegedly inspirational nude statues of men demonstrating strength, power and invulnerability and there is the further and signal matter, as Da Costa and Labriola remark, of the aesthetic glorification of the body and the recurring demonstrations in societies of collective rituals in celebration of the beauty of the body, hedonism and paganism. Thus Da Costa and Labriola ask of Fascism in Brazil and beyond Brazil: is it a primordial reflex?[106] Time may tell.

By the mid-1930s in Japan, as J.A. Mangan and Takeshi Komagome make clear, by means of modern mass education, the intense nationalism of the upper classes had diffused downwards to all the Japanese:

> it had soon convinced the descendants of peasants, who for almost three centuries had been denied swords and other arms and had been exploited by a military caste above them, that they too were members of a warrior race. Making up the great bulk of the

> conscripts, the peasants found their experience in army barracks as educational as the time spent in primary school. Both inculcated in them the glory of Japan's great military traditions and the ideal of death on the battlefield in the service of the emperor.[107]

In one regard there was continuity rather than discontinuity in this militarism. 'By the twentieth century the Emperor had become a sacred, omnipotent figurehead. He was constitutional sovereign, commander-in-chief and head of the state or quasi-religion, *Shinto*. As emperor he was expected to define the uniqueness and superiority of the "Japanese race" – to this end he was deified. The result was the emperor cult. As far as the cult was concerned there was remarkable continuity between the pre-Fascist and Fascist periods.'[108] Here once again is Fascism embodied in the person of the leader. In this regard German, Italian and Japanese Fascism possessed a common element. There was certainly at least one other. All the national agencies and agents of socialization in the Fascist era were bent to the purpose of ensuring recognition of the leader as the supreme racial icon. In Japan, the outcome was a mass, and massive, programme of indoctrination in loyalty, service and obedience to the Emperor unto death. There emerged a national ideal of martial masculinity that produced a militarized male population believing in the desirability of death in battle. As merely one small part of this outcome, the Youth Volunteer Army for Pioneering Manchuria was created, inculcated with a single-minded imperial militarism both in elementary and secondary school and in the volunteer army itself, and imbued with the idea of death on the battlefield as the supreme virtue.

Neither Germany nor Italy, nor indeed any other Fascist state, could match Japan in the completeness of its system of indoctrination into commitment to martial self-sacrifice.

> By the time of the Second World War, Japan already boasted a 50-year tradition of secular nationalism, promulgated relentlessly through every institution of Japanese life. Public education, which reached 90 per cent of Japanese children by 1900, included military training for boys and the systemic inculcation of militarism and emperor worship for both sexes. Arithmetic classes did calculations based on battlefield situations; science topics included 'general information about searchlights, wireless communication, land mines and torpedoes'.[109]

As a result the male body became 'a symbol of self-denial, a self-abnegatory offering, a sacrifice to the living deity'.[110]

The image of the Japanese Fascist Superman was not projected as a steel-muscled, powerfully torsoed, naked warrior. It was sufficient that his body in itself was sacrificial. Collectively this would be enough to ensure supremacy. Psychologically, however, he was all the Fascist Superman should be, cold, remote, insensitive and ruthless, in the pursuit of conquest. Nonetheless, Japan's Fascist educational system devoted a great deal of effort to promoting physical education and to creating a strong, fit male population prepared for war. The Youth Volunteer Army for Pioneering Manchuria provides a good example. Perhaps it is all the more significant for not being a front-line fighting force, but a volunteer agricultural force of pre-conscript male adolescents. At the same time, its civilian members, young and inexperienced though they were, acted as auxiliaries to frontier army units facing the godless Soviet Union and to the military police in their task of repressing unappreciative Chinese 'rebels'!

At the training centre of the YVAPM, the Uchihara Training Institute, under its principal, Kato Kanji: 'all the young men lived and worked together. They prepared their bodies, minds and emotions for service to the emperor. They performed Shinto rituals, sang the national anthem and martial songs and practised traditional martial arts ... Kato attached the greatest importance to "Japanese exercise" (*Yamato Bataraki*) as the expression of "the faith and ideals of the Japanese race" through the body.'[111] These volunteers were organized into battalions, companies, platoons and squads as in the regular Japanese army: their day was a mixture of military and agricultural training. Military training had a central place in the curriculum. 'Soldiers of the plough' were made not born.[112]

In the final analysis, the Volunteer Army was both a common and an uncommon army of Fascist purpose. Nevertheless their bodies were iconic instruments of Fascist imperial intention; their muscles were means of Fascist chauvinistic ambition. They were not supermen in the Aryan sense but they were men of a 'super race'[113] – an Oriental Super Race. Their bodies were shaped by ideology, imagery and action to ensure its supremacy.

According to Walter Laqueur, what made Fascism different from earlier dictatorships was the existence of a mass party – led by a leader with virtually unlimited power, adulated by his followers and the focus of a quasi-religious cult – which monopolized power by means of ruthless military and security forces, eliminated political opposition with considerable violence, possessed a doctrine that became 'an obligatory article of faith' for all citizens and projected it through powerful propaganda.[114]

Chinese Fascism had all these things so it is necessary to contradict Lacqueur in his assertion that Fascism was a European phenomenon.[115] China had no Great War but Fascism prevailed there as in Europe, because the old order seemed no longer to work, democracy had no deep roots, national resentment was running high, and there was economic breakdown and social disorder – all the other preconditions mentioned by Laqueur. China was also in moral and cultural crisis. For many Fascism seemed to provide solutions to their problems. To adapt Lacqueur on German Fascism, Chinese Fascism for a time was successful because it was China's great and only hope!

China demonstrates, as Fan Hong clearly shows, both the generalities and singularities characteristic of the nations embracing the international Fascist movement. In China Fascism in the 1930s, however incomplete in nature,[116] was forcefully represented by two associated movements: the Blue Shirts (Langishe) a replica of the Fascist youth movement in Europe, and the New Life movement, a Fascist movement with a specific Chinese dimension, a fusion of period nationalist regeneration and neo-Confucian revivalism. Among the objectives of both movements was 'the training of male … bodies for "national rebirth"'.[117]

The Nationalists under Chiang Kai-shek between 1928 and 1949, for much of the time in control of some two-thirds of the Chinese population and much of the country, unquestionably practised a Chinese-style variation of European Fascism. From the early moments of power both the party and the military found in European Fascism 'a progressive doctrine that was suited to China's restoration'.[118] Both were attracted by the strong doctrinal trinity: strong leadership, patriotic fervour and military strength. Obtaining the latter involved no less than the militarization of the entire nation to ensure survival and then superiority.

China's links with Fascism began early. In 1928 a German military mission went to China under Colonel Max Bauer who had close ties to newly emerging German Fascism. Later, following the dismal performance by his troops in his first three campaigns against the

Communists, Chiang Kai-shek imported, with the full support of Hitler, further advisers with the result that the Nationalist armies were Nazi trained and advised. Hand-in-hand with military influence went political influence. By 1931 the Nationalist party was closely following Fascist political practice in Germany and Italy. The Blue Shirts was established. It was dominated by the military and it exerted a pervasive and a powerful influence. Its aim was 'national salvation through Fascism'.[119] Implicit in this aim was unconditional obedience, loyalty and service to the Leader. The stage was set for the militarization of the Chinese male. His body was to be prepared for the ultimate expression of political fidelity – death in battle. This would ensure that spiritual degeneration would be halted. Thus, martial self-sacrifice was linked closely to the New Life movement launched by Chiang Kai-shek in 1934 which had the militarization of society as its main objective. Militarism was to promote nationalism. In this endeavour, a moral code based on traditional Confucianism was to be established, encouraged and enforced as part of a broader Fascist-inspired effort to regenerate degenerate China. Fascism *with* Confucianism would 'deliver a future to the people'.[120]

The main aim of the Blue Shirts militarization programme was 'to strengthen men's bodies ... essential for preparation for war and national rebirth'.[121] This process began early. From the kindergarten upwards children were exposed to images and implements of war, while physical exercise, team games and group activities received priority. The bookish student of the past was to be replaced by the warrior of the future. As in Japan, learning itself was militaristic in nature. Science studies, for example, concentrated on its application to war.

The Nationalist Fascist conception of the ideal society was for it to perform 'with the discipline, obedience and efficiency of a military camp'.[122] In this camp the body was to become a fit, efficient, strong instrument in the pursuit of the supremacy of the nation, the defeat of foreign aggressors and the end to national humiliation. Nazi Germany was now the admired and acclaimed model and as in Germany, youth was meticulously trained for war.

As in Germany also, the reality failed to achieve the perfection of the ideal. Superman Supreme failed to materialize in China as elsewhere. Corruption and inefficiency, student resistance, religious opposition, the need to woo the democratic West, but arguably most importantly, the requirement to unite with the Communists in the struggle against Japan, blunted the edge of Fascist effort. Control was never complete.

Nevertheless, from 1928 to 1938, when both the Blue Shirts and the New Life movement were disbanded, China experienced a sustained, ruthless and extensive attempt to ensure that a Supreme Chinese Superman emerged in the Far East.

In Italy the Fascist Superman was embodied in the physique and personality of the Duce. Institutions and media reinforced his idealized image. Austria came closest to the German racially pure Superman. The Austrian New Man was indistinguishable from the Nazi New Man. In Bulgaria there was espousal of an imposed Fascist Superman. The Bulgarians were to follow, not to lead. In reaction, espousal was not complete. Indeed, there was opposition. However, three fundamental Fascist elements *were* to be found: athletic manhood as preparation for war, associated state intervention in sport to achieve this and a zealous Fascist leadership keen to provide the means. In Denmark, the blonde, blue-eyed male gymnasts of Niels Bukh, in his view, represented the achievable physical perfection of the Aryan peoples The bodies and the actions of the bodies of his gymnasts typified a desirable Aryan masculinity. It was a short step to an acceptance of the admired discipline, order and power of Nationalist Socialism.

Spain possessed a most idiosyncratic Fascist manifestation of masculinity. There was an idealized image of the Spanish Fascist Man but it was a curious composition – borrowed partially from the indigenous tradition of the warrior-monk – austere, disciplined and stoical, and partially from the Nazi invented tradition of the steel-muscled, Nietzschean-willed, invulnerable hero.

There were no ambiguities in the idealized masculinity of the British Union of Fascism. The ideal was the warrior. As in Spain, and elsewhere, there was a mixture of indigenous tradition and international fashion – a combination in this instance of British imperial militaristic and contemporary Nazi supremacist masculinity. Both the rhetoric about, and the imagery of the BUF 'warriors of the new age' owed something to both. In addition, British Fascism had similarities to Italian Fascism in its personification of the physical superman in its leader, Sir Oswald Mosley – yet while the BUF considered violence a proper political tool, preached the virtues of the male warrior and prepared its members for war, it opposed entry into the Second World War – Fascist should not fight Fascist.

Brazilian Fascism reveals a preoccupation with the aesthetic rather than militaristic. Fascism in Brazil was uniquely Brazilian – a mixture of modern European influences and local and cultural traditions. Nevertheless, the male physique was central to this Fascism, too. The various Fascist festivals were 'testimonials to the body's imperative in political life'. A preoccupation with sport was common to all Brazilian Fascist groups, but it was less an ideological preoccupation than an aesthetic enterprise reinforcing unity through the theatrical. Body and spectacle combined to fuse élite and mass into a totalitarian community.

Both Japanese and Chinese Fascism were less concerned with projecting the male body as an idealized muscular, metaphoric icon and more concerned with it as a practical military means of achieving supremacy over other nations. In one regard, however, there was conjunction between European and Asian Fascism – in the militarization of society and in an attempt to create a self-sacrificial warrior who achieved his supreme end in death in battle. Asian male bodies were prepared for this eventuality and sport was used as a basic, and obvious, means of establishing fitness for war.

The cult of leader, paramount in Japan, less so in China, was a marked feature of Asian Fascism but neither the Emperor nor the President personified masculine physical virtue to the extent that was typical of Mussolini and Mosley. In both nations the male body was less a metaphor for power, rather it was a self-abnegatory offering. To this end, it was exercised, militarized and sacrificed. The Asian warriors of Japan and China were not hieratic icons, they were military instruments. It was their sacrifice rather than their image that represented their 'superiority'.

In summary, *Superman Supreme* concentrates on the projected image and the political purpose of the male body in global Fascism – a *neglected* element of international Fascism. As others argue, and this volume demonstrates, globally Fascism meant various things to various people, and likewise it attracted them for a variety of purposes. In one thing, at least there was, however, remarkable congruence. Virtually everywhere, it was the male body that symbolized self-sacrifice. Virtually everywhere, it was expendable. Virtually everywhere, it was a dispensable icon. Virtually everywhere, it was superordinate because it was superior in purpose – the achievement of supremacy.

NOTES

1. See Stanley G. Payne, *A History of Fascism, 1914–45* (London, 1997), Introduction.
2. Ian Kershaw, *The Nazi Dictatorship: Problems and Perspectives of Interpretation* (London, 1993), p.30.
3. Ibid.
4. Ibid.
5. Ibid.
6. Ibid.
7. Roger Griffin, *The Nature of Fascism* (London, 1994), p.vi (hereafter *Nature of Fascism*).
8. Ibid.
9. Ibid.
10. Ibid.
11. Ibid.
12. Juan J. Linz, 'Some Notes Towards a Comparative Study of Fascism…', in Walter Laqueur, *Fascism: A Readers Guide* (London, 1976), pp.7–8.
13. Ibid., p.10.
14. Ibid., p.8.
15. Ibid., p.8
16. Ibid., p.12.
17. Ibid., p.13.
18. Linz, ibid., p.33.
19. Ibid., p.33
20. Ibid., p.33
21. Ibid., p.35.
22. Ibid.
23. Ibid., p.36.
24. Ibid.
25. Griffin, *Nature of Fascism*, p.12.
26. Ibid., p.13.
27. Ibid., p.2.
28. Ibid., p.5.
29. Ibid., p.4.
30. Ibid.
31. George L. Mosse, *The Crisis of German Ideology: Intellectual Origins of the Third Reich* (London, 1966), p.315.
32. Ibid., p.315.
33. In the Foreword to Shaping the Superman, p.xii, reference was made to this point by S.J. Woolf in his Introduction (p.6) to his edited volume, *The Nature of Fascism* (New York, 1979).
34. Kershaw, *The Nazi Dictatorship*, p.39.
35. Ibid., pp.36–7.
36. See the article 'The barbarous bands who roam and rule by machete' about present Sierra Leone, by Alec Riscell in *The Daily Telegraph*, 7 August 1999, p.4.
37. Michael Wilding, *Milton's Paradise Lost* (Sydney, 1969), p.24.
38. Ibid., p.25.
39. Griffin, *Nature of Fascism*, p.26.
40. Ibid., p.32.
41. Ibid., p.33.
42. Ibid., p.34.
43. Ibid.
44. Mosse, *Crisis of German Ideology*, p.312.
45. Ibid., p.316.
46. Ibid., p.313.
47. Griffin, *Nature of Fascism*, pp.32–3.
48. Ibid., p.35.
49. Ibid., p.199.

50. Ibid., p.198.
51. Ibid.
52. Ibid., p.198.
53. Quoted in ibid., p.198..
54. Ibid., p.200.
55. Ibid.
56. Gigliola Gori, this volume, ch.1, p.45.
57. Ibid., p.47.
58. Ibid., p.41.
59. Ibid., p.52.
60. Wolfgang Weber and Paula Black, this volume, ch.2, p.63.
61. Ibid., pp.70–1.
62. Ibid., p.79.
63. Vassil Girginov and Peter Bankov, this volume, ch.3, p.82.
64. Ibid., p.100.
65. Ibid.
66. Ibid.87.
67. Ibid.81.
68. Hans Bonde, this volume, ch.4, p.110.
69. Ibid., p.113.
70. Ibid., p.115.
71. Teresa Aja, this volume, ch.5, p.119.
72. Ibid., p.142.
73. Ibid., p.121.
74. Quoted in Aja, ch.5, p.122.
75. Ibid., p.123.
76. Ibid., p.126.
77. Ibid., p.129.
78. Ibid., p.131.
79. Ibid., p.138.
80. Ibid.
81. Tony Collins, this volume, ch.6, p.148.
82. Ibid., p.145.
83. Ibid.
84. Ibid., p.146.
85. Ibid., p.145.
86. Ibid.
87. Ibid., p.146.
88. Ibid., p.147.
89. Ibid.
90. Ibid.
91. Ibid., p.153.
92. Ibid., pp.159–60.
93. Lamartine Da Costa and Plino Labriola, this volume, ch.7, p.163.
94. Roberta Da Matta quoted in Da Costa and Labriola, ch.7, p.163.
95. Ibid., p.166.
96. Ibid., p.169.
97. Ibid., pp.167, 169.
98. Ibid., p.169.
99. Ibid.
100. Ibid.
101. Ibid., p.172.
102. Quoted in ibid., p.175.
103. Ibid., p.167.
104. Ibid., p.176.
105. Ibid., p.175.

106. Ibid., p.177.
107. Quoted in J.A. Mangan and Takeshi Komagome, this volume, ch.8, p.182.
108. Ibid., p.183.
109. Quoted in ibid., p.185.
110. Ibid., p.191.
111. Ibid., p.197.
112. Ibid., p.202.
113. Ibid., p.203.
114. Walter Laqueur, *Fascism: Past, Present, Future* (Oxford, 1996), p.14.
115. Fan Hong, this volume, ch.9, p.206.
116. Ibid., p.222.
117. Ibid., p.206.
118. Ibid., p.207.
119. Ibid., p..209.
120. Ibid., p.213.
121. Ibid., p.214.
122. Ibid., p.215.

1

Model of Masculinity: Mussolini, the 'New Italian' of the Fascist Era

GIGLIOLA GORI

Fascism as a political totalitarian movement of the right was born in Italy. It was founded in Milan on 23 March 1919 with the name Fasci Italiani di Combattimento, meaning Italian Fasces of Fighting, on the initiative of Benito Mussolini. The Fascist movement came to power after the so-called 'March to Rome' on 28 October 1923 and very soon under the dictatorial government of the Duce took complete control of society. In those years, the passion for nationalism on which the Fascist ideology was based found breeding sites everywhere in the world where the wounds of the Great War were still open. Developing side by side with the model of Italian Fascism was the much more incisive model of German National Socialism.

All the regimes and movements of the right were born between the two World Wars and therefore were somehow tributary at that time to Fascist Italy. Italian Fascism, therefore, constitutes an interesting point of departure for any type of comparative investigation. In fact, after the French Revolution, Italy effected the first experiment in the institutionalization of a secular religion in Europe which contained all the major ideas of Fascism.[1] This ranged from the nationalization of the masses, to the sacralization of the symbols. The hegemonic Fascist plan included the defence of the race, in which the shaping of the New Man had ample space. These ideas, as far as Italy was concerned, later coincided with the model of the Superman represented by Benito Mussolini with whom the Italians were made to identify, with greater or lesser success.

This essay opens with a brief consideration of the predominant ideologies in Italy at the beginning of the century. These came together in the Fascist revolution. Once power had been obtained Italian Fascism built a mighty vertical organization which was structured hierarchically by the National Fascist Party. Its ideology was based on a civic religion which soon became a political religion, whereby belief in myths, rites and symbols was joined to faith in the Duce – the Man of Destiny – who was entrusted with the task of governing. People were asked to 'Believe, Obey, Fight' in the name of that faith. The intention was to mobilize the masses according to the requirements of the regime. The object was the capillary diffusion of the Fascist ideology with the aim of obtaining popular consent for every political choice of the regime. As a matter of fact, the pursuit of consent was discontinued in the course of time. It reached its apex in 1936 as a consequence of the victorious war in Ethiopia, when the myth of imperial Italy became a reality. However, it then declined because of the excessive intrusiveness of the regime crystallized in self-adulation. The death blow to the pursuit of consent came from the choices made in foreign policy: the military failure of the war in Spain; the bond with a dangerous Germany; the racial laws imposed on a fundamentally non-racist people; the participation in the wars of Hitler.[2]

This essay is concerned with the educational scheme to fascisticize, that is to transform the Italian people – traditionally individualist and lazy – into an élite race of Supermen. They had to be mindful of the glorious past of the Roman Empire and be ready to imitate its greatness, in order to found a New Civilization – destined to last forever. The scheme involved school, work, free time, culture and the arts. Its aim was to shape the character of the citizens in order to give birth to the New Italian: a virile, dynamic, bellicose man. The scheme was a source of inspiration for Hitler, who, in attempts to reorganize the German people, was inspired more than once by the Italian model and its Duce as a guide.

As a conclusion to the essay it will be interesting, therefore, briefly to compare the two realities of Italy and Germany. These bear witness not only to the cultural affinities, but also to the cultural differences of the two nations which underwent the totalitarian experiences of Fascism.

THE ADVENT OF FASCISM: IDEOLOGICAL ORIGINS

In addition to the phenomenon of Fascism, the term *fascismo* has its roots in Italian culture. It comes from the Latin *fascis* (a bundle), a symbol linked to the cult of 'sacred fire'.[3] Before the constitution of the

Italian Fascis of Combat in 1919, the symbol of the *fascis* had already been used by the interventionist movement of the Fasces of Revolutionary Action, promoted by Mussolini in 1915 after his split with the socialist party.[4] It was also used by the Futurist movement gathered into the Futurist Fasces. However, the fate of that symbol remained indissolubly linked with Mussolini and the Fascist movement which became The National Fascist Party (PNF) in 1921, continuing until the fall of the regime in 1943.[5] Within the Italian Fascis of Combat discontented veterans and irredentists joined with Futurist intellectuals and D'Annunzio's followers.[6] These came from different social backgrounds, united through the comradeship born during the war, by a burning nationalistic spirit and by the desire for radical change in society. They were exponents of 'Fascist truth' and, firmly directed by their charismatic leader Mussolini, were ready to plunge into a revolutionary adventure and equally determined to impose their creed on others. The achievement of power in 1922 was a *coup d'état* which neither the Government nor the King could oppose; at the time it was considered a temporary and necessary action to re-establish order in a nation deeply in crisis. Instead it was the first step toward the foundation of a dictatorial regime which lasted 20 years.

The success of the Fascists, who considered themselves defenders of their country and regenerators of moral values, is mainly attributed to the strong repetition of the theme 'sacrality of the fatherland' on which the civic and moral unity of the Italians was built. This was an ideology widespread in Italy with origins in the nineteenth century. In 1861, after Italian unity had been established, the problem of how to regenerate the Italians morally became of utmost importance. The Italians had lost their national identity for at least 14 centuries since the fall of the Roman Empire. The cult of the State as the supreme corporate body was now paramount. It found in Mazzini the most authoritative ideologist and, in the liberal executive class, a convinced advocate.[7]

In the first two decades of government the liberals, who rejected the revolutionary and republican aspects of Mazzini's creed, had endeavoured to win over the people to the cult of the State through school and military education[8] emphasizing the monarchic institution, fatherland memories and the heroism of the fallen. But the process of nationalization of the masses by means of the exaltation of the cult of the State, by now diffused to a large area of Europe, bore little fruit in Italy. In fact, it was a sterile seed, producing an atavistic distrust of the aristocratic managing class. The people rarely became involved in patriotic demonstrations for fear of not being able to control their strength. Moreover there was opposition from the Church of Rome, already deprived of temporal power as a consequence of the seizure of Rome in 1870. It opposed the new civic religion by all and any means. Rome's purpose was to maintain its spiritual supremacy among the Italians.[9]

At the beginning of the twentieth century, the theme of civic religion and moral regeneration of the citizens was no longer a primary concern of the government, and remained solely a matter of study and debate between intellectuals. As for the Church, it had to face the new danger of a socialist ideology, both atheistic and materialist, as exemplified by the nationalistic pagan movement led by the politician Corradini who drew his inspiration from Japan.[10] When Fascism, openly anti-Bolshevik, gained power even the Church of Rome did not oppose it, considering Mussolini's anticlericalism after all less dangerous than Marxist ideology.

The end of the First World War in which victorious Italy had sacrificed so many lives unfortunately left the matter of Fiume and Dalmazia unresolved. Both the claim on those territories together with a 'state of collective euphoria' – caused by the participation in the Great War – gave new impulse to the theme of a civic religion. This was celebrated by means of a cult of martyrdom and heroes, and revolutionary nationalism. These themes found authoritative support among intellectuals of the time, among whom Marinetti – the founder of Futurism – and D'Annunzio should be remembered.

The Futurist movement, founded in 1909 by Filippo Tommaso Marinetti, promoted values such as instinct, strength, courage, sport, war, youth, and dynamism and speed as exemplified by modern machines. In his *Fondazione e Manifesto del Futurismo* (Foundation and Manifesto of Futurism) he affirmed: 'Literature up until now has exalted thoughtful immobility, ecstasy and sleep. We want to exalt aggressive movement, feverish insomnia, running, jumping, slap and fist.'[11] Initially, Futurism was a total ideology, which incorporated art, custom, morality and politics in a revolutionary and nonconformist vision of life. It supported the Fascist movement but after 1920 Futurism became detached from it because of its disagreements with the right-wing shift of Fascism. Subsequently, Futurism abandoned any political totalitarian intention and survived as a literary and artistic school, finding followers and supporters throughout Europe. It bequeathed some values to Fascism, such as the cult of aggression, virility, youth, speed and sport, and an innovative use of language in political propaganda. Other values, such as revolutionary individualism, were rejected by the new Fascist order. Despite the declared friendship between Mussolini and Marinetti, the only Futurist intellectual who occupied and maintained a position of importance in the Fascist government was, in fact, Giuseppe Bottai.

D'Annunzio's movement was a way to understand and behave in life according to the model offered by Gabriele D'Annunzio – poet, man of letters, commander and aesthete of great charm. D'Annunzio, having placed his refined art at the service of the religious myth of the Fatherland, became its high priest – the *Vate*. He extolled the past greatness of ancient Rome, by that time forgotten, and brought new life to the political–religious ideologies of the preceding centuries. Through the adventure of Fiume in 1919, D'Annunzio realized an admirable fusion between oratorical art, patriotic mysticism and politic activism.[12] Together with his men, called legionaries in remembrance of Rome, the Vate founded a government in Fiume – the Regency of Carnaro.[13] Among his political actions have to be remembered the foundation of a Utopian League of Fiume, that pressed all the oppressed to revolt.[14]

The brief experience at Fiume, although ending with a painful abandonment of the city, notably increased the myth of D'Annunzio as the successful Superman in every enterprise and therefore capable of founding the New Italy. Mussolini, who had supported that occupation without directly participating in it, was considered a traitor because he had not taken part in the defence of the Regency of Carnaro. The Fiume enterprise, in effect, constituted the first part of a wider revolutionary plan agreed by Mussolini, which ended with the 'March to Rome' – an idea of D'Annunzio's – and culminated in the conquest of Italy.

In 1924, once in government, Fascism, stained by the assassination of the opposition deputy Giacomo Matteotti, left Italy deeply shaken and was itself in grave danger. The scorn of many settled on the figure of D'Annunzio who, with his charisma, had seemed to be the only one able to push the Italians towards the realization of the New Italy. The poet decided to retire to his residence at Vittoriale, Lake Garda. There, he withdrew into himself and became the disenchanted observer of subsequent Italian events.[15] The Duce wanted to maintain a friendly relationship with D'Annunzio, but it was always tinged with jealousy.

Mussolini felt both admiration for the man of letters and a hostility towards the man himself. This passionate ambiguity, oscillating between hate and love, lasted until the death of the poet.

In summary, the ideologies present in the first 20 years of the twentieth century, having been interwoven with revolutionary appeals, nationalistic claims, juvenile dynamism and political mysticism, favoured the Fascist movement which appropriated them. Despite the numerous 'punitive expeditions' and the associated violence committed by members of Fascist squads, Mussolini came to power without bloodshed with the 'March to Rome'. In fact, the climate of uncertainty and disorder in Italy – almost on the brink of civil war – suggested to most people a prudent acquiescence in respect of the *coup d'état*. This had been anticipated by Mussolini who had been assured of the connivance, or at least the neutrality, of the powerful. He had arranged, in reality, a 'revolution on the telephone', as Italo Balbo irritably remarked when he realized that the 'March to Rome' had been little more than a parade.[16]

THE MYTH OF THE SUPERMAN IN ITALY

During the years of the Fascist regime, the Italians suffered, almost totally, the personal charm of Mussolini, fed by unrelenting propaganda directed by himself. A man of the people and therefore able to understand the people's demands, the Duce created a myth of himself, adapting the image of the Superman of Nietzsche to the Italian *forma mentis*. After having eliminated the laws that separate good from evil, with the death of the Ethic Good, according to Nietzsche, common men had the possibility of becoming gods themselves, thus freeing their own omniscient and almighty Superman with the tools of will and intelligence. That credo was the base of the totalitarian European systems of the twentieth century as forms of absolute hegemony over life and death and good and evil.[17]

At the beginning of the century the code of the Superman was embraced in Italy – the Superman was not to allow himself to be suffocated by accepted ethics, but was to overcome them in order to give life to the New Man and to the New Italy. In 1915 the nationalistic writer Giovanni Papini, influenced by Nietzsche, had written his *Maschilita* (Manliness) in which the New Man was required to be brutal and barbarous, and abandon his romanticism.[18] That mythical master of life,

Gabriele D'Annunzio, exemplified the aspiration to Supermanism, which he pursued assiduously following a life far different from the usual pattern, indeed going 'beyond good and evil'.

Benito Mussolini himself, at this time, a young journalist and modest man of literature, also aimed at becoming a Superman. In 1908, in one of his short essays on the *Philosophy of Strength*, he underlined how Nietzsche had advocated an imminent return to the ideal, stating that 'a new kind of "free spirit" will come, strengthened by the war ... spirits equipped with a kind of sublime perversity ... new, free spirits, who will triumph over God and over Nothing!'[19]

Of the intellectual movements, Futurism most absorbed the mysticism of the Superman, accepting as Marinetti did in his romance *Mafarka le futuriste*, certain *leitmotiv* of Nietzsche such as the Will, the Superman and the Flight. The New Man, even if he could make his choices freely, was not, for the Futurists, an isolated individual. On the contrary he was 'the expression of an élite of Supermen by their own choice gathered together, united by the same attitude toward life, by discipline and by the aspiration to be the guide of the nation'.[20]

The New Futurist Man – disdainful of death and books, in love with virility, violence, and war[21] – found followers among European youth who had grown up in the shadow of sacrificial Great War myths. As for Italy, Marinetti, in his excited vision of the Italian spirit, presented the Italians as a people particularly endowed with 'creative genius, elasticity in improvisation, strength, ability and physical resistance, impetus, violence, fury in the fight'.[22] According to him, these qualities made the Italian man the noblest of all. That Utopian and racist vision was repeatedly used by Mussolini, to incite those of glorious 'Italian descent' to become protagonists in the large enterprises of the regime.

MUSSOLINI AND THE MYTH OF THE NEW ITALIAN

The Futurist international ideal of manhood was transformed by Fascism into the ideal of the New Italian, a purely national model that best suited the Fascist socialization of the Italian people, with special attention given to their uniformity.[23] Such an ideal was admirably personified by the pre-eminent New Italian – the Duce. With incessant propaganda, using all and any possible means, Mussolini, a great communicator and an expert in mass psychology, created and propagated his myth, superimposing it on the myth of Fascism so completely that, during the following years, Fascism became more and more Mussolinism.[24]

With the anti-Fascists eliminated or confined, the first aim of the Duce was to achieve the sacralization of his political ideology. It was a central purpose with which the whole population had to be associated without reservation of any kind. From 1923 to 1932 the political religion of Fascism constructed a calendar of new public holidays. These celebrated old national myths – the Nation, the Monarchy, the Great War and the Fallen Soldiers, and the new national myths – the March to Rome, the Foundation of the Fascist Movement, and the Birth of Ancient Rome.[25] To the pre-existing national symbols the new 'religion' added its own: the Littorian Fasces, the Black Shirt, the Pennants, the Skull and Crossbones, the Cudgel, the Club, the Dagger, the Roman Salute, the Hymn *Giovinezza* and the New Calendar of the Fascist era. Manipulating history in its favour, Fascism attributed to itself the greatest credit for most of the celebrated events, and steadily eliminated those in opposition to its politics and mythologies.[26] In the last decade of the Fascist government, when the political sacralization of the regime was complete, Fascism dilated its myths, particularly emphasizing those of 'Italic descent' as heirs of the Roman spirit, and founders of the empire. Meanwhile, the juvenile thrusts which had supported the advent and the affirmation of Fascism suffered a process of sclerosis and of tedious repetitive self-representation.[27] The ceremonies, parades, sports events, the Duce's speeches to vast delirious crowds, imitated more and more the coeval ones in Hitler's Germany.

Like any other religion, the Fascist religion needed its own icon. This was Benito Mussolini, whose fame was already well consolidated before the advent of the regime. Of modest origins, Mussolini, although with a limited education and a difficult youth due to his rebellious and nonconformist character, was endowed with great intuition and ambition. The determination that he put into each and every effort gave him popularity and followers from the beginning of his political career. As a child of the people he initially joined the socialist party but later broke away from it, refusing to agree with, or share, its neutralism. From 1914 as director and founder of the daily paper *Il Popolo d'Italia*, he promoted Italian participation in the First World War in which he fought with honour. After that war he used the newspaper as the voice of the Fascist movement. His personal charisma and the strength of his ideas were widely diffused by *Il Popolo d'Italia* and he set himself at

FIGURE 1.1

BENITO MUSSOLINI, ORATOR

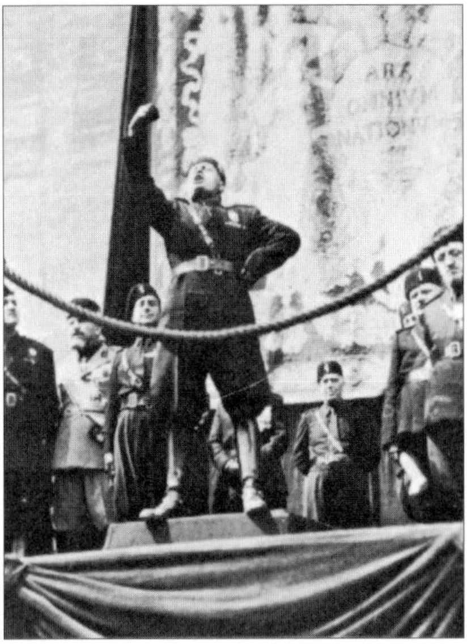

FIGURE 1.2

MUSSOLINI ON THE SKI SLOPE

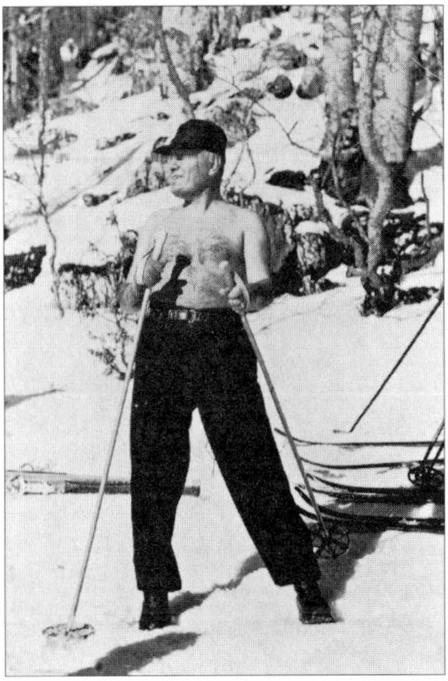

FIGURE 1.3

YOUNG MUSSOLINI'S ATHLETIC BODY

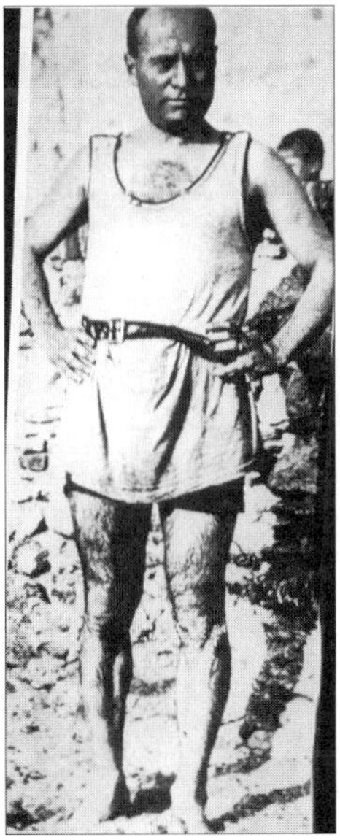

FIGURE 1.4

MUSSOLINI SHOWS OFF HIS MYTHIC TORSO, RICCIONE

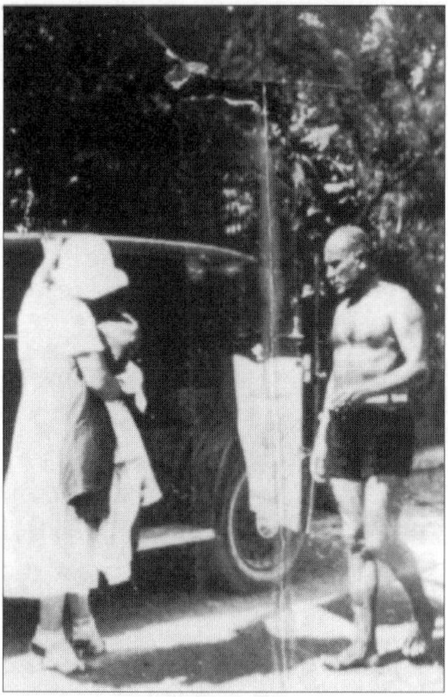

FIGURE 1.5

MUSSOLINI ON HIS WHITE HORSE

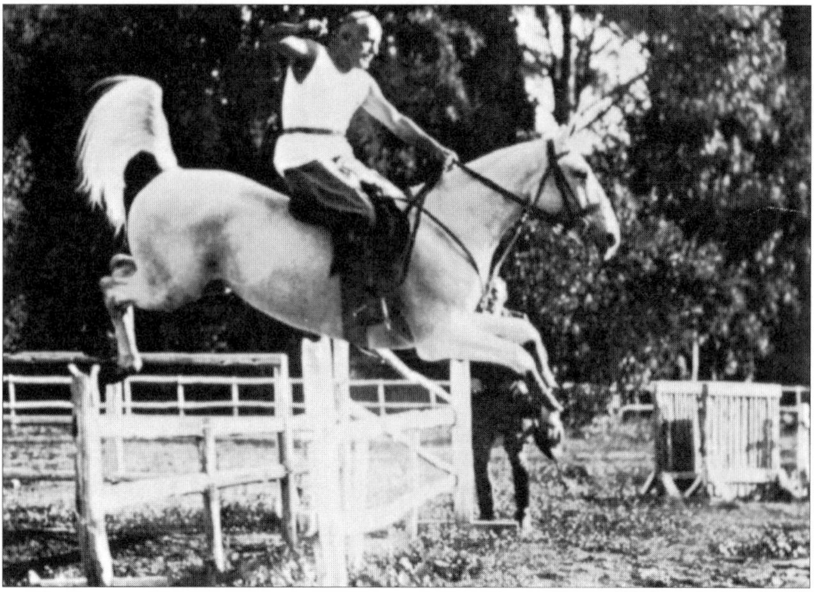

the head of the Fascist movement which with the support of the economic power of the middle classes conquered the *piazzas* and achieved power.

The myth of Mussolini the Statist, whose power he was fully aware of, saved Fascism from the crisis in 1924, which was the consequence of Matteotti's murder. Mussolini's myth also allowed him to charge himself with the moral responsibility for that murder. From 1926, after abolishing all civil liberties and centralizing all power, the Duce devoted equal care to the consolidation of the regime. This had to coexist with the realities of the Monarchy and of the Papacy. He represented himself as the perfect prototype of the New Italian, being 'the living and working model of ethical and political individuality' to which the Italians had to aspire.[28] His youth, political unscrupulousness, dynamism in action and publicized passion for speed, movement and sport were values which had been already exploited by Futurism. These differentiated him totally from the rulers who had preceded him and presented him as a modern and efficient head of state able to achieve peace, order and progress in Italy.

He lived in a time which had discovered the superiority of the photographic, broadcasting and cinematographic media over the written word, due to the simplicity with which these media mechanisms were able to reach the masses. Therefore cinema, photography and radio were mobilized to exalt the omnipresent *deus ex machina* – the Duce – the Envoy of Destiny. The extraordinary qualities of the Duce were visually dramatized in perfect Fascist style, by means of the theatrical gesture which was crude but effective. Hands on hips, legs wide apart, jaw contracted, eyes rolling, the orator Mussolini spoke to the crowd in a deep, stentorian voice. His audience, when prompted, had to answer the Duce, shouting their own assent in unison.[29] This frequent display was usually recorded on film and camera. Both portrayed the Duce from below in order to lengthen his rather stumpy figure. This powerful, elongated image was publicized all over Italy by means of newsreels and photographic services. In addition, in the 1930s notable contributions to the growth of the myth of Mussolini were provided by both the school of Mistica Fascista (Fascist Mystichystic) which focused on the cult of the Duce[30] and by the innumerable hagiographic biographies published in those years.[31] They emphasized Mussolini the self-made man. His virtues were endlessly trumpeted – heroism in war, compassion for the humble, sobriety of living, tireless effort at work and athletic dynamism.

He was even celebrated indirectly by the 'sanctification' of his father and mother. Censorship prevented the diffusion of any news which somehow might darken the bright image of the Duce. The press daily received news sheets delivered by the Duce's press office. These sheets of dispositions, the so-called *veline*, stated in precise detail what was to be published and with what emphasis. Interference with the perfect image of the New Italian Mussolini was proscribed. It was forbidden, for instance, to associate him with the negativity of illness or death. Witness the *velina* which instructed: 'Do not say that the accident to Agnelli's child occurred at the Mussolini jetty, but say that it occurred in the sea of Genoa.'[32]

In the 1930s the cult of the Duce resulted in Mussolinism, which was almost the total identification of Fascism with Mussolini. He was isolated like a god on his Olympus, and he became the one and only in command because he distrusted everyone and everything. He managed to adhere completely to the granite self-image he had constructed for himself. This phenomenon was fatal to him because it petrified the ideology that he embodied in his person but it was also fatal to the development of the Italians' civic conscience. The Italians, already accustomed to obsequiousness and delegation because of their historical past, put their destinies in the hands of a *deus ex machina*.

The propaganda induced the Italians, spellbound by the myth of the Duce, to believe that Mussolini – with the strength of his ideas, the force of his actions, the power of his 'ever young' body – would ransom them from the past and drive them on to a glorious future. The price to be paid seemed quite reasonable: the transformation urgently required to give birth to the New Italian.

THE SHAPE OF THE NEW ITALIAN

The New Italian of the New Italy was the intended outcome of his conversion to the new religion of the State. The regime devoted its maximum effort to the Italian's fascisticization, in order to mould character and develop habits according to the Fascist style, by an aesthetic fashion made incarnate by Mussolini. Unlike the liberal rulers that preceded him he neither feared the masses nor opposed them but he was convinced that they could not govern themselves. A strong leader and a strong regime were necessary. In order to convert the mass of Italians to the 'Italic descent', it was necessary to educate the masses in the new aesthetics, through both abstract symbols and the living symbol of the Duce acting on the irrationality of popular feeling.

Fascist aesthetics were now celebrated in mass liturgies. The cult of the physical beauty of the body had a remarkable impact because it was a myth which the middle class had already appreciated well before Mussolini. The same class had been fascinated by D'Annunzio's sophisticated aesthetic model but more so by the paradigm of classical beauty. In Europe from the eighteenth century onwards the idea of a well-structured mind having to correspond with a well-structured body was accepted. A beautiful body brought about conciliation between aspiration to order and aspiration to progress. This was to be achieved through the sculptural harmony of its form modelled according to the aesthetic canons of classical statuary.[33]

Fascism appropriated the cult of classical masculine beauty because this cult was functional for the Fascist plan to make Italians virile, by means of special attention being given to physical robustness and to eugenics. The virility of male bodies was, in fact, essential to reconstruct in a modern context the ancient and warlike 'Italian descent' as the National, then European and finally International model. The beauty of the Fascist as an eternally young and powerful male was contrasted with the ugliness of the non-Fascist male typified by the flabby, aged liberal bourgeois: the Jewish profiteer with his prominent nose, the Negro from Abyssinia with his too prominent features. They were the enemies to be demonized.[34] The New Italian was encouraged to assume the Fascist style, which included support for canons of male beauty advocated by the regime. He had to personify 'mens sana in corpore sano', on behalf of the Roman spirit and in the service of the cause.

After having installed a colossal hierarchical organization, the regime instilled it into its citizens from birth, because the youngest bodies and minds would accept the new creed with the innocence of their years. In that way the faithful perpetuation of the ideology was assured. Among the institutions for early childhood the foundation of the Opera Nazionale Maternita ed Infanzia (ONMI) in 1925 should be especially remembered. In it the sanitary, hygienic and preventive medical assistance for mothers and children up to three years old was of primary importance in defence of the physical and moral improvement of the race.[35] It was written: 'Everyone agrees that the Fascist education of youth into masculinity is one of the most urgent and fundamental aims of the Regime.'[36] The regime intimately insinuated itself into the Italian social fabric, endeavouring to fascisticize the world of school, work and free time. It promoted the education of the young with particular attention, because it considered the school an essential tool for both education in the Fascist creed and for pre-military training.[37] Pupils were enlisted in the Opera Nazionale Balilla (ONB), founded in 1926, to support the school in ensuring the physical and moral development of the young. Males and females from 8 to 14 years, in compulsory uniform, were organized in groups with names evoking the Roman spirit, the country and war. According to their age and sex, they were called Figli della Lupa, Balilla, Avanguardisti, Piccole Italiane, Giovani Italiane. One of the most famous slogans of the ONB was 'book and musket, Balilla perfect', in order to stress the military character of the organization.

From 1923 onwards anyone who did not continue their studies was enlisted in the Milizia Volontaria per la Sicurezza Nazionale (MVSN) and from 1930 in the Fasci Giovanili di Combattimento (FGC). These were organizations set up purely and simply to develop military character in preparation for conscription. In the universities the Gruppi Universitari Fascisti (GUF) performed the same task. After 1927 all were the direct dependencies of the Party (PNF). Sports training was combined with pre-military training. Adults were invited to enrol in the PNF and had to wear the black shirt at least to the assemblies on the 'Fascist Saturday'. At the end of 1942 the maximum expansion of the PNF was recorded. Its organizations had in total 27,376,571 affiliates from a population of about 46 million.[38]

After 1925 the free time of both intellectual and manual workers was organized by Opera Nazionale Dopolavoro (OND) – a colossal and unique organization – without apparent political pressure. In 1935 the OND owned 771 cinemas, 1,227 theatres, 2,066 companies of amateur actors, 2,130 orchestras, 3,787 bands, 10,302 professional and cultural associations, 6,427 libraries, and 994 choral schools.[39] Among the many activities proposed by the OND sport and games had ample support.[40] By 1935 no fewer than 11,159 non-competitive sport sections and 4,704 competitive sport sections existed.

In the 1930s, the expansionist aims of the Duce accelerated and therefore the aim of the regime had to be redefined. The construction of a militarized nation was combined with the model of the armed, strong and aggressive nation. Moreover, in each of the above institutions the military character of the indoctrination and of the collective physical training was accentuated in view of anticipated future wars. After the founding of the Empire in 1936 – as a consequence of the victorious war in Ethiopia – almost all of these institutions were integrated a year later into the Gioventú Italiana del Littorio (GIL).

The institutions described above publicized themselves and therefore the Fascist creed, by means of spectacular assemblies. To the usual ceremony with its rites and symbols were added demonstrations of gymnastics, athletics and sports in the name of activism and of physical power. Among those remembered are the Littoriali, Agonali, Ludi Juveniles, Campi Dux and OND contests where, in the presence of the Duce and other leaders, crowds of spectators followed the achievements of the athletes in uniform. These athletes embodied the uniformity and order of Fascist aesthetics in the geometric perfection of their choreographic executions.

As for the gymnastics training for conscripted soldiers, it had already been in existence since 1921 in the Central Military School of Physical Education equipped with ultramodern facilities in Rome. Physical activities for the soldiers, a rich and varied programme, had to be performed with a naked torso – the use of a woollen sweater was permitted in winter. These activities were performed at least once a day for approximately 90 minutes. Moreover, regimental collective competitions were regularly organized in order to verify the standard of performance reached. As the years went by the programme of training was intensified. After 1934 retired and non-commissioned officers were obliged to undergo post-military training every Sunday for ten years. Finally in 1936 conscription of all citizens aged from 18 to 55 was ordered. Fascism, as has been said already, absorbed and redefined existing cultural trends. It fully accepted the central position of sport in the training and militarization of the masses and in particular, was inspired by Futurism which supported the pre-eminence of gymnastics over books.[41] Marinetti wrote: 'Male children must, according to us, be trained far differently from female children, because their early games are clearly masculine ones – that is without affective morbidity, womanish sensibility – but lively, bellicose, muscular and violently dynamic.'[42] The Futurist state, consequently, had to occupy itself with physical, moral, intellectual and patriotic education, including daily gymnastics in schools and with the creation of many physical education institutes.[43] The publicity that Futurism wanted to give to sport is demonstrated in the script of a film entitled *Vita Futurista*, where scenes of 'morning gymnastics, fencing, boxing, Futurist assault with the sword between Marinetti and Remo Chiti and discussion by means of boxing-gloves between Marinetti and Ungari' were shown.[44]

From the beginning the regime considered exercise and sport protected and privileged, incorporating as they did aggression, violence and that 'state of collective effervescence', which Italian men inherited from the Great War, and which was essential for the formation of the disciplined, efficient New Italian man. During the Fascist years Italy was equipped with numerous stadiums,[45] gyms, sports fields[46] and academies to train the future teachers of physical education.[47] The intention was to change Italy quickly into a sporting nation, which would arouse the admiration of other peoples. As a matter of fact, the results were remarkable. In 1935 there was a total of 5,198 installations, among them gyms, sports and games fields, compared with 502 in 1928. Furthermore, in 1935 pupils practising physical education in schools totalled 470,000 against 180,000 in 1928.[48]

The sports sector was carefully controlled by either eliminating left-wing sports associations or strongly limiting the field of action of Catholic associations,[49] and in 1926 by entrusting the direction of the National Italian Olympic Committee (CONI) to men of sure political faith.[50] Moreover, in December 1928, the Carta dello Sport was issued which officially asserted the importance of physical education and sports. Both had to be practised within the organizations of the regime such as the ONB, MVSN, OND and GUF. Through Carta dello Sport total control over the varied sport federations was entrusted to the CONI, transforming it from an organ of the International Olympic Committee (CIO) to the only one responsible for Italian sport.[51] The results were flattering. At international level it is sufficient to remember that second position was attained at the Olympic Games in Los Angeles in 1932, and third place at the Olympic Games in Berlin in 1936.[52] Competition in the Rimet Cup in 1934 and 1938 also proved successful and there were victories for Italian boxers, cyclists, aviators and motorists.[53]

In the 1930s the regime, in addition to ensuring the militarization of the masses, devoted itself to successfully 'manufacturing champions' selecting the most promising athletes to train as sports professionals. The Fascist athletes were stimulated by economic rewards by way of honours and prizes and motivated by the propaganda which deified them as super heroes.[54] Known in the United States as 'Mussolini's boys', besides exporting a nationalism steadily augmented by their victories they projected the image of a strong, virile and dynamic nation, able to compete successfully against the great powers. In one of his famous speeches to Italian athletes Mussolini ordered: 'You must be tenacious, chivalrous, daring, remember that when you fight outside the borders in that very moment the honour and the sporting prestige of the nation are entrusted to your muscles and above all to your spirit.'[55]

The sports displays created cohesion and consent by attracting huge masses of spectators and flourished prodigiously. The press provided news of 30,000 sporting displays and 40,000,000 spectators in 1936.[56] There was very probably exaggeration in these statistics, but the numbers are a clear indicative of a phenomenon, participation in sport by the public and an enthusiastic, forthcoming and positive response to encouragement by the regime.

THE ATHLETIC BODY OF THE DUCE

The exaltation of the virile body as a metaphor for Fascism was common to all fascisms, but its manifestation in the body of the Duce himself was a peculiar Italian phenomenon. Mussolini came to symbolize virility, not only for the virile strength of his ideas and the bravery attributed with reason to him, but also for the power of his muscles and the talent which, it was recounted, allowed him to practise every kind of sport with success.[57]

Above all, the Duce loved machines and therefore motor racing and aeronautics. He was surely influenced by the ideas of the Futurist, Marinetti, whose art – according to the harsh judgement of the anti-Fascist Gobetti – was only 'the art of a travelling salesman of sporting objects'.[58] During the years of his government, Mussolini showed himself to the world as an outstanding athlete, demonstrated by his horsemanship, fencing, swimming, gymnastics, tennis, skiing and boxing.[59] He had himself photographed while running with soldiers, skiing down the pistes of Terminillo, swimming in the sea, harvesting grapes and reaping the corn with the farmers, and revealing his naked torso without embarrassment. 'Sporting' agricultural exhibitions, in particular, aroused the admiration of the people since, in a poor country with a rural economy such as Italy, they represented the Duce both as the common man of the people, and the aristocratic Superman of Nietzsche.

FIGURE 1.6
MUSSOLINI, PILOT

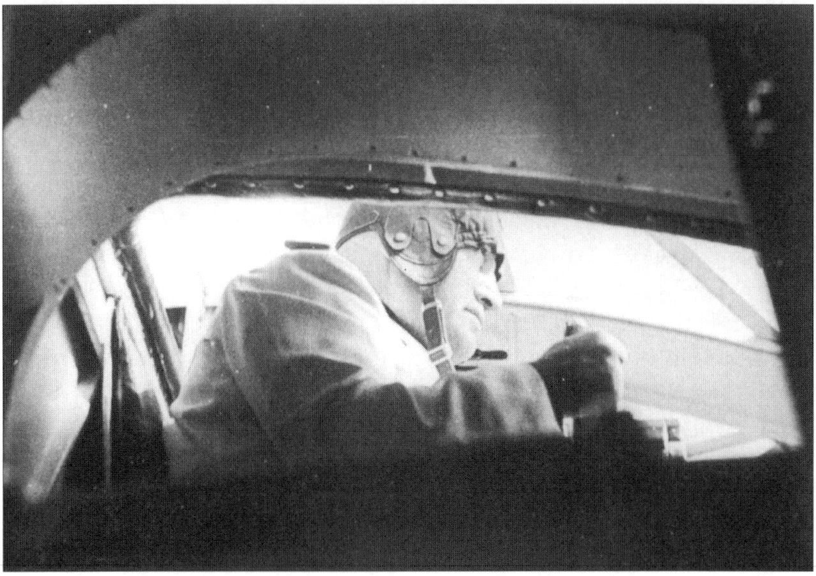

FIGURE 1.7
MUSSOLINI RUNNING WITH OFFICERS OF HIGH RANK

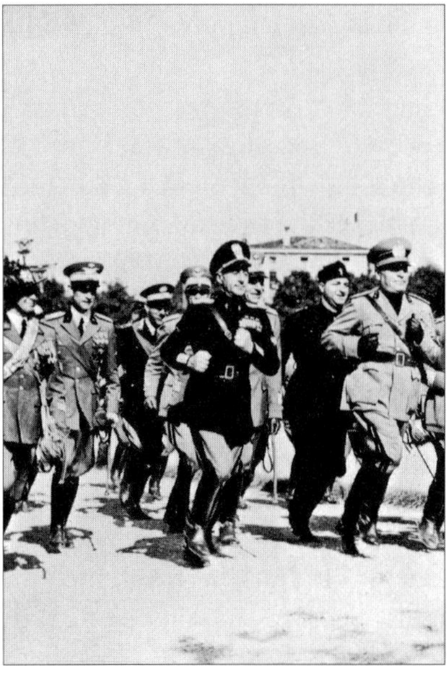

FIGURE 1.8
MUSSOLINI WALKING ON THE BEACH

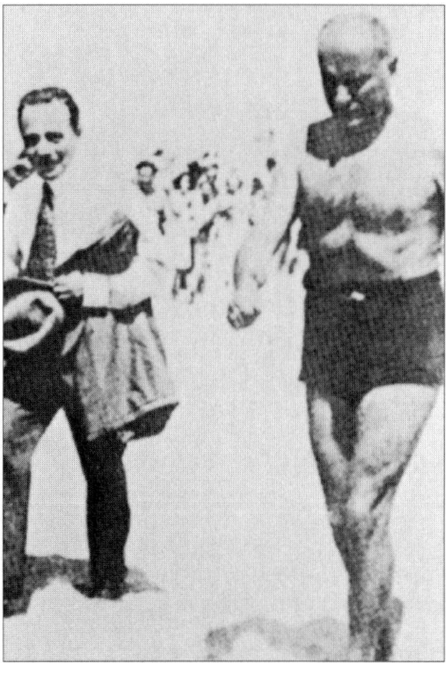

Flattering words were often applied to the athletic abilities of Mussolini but there was also some astonishment because he was not a natural sportsman.[60] As a young man, he had fenced – a practice which was widespread in Italy on account of political duels – and had been a passionate spectator at boxing matches, but with regard to other sports he was still a man of the nineteenth century, far from the model of Marinetti.[61] Nevertheless, a sickly person for most of his life, Mussolini considered physical education important for health and in sport he saw 'an effective means of inculcating discipline and team spirit into a society he considered too anarchic and individualistic'.[62] Furthermore, he sensed the importance of sport for modern societies, and being fundamentally an exhibitionist, he wanted his image to be that of the modern sporting man *par excellence*, projecting the image relentlessly at home and abroad. At his residence, Villa Torlonia, he invited the foreign press to watch his horse-riding, fencing and tennis matches – against very complaisant teachers![63] He also had his presence on beaches, on the snow and in the sky, portrayed in photos and filmed on newsreels, in order to be seen as active, virile, healthy. The Duce was not beautiful. He was short with a big bald head, a pockmarked face and a prominent jaw. However, he embodied the ideal model of virile beauty in the eyes of most Italians who, spellbound by his magnetic charm, wanted to imitate both his physical appearance and his behaviour. This was particularly evident among the leaders of the regime, among whom Achille Starace must be mentioned. He was the disliked caricature of Mussolini. Loyal defender of the Fascist style, involved in every kind of sporting activity, in 1938 Starace forced his already aged colleagues to perform physical activities difficult even for young men. In a notorious Sheet of Disposition in 1938 he in fact ordered that, on the occasion of a meeting in Rome the members of the National Directory and the Federal Secretaries must dive from a springboard, ride and swim 50 metres.[64] In short, the Duce, symbol of Fascist virility, became the source of inspiration and his athletic body was celebrated in literature, in the figurative arts and on film.[65]

VIRILITY AND FASCIST CULTURE

During its first years of life, Mussolini's ideology had been the object of cultural debate, so much so that in 1925 the intellectuals openly took sides, signing two documents – the *Announcement of the Fascist*

Intellectuals, compiled by the philosopher Giovanni Gentile[66] and the *Announcement of the Anti-Fascist Intellectuals*, compiled by the philosopher Benedetto Croce.[67] However, once its most dangerous opponents had been eliminated while maintaining a careful political control over the others, Fascism did not intervene in high culture. Optimistically Mussolini considered the past a point of departure for a glorious future. He was also eclectic and open to novelty as he had no pronounced aesthetic tastes.[68] Therefore the high culture of those 20 years, while not a particularly vital one, was not at the service of Fascist ideology.[69] Nevertheless, newspapers and magazines, as well as lowbrow popular romances and biographies, were rigorously controlled by the regime because they were broadly diffused throughout society.

Many intellectuals who supported Fascism with more or less enthusiasm, celebrated the appeal of Mussolini's personality. The playwright Luigi Pirandello, Nobel Prize winner in 1934, used to say of him: 'He, as you see, makes Italy and makes the world, he makes everyone of us as he wants; he creates us from time to time according to his whim.'[70]

The writer Curzio Malaparte composed a poem for the Duce which sketched an effective portrait of him. Here are a few lines:

O Mussolini facciadura	Oh Mussolini hard face
quando cominci a far buriana?	When do you begin to create turmoil?
Il sole sorge ed il gallo canta	The sun rises and the rooster sings
Mussolini é saltato a cavallo	Mussolini has mounted his horse.[71]

The aggressive physicality of the Duce, metaphor for his political aggressiveness, inspired Marinetti to draw this portrait of Mussolini in 1929:

> Physically he is built in the Italian way, outlined by inspired and brutal hands, forged, engraved according to the model of the craggy rock of our peninsula. Smashing, squared jaw, prominent disdainful lips spit boldness and aggressiveness on everything which is slow, pedantic, meticulous.[72]

Even the journalist Indro Montanelli, although critical of Fascist ideology in his youth, wrote an article entitled 'Mussolini e noi', which expressed well the feeling of the average Italian towards the Duce. Here is an extract:

> When Mussolini looks at you cannot be but naked in front of him. But he also is naked in front of us. There are some people who, to

> be considered somebody, need to apply for a uniform or badge; not Mussolini. His bronzed face and torso rebel against draperies and harnesses. Anxious and impatient, we snatch them from his back, contemplating only the inimitable existentialism of the man whose shaking, vibrating and beating are formidably human. The rest is not important.[73]

All the arts appropriated the physique of Mussolini – that muscular torso of bronze. The athletic body of the Duce was already well used in the 1920s but at the start of the 1930s, it received exceptional attention because it was at the centre of the propaganda spreading Fascist style among the Italians.[74]

Mussolini was depicted in books and posters, on medals and postage stamps, in the showrooms of dilettante artists and on souvenirs. The common people exalted the image of the Duce still further making his portrait even out of flowers or grains of corn.[75] His portrait was to be found in every home. It has been calculated that in the Fascist period up to 30 million postcard pictures of Mussolini were in circulation. The cult of the virile male answered the consolidated instincts of an Italian society that was deeply sexist and strongly patriarchal.[76]

In order to promote 'popular universal art' as culture for all without class distinction, the pictorial and mosaic decoration of public buildings was launched. However, ordinary people felt uncomfortable frequenting places of élite culture such as museums – confronted by Futurism as symbols of an 'obsession with culture'.[77] So-called 'militant art', that is the art openly at the service of the political ideology of the regime, was on the other hand viewed as a 'perfect means of spiritual government'.[78] Militant art was widely encouraged by means of shows, contests and prizes such as the annual Littoriali dell'Arte, the Cremona Prize and the periodic Trade Union Exhibitions. There the idealized images of the virile bodies belonging to the Duce and athletic Fascist youth, were often presented in pseudo-photographic works. In the pictures, male beauty was entirely based on beautiful models, in a repetitive representation of the healthiness of 'Italic descent'.[79] Even the figurative art of high quality in the years of the regime mainly expressed through the medium of Futurism, Novecentismo and of rationalist Modernism stuck, with some exceptions, to the themes proposed by Fascism, creating sculptures and paintings inspired by them. The main subject was always the body of the Duce, portrayed standing or sitting on horseback, dressed like a Roman

FIGURE 1.9

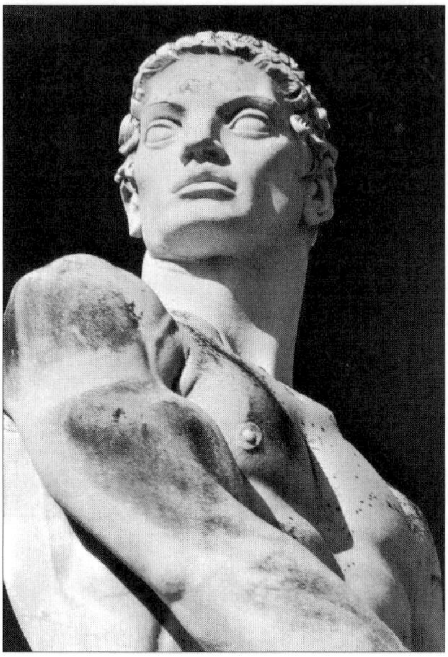

FIGURE 1.10

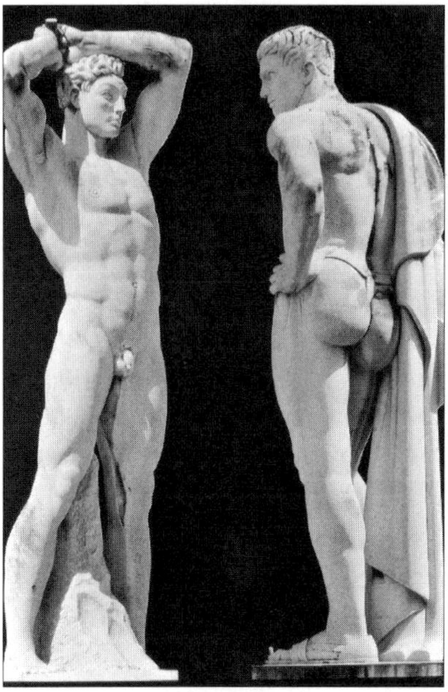

FIGURE 1.11

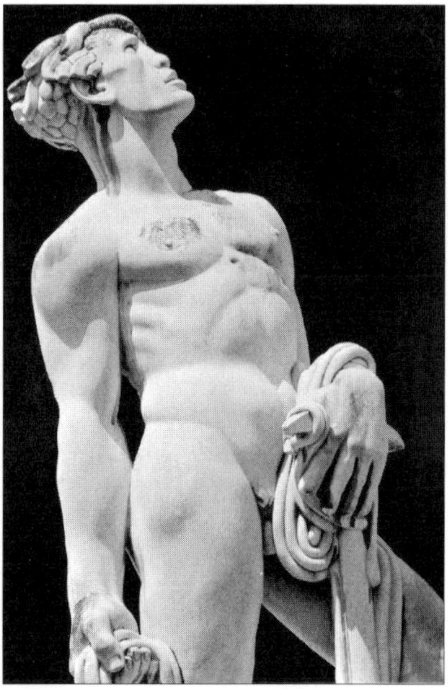

FIGURES FROM THE STADIUM OF THE MARBLES IN ROME

commander[80] or a Renaissance prince[81] and even like a revolutionary hero.[82] His image became a holy icon[83] and a public allegory.[84] In 1932 on the occasion of the decennial of Fascism an Exhibition of the Fascist Revolution was held in Rome and involved some of the best artists in the country. Special attention was given in the Exhibition to the human figure as an inspirational model for art. The figure of Mussolini became the omnipresent subject in every room as the synthesis of the Italian Spirit and of Fascism.[85]

The architecture of the regime was both monumental following the Roman style in its dimensions, and at the same time simplified into the square forms of Modernism. The virile body of the Duce and of the Fascist athlete invariably decorated the buildings. In Mussolini's Foro – an architectural complex designed by Enrico del Debbio in 1927 – the Stadium of the Marbles was one of the best examples of architecture in the Fascist style. The superior perimeter of the stadium was decorated with 60 monumental statues of white marble, representing naked athletes, symbols of the youth and virility of the New Italian. The intention of these four-metre high colossi – echoing both the Renaissance *David* by Michelangelo and nineteenth-century nudes by Ingres, Flandrin or Merson – was to evoke the Roman spirit. However they not only stimulated malicious comments from Italian women and provoked homosexual voyeurism,[86] but also irritated the Church of Rome and the respectable in general, unaccustomed to nudity exhibited too openly.[87]

Moreover, in the architectural complex of Mussolini's Foro, a gigantic obelisk of marble was erected, weighing 300 tons and dedicated to the Duce 'as the craftsman of every rebirth, and the animator of every important enterprise'. The obelisk, in recalling the granite image of the Duce, represented a phallic symbol of him and therefore was integrated into the virile context of the Foro.[88] Mussolini's Foro was also planned to accommodate a colossal statue, 80 metres high symbolizing the strength and virility of the New Italy. Obviously this semi-naked Ercole should have had Mussolini's face but after moulding the gigantic head of the Duce and his foot in bronze, it was realized the complete work was technically impossible. The plan was quietly set aside in great haste and Mussolini was said to be most disappointed.[89]

As for cinematographic art, although it had been institutionalized by the regime, it did not produce a real state cinema and only a few films were openly propagandist. Among them were *Vecchia Guardia* by Blasetti, *Camicie Nere* by Forzano, *Ragazzo* by Perilli, *L'assedio di*

FIGURE 1.12

STATUES OF BOXERS, STADIUM OF THE MARBLES, ROME

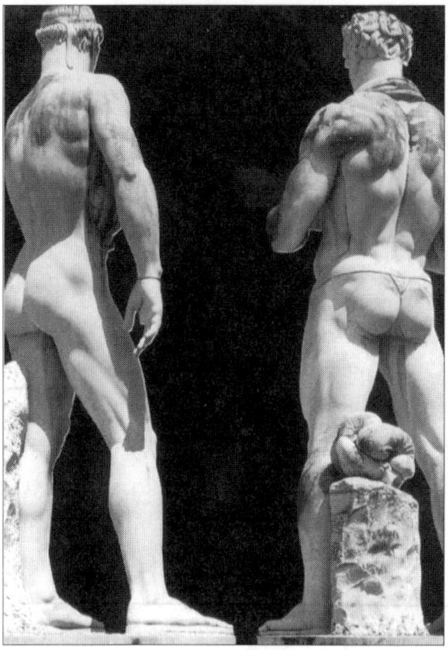

FIGURE 1.13

THIS ATHLETE'S FEATURES RESEMBLE THOSE OF MUSSOLINI. STADIUM OF THE MARBLES, ROME

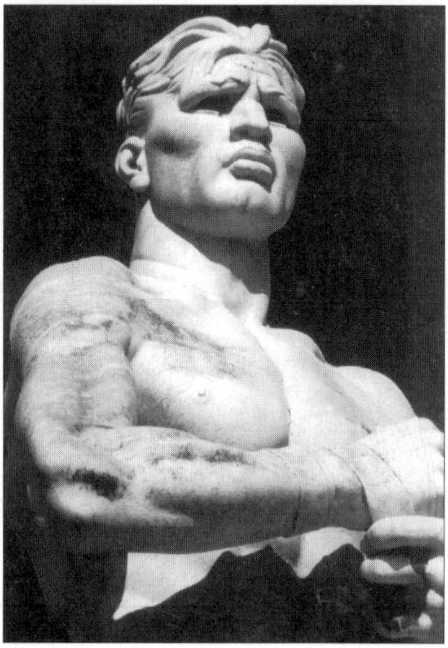

FIGURE 1.14

HANDSOME DISCUS THROWERS COMPARED

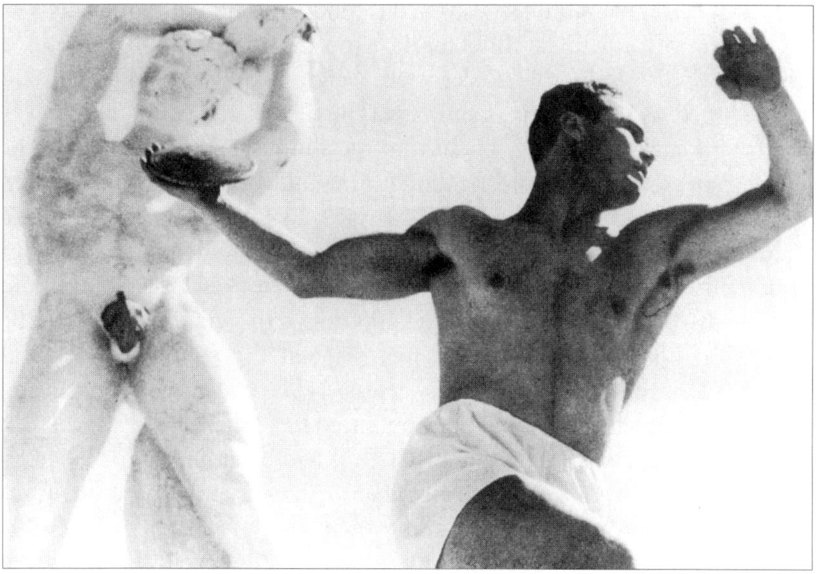

Alcazar by Genina and to an extent *Luciano Serra Pilota* by Alessandrini.[90] A few films such as *Sole* and *Terra Madre* by Blasetti expressed rural themes of Fascism. Others, such as *Rotaie* by Camerini, emphasized industrialization, but most of the approximately 700 films produced in those years were without any reference to political ideology, ideals or reality. The historical series of costume films – among which at least reference must be made to the Roman epic *Scipione l'africano* by Gallone, and the series of the so-called 'white telephones' were highly popular. At first sight the latter seemed to portray the lower and middle classes devoted to the mundane things of life. However, a closer look reveals that the non-political interests – love, family and money – of the protagonists and their pride in their own social condition, even if a modest one, complied perfectly with the aims of Fascism. It considered the citizens' indifference towards politics functional to the stability of the regime. In those films the Italian spirit and virility of the New Italian were embodied in the male protagonist. He represented, in general, a winning young man, aggressive and impetuous who resolved even the most tangled situations by sticking to the classic 'four slaps'. The actor most in demand to embody the prototype of the Italian male was Amedeo Nazzari, who, with his tall and elegant physique better embodied the Hollywood ideal of the handsome Latin than the Italian symbolized by the Duce.[91]

The duty of presenting so-called facts to society was entrusted not to film makers but to the documentaries and newsreels of the institute LUCE (L'Unione Cinematografica Educativa) founded in 1924. These documentaries used didactic situations involving industrial developments, land reclamation and archaeological discoveries. Particular attention was given to documentaries on demographic growth – with images of large and happy families – and to eugenic themes concerning the defence of the race. These showed the Fascist struggle against disease, and the strong and methodic New Italian, brilliantly participating in gymnastic and various other athletic activities.

It was left mainly to the compulsory projection of newsreels in schools, communes and Italian cinemas to ensure the maximum diffusion of appropriate images and information, already filtered in advance by the press office. The declared aim of every newsreel was the civic and moral education of the citizens. But as a matter of fact, it was a pompous and insistent set of resonances displaying Fascist parades and celebrations, with particular attention paid to the choreographic, paramilitary exhibitions of Fascist youth. In the newsreels the image of Mussolini filmed in his public or sometimes private life was dominant. Among other things, this was to show Italians living in distant countries the Duce in person, enabling them to admire his virile body, magnetism and unrestrained gestures.[92] Mussolini was fully aware of the extraordinary effect of these images and their reverberation all over the world. In 1933, in consequence he agreed to be the protagonist of an American film, directed by Thomas, called *Mussolini Speaks* in which he behaved with the boldness of a movie star. In the film's final scenes Mussolini was filmed in the Roman forum to ensure an unmistakable association with Julius Caesar. The film was mainly circulated abroad where it had some success because it presented the image of the self-made man, Mussolini, as the European political athlete whom one could trust. His usual characteristic body language made up of agitated gestures combined with hard, statuary postures produced a great effect. These were shown to the world in this film with the addition of sections of newsreels derived from the archives of the LUCE institute.[93]

In summary, Fascist culture played its full part in the plan to promote the virility of the Italians. However, they acted more like spectators than actors. There are several possible reasons. Perhaps because of an intelligently critical attitude or perhaps due to bored cynicism or even perhaps because of an atavistic idleness, men did not conform perfectly to the virile ideal of the New Italian. In fact, beyond appearances, the Italian male did not completely change – unlike men in Nazi Germany – into the strong, sculptured and obedient warrior ready to die for the cause.

FASCISM AND NATIONAL SOCIALISM, THE ITALIC DESCENT AND THE ARYAN ASCENT

With the coming to power of Hitler, Fascism had another right-wing totalitarian regime more ruthless and militaristic than the Italian. After the birth of this new Fascist regime inspired by Italy, Mussolini had to deal with a man he recognized as dangerous and with a nation historically considered an enemy of Italy.[94] Hitler had always declared himself a fervent admirer of Mussolini and of the Italian regime from which he had taken inspiration but nobody in Italy could be indifferent to the sinister spell he exerted on the German people nor to his exasperating anti-Semitism.[95] In addition, in exalting the superiority of the German race above all others the Führer contrasted the Germans directly with the Latin peoples! Consequently, during the early 1930s the Duce in no way favoured Germany. It was only after 1936, following the war in Ethiopia and condemnation by the League of Nations, that Mussolini moved closer to Hitler.

In 1938, the Italian Fascist regime, by then subjected to strong Nazi pressure, decided to issue a series of anti-Semitic laws.[96] Both the Great Council and Mussolini tried at that time to justify such policies by explaining to the Italians that they had not acted at Hitler's direction, but had followed a long–planned, coherent strategy to defend the Italian race.[97] As a matter of fact, it must be remembered that a kind of racism directed at the African black had already been in existence for some time, so that after the conquest of Ethiopia several racist regulations constituting an Ethiopian apartheid had been issued, in order to prevent the colonizers and the natives from fraternizing.[98] Anti-Semitic laws cost the regime much in terms of consent, both through the opposition of the Church of Rome and the opposition of most Italians – a melting pot of races – who were, of course, much more anti-German than anti-Semitic. The racial campaign against Italian Jews was above all a political choice by Mussolini who, even though not ideologically anti-Semitic, sought to give new vitality to the regime.[99] He offered young militant males – disappointed by the Fascist revolution – a cause through which to work off their frustrations and at the same time a reason for fighting.[100] The racial question was debated at different levels, and the Fascist racist action was supported by some intellectuals who, through publications and announcements, explained its scientific validity and its moral justification.[101] The values of 'Italic descent' were emphasized, so much so that as on the occasion of the anti-Hebrew Congress in 1938, Rome was named as the Capital of the Aryan Empire. At the same time, for the planned Roman Exhibition (E42) Mussolini substituted the word 'race' for the more generic 'descent'.[102] But if the supremacy of the Aryan race in the world was the central aim of Hitler's politics, the Duce's aim remained substantially the transformation of his people's character. While the supremacy of the Aryan race referred only to the past – mythologized in the actions of fallen war heroes and of ancient Germanic heroes – the New Italian, although heir of the ancient 'Italic descent', had to throw himself into an undefined future, which would induce the populations of different races to admire and imitate Fascist Italy, in a Utopian fascisticization of the world. In contrast to Germany, therefore, in Italy anti-Semitism had no devastating impact because only a few believed in the correctness of the racial laws and therefore they were rarely applied.[103]

At the end of the 1930s in anticipation of a war which Mussolini, however, saw as far in the future, and influenced by the mobilization of the German people – a perfect war machine – militarism took a stronger hold on the Italians. With the pro-German Starace at the secretariat of the PNF, Italian males – in the name of the glorious Italic race – had to learn to address each other comradely as *voi*. They were also to greet each other in 'macho' style with the outstretched arm – the so-called Roman salute – and to march in parade with the Roman step, a modest version of the Teutonic 'goose step'. Moreover, in order to remain purely European, to ensure the preservation of the physical and psychological characteristics of the 'Italic race', any thing considered alien to the Roman spirit, from dialects to foreign words, was banished.

In order to imitate Germany, under the control of the GIL, from 1937 onwards, the mobilization of the masses received the highest priority. Physical training and collective paramilitary drills were improved. Nevertheless, the aim of physical training remained the attainment of health, strength, discipline and will. The cult of the male body as a symbol of ruthless, sacrificial Aryan beauty characteristic of Germany, depicted graphically by Arno Breker, did not occur in Italy.[104]

Due to a typically Catholic kind of prudery, Italians viewed Nazi art with suspicion; its beautiful and muscular nudes suggested to Italian minds homoerotic sexual tendencies. Close relations between young men – created by the cult of German comradeship – and the well-known homosexuality of some in Hitler's entourage reinforced Italian suspicions. In contrast to Hitler's tall, blond athletes whose bodies appeared to be sculpted like Greek ephebes, Mussolini's boys represented a more modest physical model in which the virile ideal was not expressed by the perfect shape of their bodies but by brown, Mediterranean legs engaged in the amazingly hard task of marching in Roman step. Unsurprisingly, Italian Fascist young men seemed to most people a dull, uninteresting imitation of the Hitler Jugend, chilling in its uniform beauty and in the spectacular perfection of its parades. Yet already since the mid 1920s, when Nazism was still very far from attaining power, Fascist Italy had worked hard to obtain from young people, perfectly synchronized and choreographic execution as an obvious sign of the militaristic cohesion of the New Italians. In 1928

Lando Ferretti – man of sport and of the Party – wrote, commenting on an athletic exhibition with naked torsos: 'To watch thousands and thousands of soldiers statuesque, still and naked under their martial helmets, immediately respond as a single soldier to sharp orders is a powerful and disciplined sight that is irresistible.'[105]

Italian individualism, the fruit of secular, geographic, historical and cultural divisions, was perhaps the strongest obstacle to homogeneous transformation. Even after years of effort and indoctrination they failed to reach the same, perfect unity of German young people, who appeared to have been transformed by Hitler into wonderful automatons in such a short time. In a more general way, in spite of an insistent campaign in favour of the Fascist style, Italian people's taste was never uniform and outside the political ambit, the cultural debate could continue. In fact, whilst in Germany they burned books and rejected 'degenerate art' in order to affirm only one kind of art, 'pure art', in Italy there were numerous literary and artistic currents which proposed a variety of conceptual and aesthetic models.[106]

The two leaders, Hitler and Mussolini, although united by a strong personal charisma and by their consciousness of their roles as 'Envoys of Destiny', were completely different. Whilst Hitler played his part with terrifying conviction, Mussolini took advantage from time to time of events with an opportunism which as time went by damaged him.[107] Hitler's image, taken from northern mythology and from Nietzsche's Superman, was chilly and detached, whilst that of the Duce – which had its roots in the patriarchal and rural tradition of Italy – was emotional, self-indulgent and exhibitionist as exemplified by the continual projection of his extraordinary ability to work ('the Duce never sleeps!'), by the brevity of his thoughts, written everywhere on walls in very large letters, and above all, by his ever young and athletic virility.

However, the extrovert Mussolini, received world-wide applause.[108] In 1938 the United States, a country particularly enthusiastic about sport, allotted him first place among dictators of that time, whilst Hitler, seen by Americans as gloomy and introverted, received little support.[109]

Finally, Nazism, which had made militaristic male bodily beauty its symbol, could not avail itself of the Führer to promote its symbolism in the world. In fact, due to the irony of fate, Germany had a leader who, having little interest in sport, could not represent in any way the bodily ideal of the Aryan race. Mussolini's athletic body, on the contrary, perfectly embodied the male prototype of the 'Italic descent' even if, due to his repeated public exhibitions of his naked torso, he was somehow considered undignified if not ridiculous, above all by his ally Adolf Hitler.[110]

NOTES

1. Naturally, the Russian Revolution has to be quoted, but different ideas were professed by it, such as 'aesthetic materialism, antireligious scientism, the myth of the internationalism … and it proceeded with smaller systematic care in the institution of a collective cult'. E. Gentile, *The Cult of the Littorio: The Sacralization of Politics in Fascist Italy* (Rome-Bari, 1993), p.310 (hereafter *The Cult of the Littorio*).
2. G.B. Guerri, *Fascists: The Italians of Mussolini, the Regime of the Italians* (Milan, 1995), pp.216–25 (hereafter *Fascists*).
3. Of probable Etruscan derivation, the *fascis* consisted of an axe and numerous wooden rods tied together. In ancient Rome it symbolised power and was carried by chosen soldiers, called the *lictores*, who escorted the most important authorities.
4. The Fasces of Revolutionary Action was founded at the beginning of 1915 in order to convert Italy from neutrality to the war.
5. In the Renaissance, at the time of the French Revolution, and also in the Italian Risorgimento, the emblem of the *fascis* had returned to favour, with some variations compared with the Roman model. In its Renaissance version the *fascis* became the first symbol of the Fascist Party, whilst the Roman *lictorius fascis* was officially used in Italy in 1923. After accurate studies undertaken by the archaeologist and politician Giacomo Boni, it was adopted in order to reaffirm the Roman roots of 'Italic descent', and to counter all reference to the ideas of freedom expressed in the preceding centuries. See L. Falchi, 'The Origins of Littorio Fascis', II *Giornale di Roma* (12 April 1923). For more on the matter, see Gentile, *The Cult of the Littorio*, pp.84–90.
6. The Arditi were special assault troops who distinguished themselves in war by their bellicose spirit; the Irredentists aimed at reunifying the city of Fiume and Dalmatia with the fatherland; the Futurists were followers of the cultural movement of Marinetti; the Dannunziani were followers of the famous man of letters, D'Annunzio.
7. Giuseppe Mazzini's political mysticism was based on the binomial God–People, where people were seen as a community of believers in the religious cult of the fatherland. It is interesting to note that, besides promoting the political and moral unity of the Italians, Mazzini saw, in perspective, Rome as the centre of a future Council of European nations harmoniously united under the common religious cult of the Country. On Mazzini see T. Gandi and A. Comba, *Political Writings* (Turin, 1972). In Italy Mazzini's ideology was the base of a series of movements that, in opposition to the monarchic government, pressed for a revolution, from which the Third Italy could rise. E. Gentile, *The Myth of the New State from the anti-Giolitti Movement to Fascism* (Rome–Bari, 1982), pp.3–28; Gentile, *The Cult of the Littorio*, pp.7–12.
8. In the scholastic arena, mention has to be made of the Minister of Public Education, Francesco De Sanctis. In 1878 he introduced gymnastics in schools, the purpose of which was to educate the will of young citizens – future soldiers – by training their bodies. G. Gori, *Physical Education, Sport and Journalism in Italy: From the Unification to the first Olympic Games of the Modern Era* (Bologna, 1989), pp.71–89. The army, which was delegated to represent and defend the religion of the country, had the task of teaching the soldiers about national unity, and spreading it to their families. G. Conti, 'The Myth of the Armed Nation', *Contemporary History* (December 1990), 1149–95.
9. The year 1861, in which the Kingdom of Italy was instituted, saw the beginning of a kind of ethical war between Church and State. In that year the Pope, Pius IX, declared himself against the agnosticism of the Italian State which accepted 'infidels' in schools and offices. Guerri, *Fascists*, p.6.
10. Enrico Corradini exalted war as the crucible of heroes, and the 'living soul of the fatherland',

a cult that would celebrate the divinity of the nation. E. Corradini, 'A Nation', *The Kingdom*, 19 June 1904.

11. 'Foundation and Announcement of Futurism', *Le Figaro*, 20 April 1909. On Futurism in general, see: L. De Maria (ed.), and *F.T. Marinetti: Theory and Futurist Invention* (Milan, 1990) (hereafter *Futurist Invention*); R. De Felice (ed.), *Futurism, Culture and Politics* (Turin, 1988) (hereafter *Futurism*).
12. In September 1929 D'Annunzio, heading a group of ex-servicemen – among whom there were also officials and soldiers of the Italian army – occupied the city of Fiume in Dalmatia, with little more force than a blow of the hand.
13. The Regency of Carnaro, a kind of small nationalistic and revolutionary state, gave itself a constitution. In it, a new society centred on the trade unions was delineated, joining employers and workers. In subsequent years, Giolitti's Italian government regulated the matter with Yugoslavia, by renouncing Dalmatia – with the exception of Zara – and by declaring Fiume an independent city. D'Annunzio and his followers had to surrender and leave Fiume.
14. On 27 April 1920, an announcement was made by the aviators of Fiume in the skies of the main cities of Italy. It declared: 'With the spontaneous support of all spirits aiming at freedom, of all peoples torn by injustice and oppression, who are defeated and disappointed, the League of Fiume has been formed. It raises the flag of revolt against the League of Nations, a gang of robbers and privileged cheats.'
15. On the complex relationship between Mussolini and D'Annunzio, from 1921 to 1925, see N. Valeri, *D'Annunzio Forerunner of Fascism* (Florence, 1963), and V. Salierno, *D'Annunzio and Mussolini: History of a Cordial Enmity* (Milan, 1988). In general, on the politics of D'Annunzio, see R. De Felice, *The Politic D'Annunzio 1918–1938* (Rome–Bari, 1978).
16. Guerri, *Fascists*, p.90. The famous aviator Italo Balbo, who supported Mussolini from the beginning, had surges of prestige during the regime. On Balbo, see ibid., pp.78–83.
17. On the myth of the Superman: M. Carrouges, *La Mystique du Surhomme* (Paris, 1948), *passim*; B. Welte, 'Nietzsche Superman: Ambiguous Duplicity', G. Renzo (ed.), *Friedrich Nietzsche and the Destiny of Man* (Cittanuova, 1982), pp.23–41.
18. G. Papini, *Masculinity* (Florence, 1915), p.41.
19. Guerri, *Fascists*, p.43.
20. G.L. Mosse, 'Futurism and Political Culture in Europe: A Global Perspective', De Felice, *Futurism*, p.17.
21. 'We exalt patriotism and militarism; we laud war, as the only cleanser of the world, the proud flame of enthusiasm and generosity, the noble bath of heroism ...' P. Hulten, *Futurism and Futurisms* (Milan, 1986), p.18.
22. These words are taken from an item by Marinetti of December 1915, eloquently titled *Italian Pride*, De Maria, *Futurist Invention*, p.503.
23. Futurism was exported to Russia, where it prospered, and to other countries including Germany, Scandinavia, Great Britain, Spain, Portugal, Japan and Mexico.
24. Mussolini was an admirer of Gustave Le Bon, the scholar of mass psychology. His *Psychologie des Foules*, and *Psychologie des Temps nouveaux* were frequently read by Mussolini. See S. Moscovici, *L'Age des Foules: un Traité Historique de Psychologie des Masses* (Paris, 1981), p.93. The Duce said he had experimented on the grounds that 'the tendency of modern men to believe was absolutely unbelievable!' Guerri, *Fascists*, p.172.
25. That celebration, which was held on 21 April, exalted the forces of production and work, in substitution for the 1 May celebration, which was abolished, being associated with the left wing.
26. The celebration of 20 September, commemorating the victory of the State over the Church of Rome in 1870, was abolished by Mussolini. He did not want to aggravate further the problems of coexistence between two different religions, the Fascist – new and nationalist – and the Catholic – ancient and international, which had its Holy Centre in the very heart of the capital of Italy.
27. On the sacralization of Fascist ideology see Gentile, *The Cult of the Littorio*, pp.63–103.
28. R. Cantalupo, *The Managerial Class* (Milan, 1928), pp.74–5.
29. Mussolini's style of speech in the form of questions and answers had imitated the style

introduced by D'Annunzio during the enterprise of Fiume. On the Duce's language, see M. Saracinelli and N. Totti, *The Duce's Italy: Information, School, Habits* (Rimini, 1983), pp.157–73 (hereafter *Duce's Italy*).

30. For further information on the Fascist mystics, see M.L. Bretri, 'Between Politics and Culture: the School of Fascist Mystic', *Contemporary History*, 1–2 (1989), 377–98.
31. On the biographies of the Duce, see L. Passerini, *Imaginary Mussolini: The History of a Biography 1915–1939* (Rome–Bari, 1991), pp.153–234 (hereafter *Imaginary Mussolini*).
32. G. Manacorda, *Literature and Culture of the Fascist Period* (Milan, 1974) (hereafter *Literature and Culture*), p.241. On censorship in general and on the *veline* for the press, ibid., pp.232–46.
33. G.L. Mosse, 'Fascist aesthetics and society', A. Del Boca, M. Legnani, M.G. Rossi (eds.), *The Fascist Regime: History and Historiography* (Rome–Bari, 1995), p.110 (hereafter *The Fascist Regime*). See also L. Casini, *The Rediscovery of the Body* (Rome, 1990), passim.
34. Mosse, *The Fascist Regime*, p.111.
35. On the ONMI, see: S. Fabbri, *The National Organisation for the Protection of Maternity and Infancy* (Milan, 1933); C. Saraceno, 'Shaping Maternity and Paternity', *The Fascist Regime*, pp.491–7. Since 1927, the ONMI had control of the health resorts, offering the neediest children a period of life in the open air at the seaside or in the mountains. From 1931 to 1938, no fewer than 4,262,015 young guests benefited from the Fascist health resorts.
36. L. Ferretti, *The Book of Sport* (Rome–Milan, 1928), p.189.
37. From 1923 to 1936 the school system, from primary school to university, doubled the number of affiliates. Guerri, *Fascists*, pp.156–7.
38. Ibid., pp.198–9
39. Ibid., p.178. On the organization of the ONB, see: E.R. Tannenbaum, *The Fascist Experience: Culture and Society in Italy from 1922 to 1945* (Milan, 1974); V. De Grazia, *Consent and Mass Culture at the seaside and in the mountains.* From *In Fascist Italy* (Rome–Bari, 1981).
40. The popular games of OND were: bowling, little-drum game, elastic-ball game, pulling the rope, volley-ball, rowing with fixed seat, stratto-ball game, chess. R. Stefanelli, *Dopolavoro* [After Work]*: Practical Norms for Executives* (Turin, 1940), pp.75–90.
41. Marinetti expressed his sympathy with physical culture to Italian students, by declaring that Futurism was: 'the cult of progress and speed, of sport, physical strength, rash courage, heroism and danger, against obsession with culture, classical studies, museum, literature and ruins'. De Maria, *Futurist Invention*, pp.328–40.
42. Ibid., p.370.
43. Ibid., p.340 and p.372.
44. F.T. Marinetti, 'Some parts of the film *Futurist Life*, IV point'. *Futurist Italy* (15 October 1916).
45. Among others must be mentioned, due to their monumentality, the stadium of the Littoriale in Bologna (1926), the Berta stadium in Florence (1929), the Marbles stadium in Rome (1932), the Mussolini stadium in Turin (1933), the cycle racing track Vigorelli in Milan (1933) and the Victory stadium in Bari (1934).
46. In 1928, the Littorio stadium designed by D'Albora became the standard and was replicated in every commune in Italy, with financial support from the state. In 1930, there were 3,280 stadiums mainly in the north. F. Fabrizio, *Sport and Fascism: Sport Politics of the Regime 1924–36* (Rimini–Florence, 1976), pp.22–4 (hereafter *Sport and Fascism*).
47. In 1928 the Royal Fascist Male Academy of Physical and Juvenile Education was founded in Rome and in 1932 the Female Academy was founded in Orvieto.
48. 'Statistical comparative outlook in the years 1928–35 (ONB)', *Fascist Sport,* IX, 4 (1936), 10. See also P. Ferrara, *Italy in the Gym: History, Documents, Images of Gymnastics from 1833 to 1973* (Rome, 1992), p.241 (hereafter *Italy in the Gym*).
49. In 1924 the Federation of the Catholic Sport Associations (FASCI) disbanded voluntarily. In 1927 the YMCA and the Boy Scout Association were suppressed by the authorities. Nevertheless some gymnastic sections of the Catholic Youth resisted until 1931 even though operating with many restrictions, F. Fabrizio, *History of Sport in Italy: From the Gymnastics Societies to Mass Associations* (Rimini–Florence, 1977) (hereafter *History of Sport*), pp.104–12; Ferrara, *Italy in the Gym*, pp.234–7.
50. Fabrizio, *History of Sport*, pp.113–20; Ferrara, *Italy in the Gym*, pp.234–7.

51. Fabrizio, *Sport and Fascism*, pp.39–42.
52. On the 1936 Olympic Games, see G. Gori, *The Athlete and the Nation: Essays of History of Sport* (Rimini, 1996), pp.97–139.
53. Among them we quote Carnera, Bindi, Guerra, Bartali, De Pinedo, Balbo, Nuvolari.
54. In 1933 two prizes, the medal for athletic merit and the stars for sports merit were instituted. Made in gold, silver and bronze, they were used to reward the athletes and the presidents of the sport federations who were victorious in international and national contests. See PNF, Sheet of Orders n. 175, 20 December, XII (1933).
55. That speech made on 28 October 1934, is quoted by G. Vaccaro, 'Giorgio Vaccaro illustrates the methods and goals of Fascist sport', *Fascist Sport*, V (1935), 11.
56. A. Banti, 'The Importance of Sport Displays', *Fascist Sport*, I (1936), 31.
57. In the 1920s the myth of Mussolini the 'great seducer' was exalted only as a possibility, for it conflicted with the Duce's so-called austere life. Later on it was accepted, because it became somehow compatible with the Latin male stereotype of the good husband and the good father. After that, the virile Fascist man adopted the dictum 'many women, much honour!' Passerini, *Imaginary Mussolini*, pp.3, 5–6.
58. P. Gobetti, *Liberal Revolution*, IX (1924), 34.
59. According to Mussolini, boxing was 'an exquisitely Fascist means of self-expression'. D. Mack Smith, *Mussolini* (Milan, 1981), p.149.
60. '[He is] Dominator and multiplier of the enormous energies of his athletic body, by using method, enthusiasm and discipline every hour of every day. [He is] the virile and generous personification of triumphant Italian sport', L. Ferretti, 'Mussolini, First Sportsman of Italy', *The Fascist Sport* (1933), 3. See also: C. Dell' Ongaro, *Mussolini and Sport* (Mantova, 1928); A. Cotronei, 'Caesar the Gladiator', *Il Popolo d'Italia*, 28 October 1934; F. Fabrizio, *Sport and Fascism*, pp.114–19.
61. A. Papa and G. Panico, *Social History of Football in Italy: From the Pioneers Clubs to the Sporting Nation 1887–1945* (Bologna, 1993), p.135.
62. D. Mack Smith, 'Win, Win, Win', *FMR*, XXVI (1984) (hereafter 'Win', *FMR*), 112.
63. J.M. Hobermann, *Politics and Sport: The Body in the Political Ideologies of the Eighteenth and Nineteenth Century* (Bologna, 1988), p.137 (hereafter *Political Ideologies*).
64. L. Preti, *Youth, Youth* (Milan, 1972), pp.109–10.
65. On the cultural movements during Fascism see: Manacorda, *Literature and Culture*; M. Biondi and A. Borsotti (eds.), *Culture and Fascism: Literature, Arts, Performance in the Two Decades* (Florence, 1996) (hereafter *Culture and Fascism*).
66. Gentile, with his idealism, his religious background and his conception of the ethical state, was the philosopher of early Fascism; in the 1930s his star progressively declined.
67. The liberal Croce, by editing the magazine *The Critic*, became the spokesman for those who believed in freedom.
68. In fact Norberto Bobbio, who substantially modifies the idea of blind enslavement to the Italian culture, Fascism, affirms: 'Whoever looks today at the cultural panorama of those years … above all at literary, historical and philosophical culture … finds it hard to realise that in Italy there had been such an earthquake as Fascism was, or was said to be …' (quoted in Guerri, *Fascists*, p.154).
69. G.L. Mosse, *Fascism toward a General Theory* (Rome–Bari, 1996) (hereafter *Fascism*), p.65.
70. Passerini, *Imaginary Mussolini*, p.166.
71. C. Malaparte, 'L'arcitaliano (The True Italian)', *The Voice* (Rome, 1928).
72. De Maria, *Futurist Invention*, p.575.
73. Manacorda, *Literature and Culture*, pp.160–1.
74. 'The Duce's portraits are in thousands. They will reach fabulous numbers; they cannot be counted any more.' F. Sapori, *Art and the Duce* (Milan, 1932), p.135.
75. Numerous photos of the Duce's portraits, including those constructed from petals of flowers and grains of wheat, are in L. Malvano, *Fascism and Politics of the Image* (Turin, 1988).
76. C. Bianchi 'The Heroic Nude of Fascism', in S. Bertelli and C. Grottarelli, *Alexander's Eyes: Sovereign Power and Sacredness of the Body from Alexander the Great to Ceausescu* (Florence, 1990) (hereafter *Alexander's Eyes*), p.162.
77. De Maria, *Futurist Invention*, p.340.

78. M. Sironi, 'Announcement of mural painting', *Column*, I (December 1933), 10.
79. G. Armellini, *The Images of Fascism in the Figurative Arts* (Milan, 1980), p.165 (hereafter *Images of Fascism*). On the Cremona Prize, instigated in 1939 thanks to the initiative of the leader Farinacci, see ibid., pp.175–6.
80. Among the artists we quote: Albino Manca, who carved the Duce's bust dressed as a Roman emperor; the painter Emilio Florio, who represented him completely naked, as a kind of Roman wolf, with the twins Romulus and Remus at its feet. The relief by Publio Morbiducci, *The History of Rome through its Buildings*, was a kind of modern Trajan's Column, where Mussolini was depicted as the commander, erect in the stirrups on his horse.
81. As an example, Giuseppe Graziosi portrayed the Duce in an equestrian statue, which recalled both the *Gattamelata* by Donatello and the *Colleoni* by Verrocchio.
82. The subject of the Duce riding a horse, with his cloak lifted by the wind, was depicted in a painting by Primo Conti and in a sculpture by Cleto Tomba. They imitated the famous picture *Napoleon at the Grand San Bernardo*, by David.
83. Mussolini was 'sanctified' in Montreal, by an 'ingeniously blasphemous fresco' painted on the apse of the Catholic church of the Lady of the Defence. The painter Guido Nincheri entitled it *Mussolini Surrounded by the Quadrunviri, the Duke of Abruzzi and Marconi*.
84. The Futurist, Ferruccio Vecchi, in his sculpture *The Empire Rises from the Duce's Head*, represented Mussolini's head as it was giving birth to the Empire, sculpted as a strong, virile and athletic naked figure, having the same features as the Duce.
85. More broadly on that Exhibition, see Gentile, *The Cult of the Littorio*, pp.213–35
86. On the athletes of the Stadium of Marbles, as ambiguous symbols of Mediterranean bisexuality, see A. Arbasino, 'Youth, Youth', *FMR*, YXVI (1984), 96–8. On Mussolini's Foro, today the Foro Italico, see: M. Paniconi, 'Information and Data on Mussolini's Foro', *Architecture*, XII (1933); E. Del Debbio, 'The Figurative Arts', *Panoramas of Fascist Realizations*, VII (1938–1942).
87. It was very soon decided to hide the sex of most statues, applying a rudimentary fig leaf in cement, out of respect for Catholic sensibility.
88. C. Cresti, 'Forum Beniti', *FMR*, XXVI (1984), 106.
89. Mack Smith, 'Win', *EMR*, 118.
90. A. Catania, 'L. Freddi and the Book of Solitude', *Culture and Fascism*, p.296.
91. On cinema and Fascism: G.P. Brunetta, *History of the Italian Cinema: The Cinema of the Regime 1929–1945* (Rome, 1993).
92. Saracinelli and Totti, *Duce's Italy*, pp.78–81.
93. M. Isnenghi, 'The Body of the Duce', *Alexander's Eyes*, p.171.
94. Among newspaper headlines: 'In the footsteps of fascism, Hitler, chancellor of the Reich, heads the power of the young innovating forces of Germany', *Il Resto del Carlino*, 31 January 1933; 'Hitler affirms that the success of the national socialist idea is due to the glorious example of Rome', *Il Popolo d'Italia*, 1 February 1933.
95. A. Krüger, 'Fasces and Hooked Crosses', *Lancillotto and Nausica: Critic and History of Sport*, I–II (1991), 88–101.
96. In order to defend the Italian race, certain laws were passed: Law of 17 December 1938; Law of 29 June 1939; Law of 13 May 1940. By then the natives of Libya, Eritrea, Somalia and Ethiopia had a civil status lower than that of the colonizers.
97. 'The Great Council of Fascism points out that Fascism has operated for ten years, and still operates, a positive policy directed at the quantitative and qualitative improvement of the Italian race – improvement which could be seriously compromised by interbreeding and degeneration. The Hebrew problem is only the metropolitan aspect of a problem of a more general character.' And Mussolini affirmed: 'The racial problem has not blown up suddenly; empires are conquered by weapons and they are kept by prestige; we need a strong racial consciousness which states not only the differences, but also the very clear superiorities.' A. Del Boca, 'The Racial Laws in Mussolini's Empire', *The Fascist Regime*, pp.388–9.
98. In 1936 the Minister for the Colonies, Alessandro Lessona, had issued instructions to avoid every kind of fraternity between the two races. In 1937 he summarized Fascist racial politics as: 'a) a clear and absolute separation between the two races; b) collaboration without promiscuity; c) humanity in line with past errors; d) implacable severity with future errors.'

Ibid., pp.336–7.

99. Among his lovers, two Jewish women of great culture – Angela Balabanov and Margherita Sarfatti – have to be quoted. They would have been unacceptable partners for Hitler! P. Chessa, *Renzo De Felice: Red and Black* (Milan, 1995), p.153 (hereafter *Renzo de Felice*).
100. Ibid., pp.156–7.
101. Racist announcements are in Manacorda, *Literature and Culture* pp.247–53. On Italian racism see also M. Tarchi, 'Julius Evola and Fascism: Notes on an Unusual Route', *Culture and Fascism*, pp.123–42.
102. This substitution was contained in the written project for one of the sections – Orthogenesis of the Fascist Race – of the E 42 Exhibition, co-ordinated by Pende. This exhibition, however, was never held due to the war. Malvano, *Fascism and Politics of the Image*, p.156 and p.172.
103. Chessa, *Renzo de Felice*, pp.149–63. In general, on the Hebrew problem, R. De Felice, *History of the Italian Hebrews Under Fascism* (Turin, 1961).
104. G.L. Mosse, *Sexuality and Nationalism* (Rome–Bari, 1966), p.199 and G.L. Mosse, *The Image of Man: The Creation of Modern Masculinity* (New York, 1996), *passim.*
105. Ferretti, *The Book of Sport*, p.127.
106. Armellini, *Images of Fascism*, pp.159–76.
107. U. Silva, *Ideology and Art of Fascism* (Milan, 1973), p.68.
108. S. Pivato, 'Sport et rapports internationaux: le cas du fascisme italien', P. Arnaud and A. Wahl (eds.), *Sport et Relations Internationales* (Metz, 1994), pp.64–72.
109. Passerini, *Imaginary Mussolini*, p.179.
110. Hoberman, *Political Ideologies*, p.146.

Muscular *Anschluss*: German Bodies and Austrian Imitators

WOLFGANG WEBER and PAULA BLACK

In 1991 an Austrian local radio station broadcast a programme 'Gymnastics and Politics in the Austrian Province of Vorarlberg'. In it the former press officer of the Vorarlberg Gymnastics Association, Kuno Fend, described his motives for joining a gymnastics club in the 1920s:

> I became a gymnast exclusively because I wanted to train my body, not to do politics. There were no political motives in gymnastics, in the training sessions we practised on the apparatus. Yes, we sang some nationalist songs at the beginning of the sessions, but this was not political, it just showed our love for our German culture.[1]

This is an investigation of the myth of the non-political nature of Germanic body culture in Austria. As Kuno Fend illustrates above, certain contemporary Austrian gymnasts still believe in the possibility of a pure body culture, existing in a vacuum, far removed from the influences of day-to-day politics. This must, however, be recognized as an ideological standpoint, in contradiction to sociological work on the body which has shown how body projects reflect the social characteristics of the society in which they are embedded.[2] The body can no longer be considered a 'natural' phenomenon, and the portrayal of the body as ideologically neutral is in itself a political construction. In order to decode the metaphor of the non-political body culture inherent in Austrian gymnastics it is necessary to consider the historical and ideological roots of the German Gymnastics Movement in Austria, investigate its collaboration with the Nazi movement in inter-war Austria, examine the involvement of Austrian gymnasts in the illegal NSDAP, and finally explore their work for an *Anschluss* of Austria to Germany. All of these activities were carried out in the name of the welfare of the greater German nation through the politicization of physical exercise in order to strengthen the male body in readiness for struggle. In addition to investigating the historical context within which this ideology arose, other sociological points are made. The nature of this body which was to be prepared for struggle is a highly constructed and specific body form. It reflects gender and class characteristics and is justified by recourse to Darwinian theory. These points are elaborated in a historical outline of German gymnastics in Austria.

POLITICAL HISTORY OF GERMAN GYMNASTICS IN INTER-WAR AUSTRIA

In German the term *Turnen* (gymnastics) describes a specific form of body culture, which was introduced at the beginning of the nineteenth century by Friedrich Ludwig Jahn[3] in Prussia. Jahn's *Turnen* is characterized by a strong emphasis on the ideological benefits of sport. He demanded from his pupils not just the training of the body, but also the training of the mind. In his opinion the task of gymnastics was to prepare the German people physically and mentally for a rebellion against the French occupation troops in Germany and to unify the various German states existing at that time into one national state under the leadership of the Prussian king. For this reason his training sessions were organized along paramilitary lines: gymnasts had to undertake walking, marching, swimming, riding, shooting and fencing.[4] At the end of each training session Jahn assembled the gymnasts at a place which he called after an old Germanic word *Thing* (square). There he read from his *Deutsches Volkstum* (German character) which he published in 1810. This is a work replete with racial intolerance and Darwinist assertions. In just one illustration in *Deutsches Volkstum* Jahn stated: 'The purer a nation is the better; the more mixed it is the worse … Deficient nations and deficient languages must disappear or be exterminated.'[5]

This political nature of Jahn's sport is fundamental to it and to an understanding of it. It was transmitted down the decades and formed the ideological foundation on which Austrian gymnasts in the inter-war period constructed their activities. Nevertheless, Kuno Fend stressed in his interview that Jahn's work for a unified Germany was in no way political:

> No, Jahn's sport is not political. It was born out of the French wars of that time, out of the liberation struggle the Germans fought

> against Napoleon. If the French hadn't occupied Germany there wouldn't have been a need for this war. It is not politics if you want to set free your people from the dictator Napoleon. Don't we have the right to fight dictatorship? The world just wants to deny the German people's right to keep their freedom by fighting. This is what they want. And then they turn the tables and call it political, if we fight for our national freedom.[6]

In Fend's perception Jahn's sport could not be political, because he was fighting for all Germans. In contrast, political parties, which usually represent social classes, are political because they only represent a certain section of society. The gymnasts still claim to speak for the whole nation and consequently do not see themselves as political. This is despite the fact that their members were predominantly drawn from the middle classes. In reality, of course, politics deal with society, its economic, structural and social organization. Narrow definitions of politics such as Fend's were one reason why Austrian gymnasts became Nazi supporters in the inter-war period, because as far as they were concerned, Hitler was not political but only advocated the German people's right 'to defend their freedom'. After the collapse of the Habsburg Empire and the creation of the new Republic of German–Austria in the autumn of 1918 there was a political need to reorganize the structure of the German gymnastics movement in Austria. By then it was separated into four main factions: the Social Democratic Arbeiter-Turnerbund Österreich, the Conservative Christlich-deutsche Turnerschaft für das Gebiet Deutsch-Österreich and the two German nationalist associations Turnkreis XV Deutsch-Österreich and Deutscher Turnerbund (1889). Efforts to create a single Austrian-wide umbrella organization for all of the four politically divided gymnastics associations were in vain. The Social Democratic and the Conservative federations were refounded after the First World War. Only the German nationalist gymnasts brought their sections together successfully. On 7/8 September 1919 they founded the Deutscher Turnerbund (1919) (DTB) as the umbrella organization of all nationalist gymnastics clubs in Germany and Austria. Their goals, they declared, were 'the creation and strengthening of mental and physical fitness and of the tribal identity of the German people'. Gymnastics should be the preservation of 'health, power and agility', the creation of 'intellectual and moral values' and the improvement of the German people's ability to defend themselves. The ideological basis on which the activities of the DTB were founded were the so-called three Aryan wisdoms 'Purity of Race, Unity of People, Freedom of Thought'. To make sure that its members were not 'seduced' by outsiders the DTB added several regulations to its statutes. Firstly, it forbade people of Jewish religion to join its clubs, because they were seen as a substantial enemy of Germans. This regulation became known as the so-called 'Aryan paragraph'. Secondly, the DTB excluded 'supporters of international movements', because due to their ideology they could not support the German nation; thirdly, the organization banned 'all party politics' within its clubs and finally, it only allowed its clubs to participate in 'competitions with other sports organizations if members of Germanic tribes attend and German character and German sentiment are not diminished'.

In fact, in attempting to realize these requirements, the DTB acted most inconsistently. There were several reasons. The regulation relating to participation only in sports competitions where Germanness was not in danger of being 'contaminated' proved to be very difficult for gymnastics clubs to implement in the West Austrian province of Vorarlberg, which has a common border with Switzerland, Liechtenstein and Germany. Many of its first gymnastics instructors were either Swiss or German. Vorarlberg gymnastics clubs attended several Swiss and German sports festivals. These links were decisive for the establishment and the further development of gymnastics in Vorarlberg. In the view of the DTB, Switzerland was not a Germanic state due to its multi-ethnic constitution and it forbade the Vorarlberg clubs to attend Swiss gymnastics festivals. The DTB also prohibited its members from attending gymnastics festivals organized by the Deutsche Turnerschaft (German Gymnastics Association) because Jewish people were members of its clubs. However, in 1923 the DTB forbade a group of Vorarlberg gymnasts to attend the central festival of the Deutsche Turnerschaft in Munich because Jewish people and foreigners would be participating; while at the same time it sent its national gymnastics trainer to Munich. When Vorarlberg gymnasts attended the Swiss and German national gymnastics festivals in Lucerne and Cologne in 1928, they were expelled from the DTB. The sixth guiding principle of the DTB, published in 1919 demanded that proof of 'national knowledge' had to be provided at gymnastics competitions, which was not usually done at Swiss or German gymnastics festivals. Principle number six on many occasions prevented the participation of foreign gymnastics clubs at Austrian sports competitions. In 1923, for example, the Austrian Vorarlberger Turngau, a sub-organization of the DTB, held its annual festival. It included ten 'national questions' which had to be answered by the gymnasts after the practical exercises. Both, practical exercises and ideological answers were marked by referees who then awarded an overall mark which decided the ranking of the individual gymnast. The questions in 1923 mainly referred to events in German history and the DTB's organizational structure. The Swiss gymnastics clubs, which had traditionally participated in Vorarlberg sports competitions since the nineteenth century, withdrew their entry for the 1923 festival because 'in relation to proof of national knowledge all sorts of things were demanded from them by the Vorarlberg side'.[7]

The DTB's ban on 'supporters of international movements' from joining their clubs was also handled erratically. In 1925 the Austrian decorator Heinrich Reisecker joined the DTB club Turnverein Feldkirch. Reisecker spent the World War One years in Swiss exile. There he was in contact with Wladimir Iljitsch Lenin. In 1920 he went to Linz, capital of the Austrian province of Upper Austria and co-founded the province's branch of the Austrian Communist Party. In the early 1920s he left Upper Austria to settle down in Vorarlberg where he became one of the most influential activists from the local Communist Party. Although he was well known as a Communist, the board of the Turnverein Feldkirch had no objection to his membership of their club. Reisecker was never banned, even between 1933 and 1945 when the Austrian Communist Party was illegal and carried out an undercover fight against the Fascist regimes of Austria and Germany.[8]

As the example of Reisecker shows, the DTB was willing to ignore the political beliefs of individuals. It did not when it came to its sub-organizations. A few weeks after the end of World War One the majority of the board of the German nationalist Turnverein Hoechst in the Austrian province of Vorarlberg changed its political beliefs dramatically. Five out of seven functionaries declared themselves to be Social Democrats and no longer German Nationalists. The club's annual general meetings from 1919 to 1921 re-elected this board. In 1921 the two remaining nationalist functionaries provoked a conflict which ended in the disbandment of the Turnverein. The property of the club was passed by the state to the nationalist Vorarlberger Turngau, a member of the DTB. The Vorarlberger Turngau entrusted the two nationalist functionaries with the re-foundation of a nationalist club in Hoechst, which they did successfully. With the support of the Austrian Labour Party the former Social Democratic functionaries founded a new gymnastics club too, but it did not develop as well as the nationalist one. The Labour gymnasts suffered from lack of funding and consequently of gymnastics apparatus and training sites.[9]

Regarding the ban on 'party politics' in the DTB statutes the Deutscher Turnerbund was not nearly as consistent as in the case of the Turnverein Hoechst. When the DTB gymnasts passed this regulation in 1919, they stressed that their own ideology and work could not be political, because they were only working for 'the creation and strengthening of mental and physical fitness and of the tribal identity in the German people'. In contrast to the internationalist parties of the Social Democrats and the Conservatives, which were organizing the German people along class and religious lines, the DTB aspired to the unification of the Germans irrespective of class or religion. Its work was devoted to the entire German nation and therefore, in its eyes, could not be political. After the German nationalist parties suffered several defeats in the elections for the Austrian parliament between 1919 and 1923,[10] the DTB reconsidered its regulation on party politics. In a leading article in the gymnastics magazine *Turnen und Sport* the chairman of the DTB district Styria–Carinthia, Dr Robert Hesse, called upon the gymnasts to 'join the nationalist parties'. The gymnasts' task would be to 'take care that the hazards of day-to-day politics do not lead the parties astray, do not remove them from the nationalist goals'.[11] In Hesse's view gymnasts were the guarantors of the non-political mission of the German nationalist movement in Austria. The national chairman of the DTB, Klaudius Kupka, supported this view. Almost a week before the general election for the Austrian national parliament in October 1923, Kupka wrote in a gymnastics journal: 'We nationalist gymnasts have to perform our duty also in political life, outside our association life. We shall not stand aside and by abstention help our rivals in Vienna, for example, the Social Democrats and their allies, the Jews and the Czechs, to win.'[12] The clear political view expressed in Kupka's statement did not necessitate rewriting the DTB statutes. The Deutscher Turnerbund understood the value of keeping the myth of its non-political mission alive. The following resolution of the Upper Austrian Inn-Traun-Gau, a DTB sub-organization, illustrates how it managed to do this.

In its resolution in 1923 the Inn-Traun-Gau stressed that due to their statutes gymnastics clubs and the DTB had to distance themselves from day-to-day party politics. The task of individual gymnasts, however, was to make sure that 'they engage in public life, everyone according to his own energies and his suitability. Our motto Purity of Race, Unity of People, Freedom of Thought has to be real … In public life this is only possible through engagement in politics and, given the facts, on the side of the nationalist parties.'[13] Though political parties were still a necessary evil for the DTB, the primary goal of its politics remained 'to become a people without parties'.[14] Under the 'current constitutional conditions in Germany and Austria' political parties were a necessity, 'the nationalist parties are substantial because there are non-nationalist parties, too'.[15]

After this decision to engage in party politics in principle had been taken the DTB defined what a nationalist party was. Its task should be 'to protect and to patronize the activities of organizations which work on the moral, mental and physical education of the German people; furthermore to make sure that the nationalist principles are not in danger of being questioned in case non-nationalist powers in legislation and administration influence the fate of the people'.[16] These demands were met by three parties in inter-war Austria: the Großdeutsche Volkspartei (Greater German People's Party), the Landbund and the NSDAP. Consequently, Austrian gymnasts engaged in the propaganda activities of these parties. Dr Robert Hesse, for example, chairman of the DTB district Styria–Carinthia, was vice-president of the Großdeutsche Volkspartei. The president of the DTB sub-organization Vorarlberger Turngau, Alfred Wehner, led the Vorarlberger branch of the Großdeutsche Volkspartei. From the mid-1920s onwards gymnasts also worked for the NSDAP. They were co-founders of local branches of the NSDAP in, for example, the West Austrian towns of Bregenz, Dornbirn and Feldkirch, and they had a prominent role in the building of the Austrian SA (Sturmabteilung, stormtroops).[17]

The forerunner of the Austrian SA was the so-called Patriotic Protection Association (Vaterlaendischer Schutzbund), a German nationalist organization founded in the mid-1920s. Its main tasks were to guard the Austrian constitution, support the state security forces, defend against a potential putsch, protect individuals, property and public events.[18] To these ends its members engaged in paramilitary training. In 1931 the Schutzbund was reorganized as a National Socialist subsidiary and renamed Sturmabteilung. A considerable number of its activists came from DTB clubs. This was possible because the DTB had practised a particular form of gymnastics which it called *Wehrturnen* (military gymnastics) after 1919; and because of common ideological features discussed later. The exercises in military gymnastics were similar to those practised by the SA, for example, throwing hand-grenades, cross-country running, parading and marching. The newly formed SA squads suffered from a lack of infrastructure such as training grounds or halls. For this reason they hired the halls of nationalist gymnastics clubs or even joined the relevant teams within the clubs. Especially in the Austrian countryside where communities were comparatively small this meant that military gymnastics squads could be virtually equivalent to an SA unit; 42 per cent of the military team of the West Austrian Turnverein Dornbirn, for example, were members of the local SA branch.[19]

In the mid-1920s some factions in the DTB criticized the fact that the German nationalist movement in Austria was represented by several parties. This was seen to contradict the DTB's motto 'Unity of the People' and was also a disadvantage for the German Nationalists in the political fight against the Social Democrats and the Conservatives. Therefore it was time for there to be 'only one nationalist party which includes all classes and estates of the people'.[20] In the following years a struggle to be the sole legitimate representative of the German nationalist population in Austria took place between the Großdeutsche Volkspartei and the NSDAP. By the early 1930s the NSDAP had won. In 1931 the DTB board and the leader of the Austrian SA (stormtroops), Hermann Reschny, met to exchange ideas. After this meeting Reschny declared that the Austrian NSDAP would 'refrain from founding its own National Socialist gymnastics and sports clubs, because due to the German nationalist Aryan principles of the Deutscher Turnerbund there are no intentions to withdraw NSDAP members from the Turnvereine'.[21] In May 1933 the Vorarlberg branch of the Großdeutsche Volkspartei recommended to its members that they join the NSDAP 'because this movement supports the main demands of the Großdeutsche Volkspartei especially the will of the Anschluss and anti-Semitism'.[22] The same can be said for the DTB: it also practised strong anti-Semitism and since its foundation in 1919 it had stood for an *Anschluss* of Austria with Germany. In addition its members had a sociological structure comparable with that of the NSDAP.

COMMON IDEOLOGICAL, SYMBOLIC AND SOCIOLOGICAL FEATURES OF THE NSDP AND THE DTB

Amongst others, the DTB declared Purity of Race to be a binding principle of its work. To preserve this racist value all DTB clubs had to add the so-called Aryan paragraph to their statutes. It forbade all individuals of Jewish religion to become members of a German *Turnverein*. The 'Aryan paragraph' was the reason why Austrian gymnastics clubs left the Deutsche Turnerschaft at the end of the nineteenth century. Until 1904 the majority of Austrian gymnastics clubs belonged to the Deutsche Turnerschaft. They formed its district Turnkreis XV Deutsch-Österreich. In 1901 the Turnkreis XV 'aryanized' its statutes which meant that from then onwards it was obligatory for all of its member clubs to include the Aryan paragraph in their club programme. The Deutsche Turnerschaft did not agree with this policy and expelled the Austrian clubs. They founded several independent gymnastics federations before 1914. After the First World War they continued with the DTB. The DTB saw itself as the sole legitimate successor of these organizations and practised a strong anti-Semitic policy. In 1923 the Styrian German Sports Club Leoben was expelled from the Styrian Football Association because it refused to play a match in the Austrian championship against the Viennese Jewish football club Hakoah. The DTB praised the Leoben football players for this decision and criticized the Styrian Football Association in their journal:

> Let's hope that there are more sports clubs in Styria which will not understand the Football Association's ugly favouring of the Jews … Sportsmen unite in all fields in Aryan sports federations! … Don't let yourselves be pushed together with the Jews, the deadly enemy of our people. Found Aryan federations, refuse the Jews entry to your clubs![23]

The DTB was as uncompromising in its demand for an *Anschluss* of Austria with Germany. Its clubs were urged to celebrate the DTB principle Unity of People in its parties and festivals. In 1923 the organizers of the annual Vorarlberger Turngau gymnastics festival declared as their goal: 'A national uprising and a lasting strengthening of our will to survive through the difficulties of the time and to continue to gather our energies until the one big moment when our leaders will call us to help in the rebuilding of the great and unified fatherland which will encompass all German tribes.'[24]

At a DTB district festival in Bregenz in 1924 the town mayor Dr Ferdinand Kinz reminded the gymnasts in his opening speech that their task was 'to clear the way on which our separated national comrades in the North and in the South, in the East and in the West will be able to move into the great unified parental home'.[25] Almost a decade later Dr Hermann Schmid, the ideological secretary (*Dietwart*) of the Turnverein Bregenz, expressed the same sentiments as Kinz, but much more directly, at a midsummernight celebration in 1933. Schmid said, 'Our fatherland is only the great German fatherland. This ground on which we stand is German and has to stay German. We will remain faithful to our German brothers who fought with us in the World War shoulder to shoulder. *Heil Alldeutschland*!'[26]

In Austria, anti-Semitism and the vision of a Greater Germany were two ideological constants which were shared by the DTB and the NSDAP. This correspondence also expressed itself at the symbolic level of both movements. In 1919 the DTB chose a swastika with round beams as the emblem of its organization. It symbolized the four capital Fs of the gymnasts slogan 'Frisch–Fromm–Froh–Frei' (Fresh–Pious–Cheerful–Free). The four Fs were arranged from left to right around a central point which gave them the look of a swastika. At a common meeting of Austrian, Czech and German National Socialists in 1920 Adolf Hitler declared a swastika with angular beams to be the emblem of the Nazi movement.[27] These similar emblems led to rumours in the early 1920s that there was strong collaboration between the DTB and the NSDAP. When the Vorarlberger Turngau held its annual gymnastics festival in 1923 the local press hinted that this sporting event was simply a swastika party and that in fact the sports activities would only be an excuse for party politics. The festival's organizing committee released a press statement in which it stressed that 'the swastika was the emblem of the DTB long before it became the heavily criticized party symbol of our current days. The DTB rejects any kind of politics in its own ranks, the DTB is national, but it has nothing to do with the modern National Socialist movement which has the swastika in its party badge.'[28] Some years later, in 1934, the DTB emblem was banned by the Austrian government as a political symbol.[29] The reason was that after the banning of the Austrian NSDAP in 1933 the illegal Nazis wore the gymnastics symbol as an unofficial party badge. Consequently, the

Austrian government forbade the nationalist gymnastics clubs to decorate their training halls and their equipment such as club banners and publications with the round-beam swastika. At sports competitions the decorations had to be in the Austrian colours Red–White–Red.

TABLE 1

PROFESSIONAL PROFILE OF DTB AND NSDAP IN DORNBIRN

Professional position	NSDAP	Turnverein Dornbirn
	n=76 men %	n=538 men %
Employees	32.9	29.9
Workers	10.5	5.0
Craftsmen	38.6	30.6
Self-employed	17.1	32.3
Farmers	1.3	1.1
Others	0.9	1.3

In addition to these ideological and symbolic similarities the DTB and the Austrian NSDAP shared some sociological features. Gymnasts and Nazis recruited their supporters mainly from the middle classes. The professional profile of the local DTB and NSDAP branches in the West Austrian town of Dornbirn in 1932/33 is shown in Table 1. If these data are compared with the population of Dornbirn, differences in the percentages of 'farmers' and 'self-employed' occur.[30] In 1934, 10.1 per cent of the Dornbirn population worked in agriculture. Gymnasts and Nazis recruited about 1 per cent of this stratum. On the other hand approximately a fifth to a third of their ranks were self-employed, where the total proportion of this stratum in the Dornbirn population was 3.7 per cent. Overall it is clear that both the Nazi and the nationalist gymnastics movements consisted of middle-class supporters, which was one reason why individuals were members of both organizations. In 1932 the NSDAP had ten local branches in the Austrian province of Vorarlberg with 550 members; 143 of these Nazis were also members of their local gymnastics clubs.[31] As the following example shows, NSDAP and gymnastics clubs collaborated in recruiting new members.

On 25 May 1932 the Turnverein Feldkirch and the local NSDAP branch organized a commemorative ceremony for Albert Leo Schlageter in the gymnastics hall. Schlageter was a German nationalist who carried out bomb attacks against the French occupation troops in the Ruhr district after the First World War. In 1923 he was captured and executed by the French. The National Socialists made him a martyr for their movement and commemorated his death in several events. A few days after the ceremony in Feldkirch six men joined the Feldkirch NSDAP branch, among them five gymnasts. Not only ordinary gymnasts, 'seduced by politics', worked for the NSDAP, but also high ranking functionaries of gymnastics clubs, as the example of the Austrian province of Vorarlberg shows. The NSDAP *Gauleiter* of Vorarlberg, Anton Plankensteiner, was president of the Turnverein Dornbirn. The leader of the Vorarlberg SA (stormtroops), Eugen Koelbl, led the military squad of the Turnverein Dornbirn. The president of the province's Hitler Youth, Otto Weber, was a gymnast too, so was Rudolf Gunz, one of two NSDAP MPs to the Vorarlberg local parliament. Half of the chairmen of the Vorarlberg NSDAP local branches in 1932 were gymnasts.[32] This very close relationship between the Hitler party and DTB clubs did not end when the NSDAP in Austria was banned in 1933. On the contrary, gymnasts went underground and supported the illegal Nazi activities.

In July 1934 the Austrian NSDAP organized a coup against the government. It started from a gymnastics hall of the DTB in Vienna. The Austrian Chancellor Dr Engelbert Dollfuss was murdered by Nazis. On the side of the putsch organizers 17 gymnasts died and five were executed after the failure of the putsch. As a first reaction to these events the Austrian government banned all DTB activities until October 1934: its gymnastics halls were closed and all DTB clubs were put under police supervision. In autumn 1934 the ban was lifted on the condition that the gymnastics clubs accepted a person of trust, named by the Austrian government, who supervised their activities and reported any anti-Austrian activity to the state authorities. Despite these strict requirements the DTB clubs continued to support the illegal NSDAP. Their activities included disrupting so-called Austrian patriotic rallies by shouting *Heil Hitler* or singing the German national anthem, building and maintaining the illegal party structures of the NSDAP, carrying out bomb attacks against Austrian state property and kidnapping.

In August 1934 the security agencies exposed the illegal SS of the Vorarlberg province. This was only made possible because the authorities had a contact in the SS. The Austrian SS was founded in January 1930 by the Viennese *Gauleiter* Eduard Frauenfeld. In its early years it did not develop very well. In Vorarlberg the only two SS branches were founded from Germany in 1931–32. They had up to 40 members. A third of their officers were members of the Turnverein Bregenz. The main tasks of the Austrian SS, which was sponsored by Hitler's Germany, was to keep the NSDAP functionaries, Austrian public life and police forces under surveillance. It also had to make sure that it was represented in the best circles and that it recruited new members from this section of the population. In addition to this surveillance squad the Austrian SS had a combat unit. It was responsible for most of the illegal Nazi propaganda activities, amongst them the putsch in July 1934. Its members were pledged to absolute obedience. On 30 May 1933 Siegfried Haemmerle, a gymnast and an SS member, was captured by the Austrian police. He had distributed Nazi leaflets and brochures without permission. In the interrogation that followed his imprisonment Haemmerle was asked if he did not know that he had committed a crime. He responded, 'I don't care if this is prohibited or not. When we get orders from headquarters we have to carry them out, no matter what happens. We are obliged to blind obedience. If we get punished we have to accept it.'[33]

Haemmerle was involved in other criminal offences too. Weeks before the exposure of the Vorarlberg SS, rumours in NS circles said that a contact of the Austrian government had infiltrated the SS officers and this was substantiated. Haemmerle and other remaining SS members kidnapped this officer and took him to Germany where he was put in front of a NSDAP party court. He was found guilty and imprisoned in the NS penal camp Lechhausen. From there he fled back to Austria in autumn 1934. Four out of seven men involved in his kidnapping were members of a Vorarlberg gymnastics club.[34]

The example of Vorarlberg also shows the extent of the engagement of DTB gymnasts in illegal NS propaganda; 715 out of 3,300 DTB gymnasts in Vorarlberg were punished for illegal NS activities between 1933 and 1938. The offenders came from 14 out of 32 DTB clubs in the province. Six of these clubs were banned because of their central role in undercover Nazi propaganda. Seventy-one Vorarlberg gymnasts fled to Hitler's Germany to avoid imprisonment. There they joined the so-called Austrian Legion, a paramilitary troop which was recruited by the NSDAP and trained for an invasion of Austria. In 1934 an illegal SS branch was founded from the Turnverein Goetzis. Ninety per cent of the Vorarlberg Hitler Jugend (Hitler Youth, HJ) were recruited from the youth squads of the DTB clubs. Vorarlberg gymnasts collected membership subscriptions for the illegal NSDAP and they distributed illegal NS leaflets and newspapers.[35] These criminal offences were carried out before or after weekly training meetings. The HJ in the West Austrian town of Feldkirch, for example, handed out NS press material to its members after the training sessions of the youth squads of the local Turnverein. This material was mainly of German origin, but in 1936 the Vorarlberg HJ produced its own illegal magazine entitled *The Fanfare*, which contained news of local and national NS circles. Funding came partly from the Austrian HJ headquarters in Vienna and partly from Germany. The main leaders of the Vorarlberg HJ were based in the German town of Lindau, a few miles from the Austrian border. From there they directed the HJ activities. These included collecting membership subscriptions, distributing NS leaflets, smuggling NS propaganda material into Austria, weekend camps with scouting games and drill, and political schooling at secret meeting points in the woods, in shelter huts in the mountains or at somebody's home. The overall goal of these activities was to 'keep Hitler's idea alive among National Socialist youth' and 'to strengthen our comradeship in the spirit of Hitler'.[36] Absolute physical dedication was demanded from HJ members. At an illegal training camp at Whitsuntide 1937 the German HJ leader Kurt Clemens spoke to Vorarlberg Hitler youths and demanded that they stand together and not lose heart, even if one or the other was imprisoned. If this happened they could always go on hunger strike which had already helped in the past. The average age of the Vorarlberg HJ was 17; about a third were unemployed, the rest trainees, apprentices or schoolboys. The social background of their parents was petit bourgeois, almost 10 per cent had single parents. The vast majority were Austrian, but 8 per cent were German, Czechoslovak or Yugoslav citizens.[37]

The DTB and its clubs were very concerned to prevent the involvement of its gymnasts in National Socialism. The board of the Turnverein Goetzis distributed a circular in 1933 in which it asked its members to distance themselves from any party politics inside and outside the club, to keep strict control of themselves and to follow the instructions of the state authority. However, the ideological superstructure of German gymnastics in Austria meant that initiatives such as this failed; 63 per cent of the Goetzis gymnasts, for example, were punished for illegal National Socialist activities. In 1934 its members founded an illegal branch of the SS; in 1935/36 young members founded a branch of the HJ and of the BDM (Bund deutscher Mädchen), which was the female HJ.

The crucial role gymnasts played in the NSDAP activities between 1933 and 1938 in Austria became obvious again after the occupation of Austria by Hitler's Germany in March 1938. The secretary of the Turnverein Dornbirn wrote in his annual report in October 1938:

> It has to be mentioned that we collaborate with the party (NSDAP) and its units on the friendliest terms, although we lost the best people after the *Anschluss* to the party and many of us can hardly find time for our club business because we are too busy with party affairs; but even this will change once the new state is established and the *Ostmark* catches up on the advantage the Old Empire (*Altreich*) has over us.[38]

These hopes were not fulfilled. The National Socialist state had no interest in keeping the autonomous life of its former collaboration partner alive. The Nazi government forced the DTB to disband. Its clubs were transferred into the united NS-Reichsbund für Leibesübungen (Reich Association for Physical Education) where they became part of the one and only German national body, led by the NSDAP.

CONCLUSIONS

The DTB and NSDAP shared common features in their ideological superstructure and their sociological profile. In addition to drawing their support predominantly from the middle classes, their theory and practice was based upon anti-Semitism and the vision of a Greater Germany. For these reasons political collaboration between the NSDAP and the DTB took place in the 1920s and 1930s. Gymnastics clubs not only put their cadres at the disposal of the NSDAP, they also supported the Hitler party with their infrastructure and organized common events in their gymnastics halls. This coalition continued even after the banning of the NSDAP in 1933. Gymnasts dedicated their body and mind to an *Anschluss* of Austria with Hitler's Germany and played a crucial role in the illegal Nazi activities between 1933 and 1938.

In order to explain these activities and the link between the two movements it is necessary to investigate the social and ideological characteristics which they shared and the ways in which these were linked to projects involving the body. Certain key features of both organizations relate to the gendered nature of their idealized body image and political organization; their reliance on a Darwinian evolutionary theory to justify their political projects of the body; and the class structure of their organizations. Despite the rhetoric of unification and reference to the 'German people' or to 'the Nation', in reality the people or the nation referred to was not inclusive, but exclusive. This nation, or by analogy this body, is actually a heavily gendered concept and one that relies on a particular view of the citizen in terms of class, ethnicity, sexuality, physical capabilities and so on. This point was made clear by Jahn, the originator of the gymnastics movement who referred to the desirability of the 'pure' nation.[39]

In class terms, both the DTB and the NSDAP recruited their members from the middle classes, as did the NSDAP in Germany. Using the example of Dornbirn, it is clear that both the gymnastics clubs and the NSDAP included a higher proportion of the self-employed than in the population as a whole. In contrast, their membership under-represented agricultural workers in comparison with the local population. This predominance of the middle classes had implications for the approach to the body and for corresponding political affiliations. P. Bourdieu has pointed out that the working class and the middle class have differing approaches to the body.[40] For Bourdieu the body is not a finished biological entity, but represents an unfinished product. The body is key to the production and reproduction of class in that it is the bearer of physical capital, the location of the habitus, and the displayer of taste.[41] Each class has a specific relationship to these factors, and applies differing approaches to the way in which the body becomes a culturally complete product. For the working class, the body is regarded instrumentally. This means that for them, the body is a means to an end. The physical capital of the body is converted into economic capital. Through the necessity to work, and the intensity of labour, this economic capital becomes the focus, and the body remains a tool to achieve a basic standard of living. Here it becomes clear that the agricultural labourers in the Dornbirn example would be little attracted by a body culture which required investment of time and physical capital and yet was not converted into economic capital. The demands of agricultural labour leave little time, or physical reserves, for engagement in body projects which does not result in economic benefit. The habitus of this section of the working class would also predispose them to an instrumental view of the body and in so doing make it unlikely that their taste would be displayed by unproductive body cultures such as gymnastics.

In contrast, Bourdieu outlines the tendency for the middle classes to interweave their self identity with the control and display of the body. For the middle classes, with access to higher economic rewards through a smaller expenditure of physical labour, the time and energy required to view the body as a project in itself are available. When the body becomes an end in itself, it also becomes an important means of displaying taste through achievement of a specific body shape, the display of commodities associated with the body, and engagement in a particular lifestyle. The over-representation of the middle classes amongst the Turnvereine and the NSDAP appears to support this view of body projects in relation to class. In making a fetish of the body, members of both organizations displayed a middle class habitus. In linking the role of the body to a political project, they were engaged in reproducing not simply physical characteristics, but also corresponding ideologies. It is clear then that the association of gymnastic organizations and activities with a political aim was a tool to mobilize the middle classes rather than a means of preparing the working class for struggle. It is also evident that the ideology of the 'German body' in fact disguises differences in class within this body culture.

The view of the body drawn upon and the activities selected to prepare the body and mind for political action also display a heavily gendered concept of the idealized body. The advent of 'military gymnastics' which included activities such as throwing hand-grenades, parading and marching seems designed to militarize gymnastic activities. Jahn's original training sessions were also organized along paramilitary lines and included marching, shooting and fencing. These activities were intended to prepare the male body for action, and also to create a specific form of masculinity, one that is allied to hegemonic masculinity. Defining a healthy body and mind as one which has engaged in certain activities in order to achieve a particular level of fitness produces two results. Firstly, masculinity is differentiated from femininity in terms of the nature of bodies produced, and the activities suitable for each gender. Secondly, masculinity is defined in one particular form, that of hegemonic masculinity.[42] Sport has long been both a constituent of this form of masculinity and a means by which it is displayed.[43] Hegemonic masculinity is a 'White' masculinity in that hegemony establishes a central position for the most powerful groups, in this case in relation to ethnicity. Some ethnicities themselves are defined through this process in reference to what are regarded as feminine qualities.[44]

Here again the myth of a people's unity is exposed as an attempt to create a hegemony based on the visibility of one body form and a rendering of the 'Other' invisible. The body so far discussed has been masculine and middle class and hence those who differ from this ideal become 'Other', defined by the idealized body culture and vulnerable to victimization. This policy of persecution and exclusion was legitimized by reference to a further ideological construct: that of Darwinism.

Darwinism supports the attempt to channel the animalistic tendencies of humans into a more 'civilized' or organized form. Darwinism also underpinned the attempts by the NSDAP and the DTB to position the body as a product of nature. Consequently, gymnastics festivals were held outdoors, at a central place in a village or town, starting off with a procession of the participants in white gymnastics uniforms through the streets. All disciplines such as wrestling, fencing or team gymnastics were performed outdoors on the festival field (*Festwiese*). In addition, gymnastics clubs organized regular club hikes throughout the year, and weekend camps were held in the woods or mountains. This enabled the creation of the mythology of the gymnast as closer to nature. By defining nature and culture in opposition to each other, nature can be constructed as pure and associations with it as physically and morally enriching. Darwinism, in addition to constructing the body and its expression as natural, was also used to reinforce a linear view of history. Though Darwin himself did not propose the inevitability of any particular form of evolution, his work has been interpreted in order to justify this view. Nazi propaganda defined the body as natural and evolution as progressive. The DTB itself was based upon the so-called Aryan wisdoms, one of which was Purity of Race. In this way the Aryan body and the closely regulated gymnast's body could be placed at a point on the evolutionary scale higher than those bodies which did not fit this idealized body image. The body here not only becomes evolutionarily superior, it also lies beyond the control of social and cultural factors. The naturalization of bodies may be extended to naturalize social conditions and social relations.

The ideology of inclusiveness advocated by Austrian gymnasts in their denial that their activities could be defined as political, and in the belief that as they worked for a unification of the Austrian and the German people they were not representing sectional interests, is shown to be a fallacy. The body, the State, and the people were linked by analogy, by the use of symbols and by reference to a sophisticated set of ideological constructs. However, this analogy, contrary to claims of unification, actually served to exclude certain categories of people. The healthy body and mind are defined in reference to class, to hegemonic masculinity, and to racist interpretations of Darwinism through a political project. Contrary to gymnasts' claims, the body does not exist as a 'natural' entity beyond the influence of social and political factors. The example of the Austrian gymnastics movement shows how sport, the body and politics are closely linked, and provides a historical context within which this can be illustrated.

NOTES

1. Radio Vorarlberg, 1 June 1991.
2. C. Shilling, *The Body and Social Theory* (London, 1994) (hereafter *Body and Social History*). M. Featherstone, 'The Body in Consumer Culture', *Theory, Culture and Society,* 1, 2 (1982), 18–33.
3. For Jahn see Christiane Eisenberg, 'Charismatic Nationalist Leader: Turnvater Jahn', *International Journal of the History of Sport*, 13 (1996), 18–27.
4. Ibid., 18.
5. H. Ueberhorst, *Zurück zu Jahn? Gab es kein besseres Vorwärts*? (Bochum, 1969), p.23 (hereafter *Zurück zu Jahn?*).
6. Radio Vorarlberg, 1 June 1991.
7. *Turnen und Sport*, 13 (1924), 27 March, 50.
8. J. and W. Weber, *'Jeder Betrieb eine rote Festung!': Die KPOe in Vorarlberg 1920–1956* (Feldkirch, 1994), pp.110, 121, 132, 159, 160–2, 169, 170, 173, 179, 202, 223, 252.
9. For details see W. Weber, *Von Jahn zu Hitler: Politik- und Organisationsgeschichte des Deutschen Turnens in Vorarlberg 1847 bis 1938* (Constance, 1995), pp.213–14 (hereafter *Von Jahn zu Hitler*).
10. Overall they lost about 5 per cent of their electorate, see E. Weinzierl and K. Skalnik, *Österreich 1918-1938: Geschichte der Ersten Republik*, Vol.2, p.1092.
11. *Turnen und Sport*, 4 (1924), 24 January, 13.
12. *Turnen und Sport*, 20 (1923), 18 October, 1.
13. *Turnen und Sport*, 7 (1924), 14 February, 30.
14. *Turnen und Sport*, 9 (1924), 1 March, 33.
15. *Turnen und Sport*, 4 (1924), 24 January, 13.
16. Ibid.
17. Weber, *Von Jahn zu Hitler*, pp.118–20, 138, 159–60.
18. *Vorarlberger Landesarchiv*, Bregenz/Austria VLandreg. I-146/1925 (hereafter *VLA*).
19. *VLA*, VLandreg. Ia-1124/1934.
20. *Turnen und Sport*, 4 (1924), 24 January, 14.
21. *Zur Abwehr der klerikalen Angriffe gegen den Deutschen Turnerbund* (Vienna, 1929), p.17.
22. *Vorarlberger Tagblatt* (1933), 8 May.
23. *Turnen und Sport*, 21 (1923), 25 October, 86.
24. *Turnen und Sport*, 5 (1923), 5 July, 21.
25. *Turnen und Sport*, 26 (1924), 25 July, 104.
26. *VLA*, BH Bregenz III-1516/1935.
27. A. Graenz, 'Das Hakenkreuz', in A. Schilling, *Dr. Walter Riehl und die Geschichte des Nationalsozialismus* (Leipzig, 1933), pp.378–80.
28. *Turnen und Sport*, 5 (1923), 5 July, 1.
29. *Österreichisches Staatsarchiv*, Archiv der Republik, BKA Zl.215.770–GD2.
30. Dornbirn results of the national census in 1934: industry and business 59.5%, trade and traffic

11.8%, agriculture and forestry 10.1%, unemployed 8.8%, self-employed 3.7%, public employees 2.8%, no information 2.2%, banking 0.8%, domestic services 0.3%, in: *Dornbirner Schriften XI. Beiträge zur Stadtkunde*, 56.

31. Weber, *Von Jahn zu Hitler*, pp.270–1.
32. Ibid. p.272.
33. *VLA*, BH Bregenz III-423/1936.
34. *VLA*, BH Bregenz III-4214/1934.
35. Weber, *Von Jahn zu Hitler*, pp.101–84, 188–208, 211–33, 234–45, 250–5, 259–64.
36. *VLA*, BH Bregenz III-2322/1934.
37. For details about the Hitler Youth see Weber, *Von Jahn zu Hitler*, pp.112–52, 157–75, 188–97, 234–45, 250–5.
38. Turnverein Dornbirn, Chronicle 1939.
39. Ueberhorst, *Zurück zu Jahn*, p.23.
40. P. Bourdieu, 'Sport and Social Class', *Social Science Information*, 17 (1978), 819–40 and P. Bourdieu, *Distinction: A Social Critique of the Judgement of Taste* (London, 1984).
41. Bourdieu defines habitus as 'the strategy generating principle enabling agents to cope with unforeseen and ever-changing situations … a system of lasting, transposable dispositions which, integrating past experiences, functions at every moment as a matrix of perceptions, appreciations and actions that makes possible the achievement'. P. Bourdieu, *Outline of a Theory of Practice* (Cambridge, 1977), pp.72, 95. The habitus is essentially corporeal in that it exists and is displayed through bodily actions. Physical capital refers to the body's possession of status, power and the potential to transform this physicality into other forms of capital. Taste is the development of preference for lifestyle forms which are actually limited by material factors. Taste is the manifestation of the habitus. C. Shilling, *Body and Social History*.
42. R. Connell, *Masculinities* (Cambridge, 1995).
43. A. Parker, 'Sporting Masculinities: Gender Relations and the Body' in M. MacAn Ghaill (ed.), *Understanding Masculinities: Social Relations and Cultural Arenas* (Buckingham, 1996).
44. E. Said, *Orientalism: Western Conceptions of the Orient* (Harmondsworth, 1995).

3

Fascist Political Athletes and the Body Politic: Bulgaria Reborn

VASSIL GIRGINOV and PETER BANKOV

The study of Fascism in Bulgaria is a contentious issue, one which reflects different ideological interpretations given to the period between the 1920s and 1944. The theme of sport and Fascism is no exception as the academic studies of that time are scarce. Most of the post-Fascist analyses tend to describe the struggle of the Communist sports clubs against a monarcho-Fascist dictatorship and fail to elaborate on the nature of its ideology and practices. With the end of the Communist era in 1989, a radical view emerged suggesting that Fascism never existed in Bulgaria. This is not true. Although, Bulgaria's variant of Fascism was not as total as elsewhere, inspection of the country's history provides persuasive evidence of the domination of the Fascist ideological doctrine, the efforts of various government administrations and institutions to ensure its acceptance in society and their aspiration to create an 'Aryan' manhood. Thus, a number of interrelated questions need to be answered concerning the anthropological and ideological premises for the emergence of the Superman as a dual metaphor for the *political athlete*, and for the body as a *politicum*, as well as the impact of the relationship between Italian–German Fascist doctrine (as countries of origin) and recipient Bulgarian culture.

This essay, therefore, will aim to provide some answers to these questions in the form of three arguments:

(i) the ideological and social preoccupations of Bulgaria's Fascist sport sprang from the common sources of the pre and post First World War moral and material crises and from the specific historical links between German corporal education and Bulgaria's sports movement;

(ii) in relation to sport, the theory and practices of Bulgarian Fascism (representing the case of a culture-bearing race as opposed to the

Aryan culture-creating race), endorsed not all but certainly some of the major ideas of Fascist ideology: nationalism; super-patriotism, the use of violence to impose views on others, anti-Communism, and *völkisch* (people's) education;

(iii) the rise of the totalitarian political athlete and body politics was grounded in the notion of national self-assertion and the ideological struggle between Fascism and Communism and, as such, had its continuation in the theory and practices of the Communist state established after 1945 in Bulgaria. It was said that the Italian Fascists made the Italian trains run on time; Hitler and the Nazis made the nation run in unison into disaster; and it can be added that Tsar Boris III[1] and the Bulgarian Fascists did the same, albeit in disharmony.

ON THE GENESIS OF BULGARIAN FASCISM AND THE CONCEPT OF APOLLONISM

The preconditions for the emergence of Bulgarian Fascism can be traced back to the development of the Bulgarian state and political democracy at the end of the nineteenth and in the beginning of the twentieth centuries. Bulgaria began the journey towards a free bourgeois society in 1878 with the ambition to gain back its cultural and territorial identity after five centuries of Ottoman domination and seven years of brutal Western intervention (German, British and French after the 1878 Berlin Treaty), which imposed ethnic and constitutional division on the country. The drive for the unification of Bulgarian lands, and the consolidation of the nation (further reinforced by the nostalgia for the once Great Bulgaria[2] which had spread across three seas) became a national ideal, and has clearly dominated Bulgarian policy ever since.

Eventually, in 1885 Bulgaria gained its unity. It was declared a constitutional monarchy, and a 22-year-old officer from the German army, a member of the Battenberg dynasty was proclaimed the first Bulgarian Prince and entrusted with considerable power.[3] The country's further historical development was marked by continuous military conflict and disaster – two coups and two consecutive wars – the Balkans War from 1912 to 1913 and the Great War from 1915 to 1918. In all instances the army continually made a critical appearance on the political scene. Although in the Great War Bulgaria was defeated and suffered huge material and moral losses, as N. Gentchev comments: 'the army – this reactionary institution – haunts ubiquitously political life, plays a fatal role, and prepares a reactionary phalanx of political figures and military personnel, who look with disdain on the traditions of bourgeois democracy'.[4]

Naturally, the first organizations championing 'tough power' based on open political terrorism against Bolshevism were the Military League, the Union of the Reserve Officers and the organization Kubrat.[5] All three were well connected with the monarchy and aimed to defend the foundations of bourgeois society after the national catastrophe brought about by the Great War. Bulgaria's many years of uncertainty, frustration, national humiliation and human and material suffering, coupled with the failure of bourgeois democracy to provide the basic necessities of life, created anxiety, anger and a demand for order, stability and social and economic efficiency, needs which were particularly appealing to the young working class and the military. Right wing revolutionaries called for a new social order capitalizing on nationalistic fervour, and mounted a military Fascist coup on 9 June 1923. More than 20,000 people were exterminated, and with their demise the Fascist regime of Al. Tzankovwas established.[6]

Bulgaria's social and political reality after the Great War as a defeated German ally was predetermined to a large extent by the 'slavery' clauses of the 1919 Neuilly Treaty.[7] 'The most fruitful lands of south Dobrudja, western Thrakia, and other western outlying districts were cut off from the rest of the country and unbearable reparations equal to 20 per cent of the national wealth were imposed, in addition to the old foreign debts.'[8] Bulgaria was denied a regular army; specific guidelines were established regarding the character of voluntary sport organizations and even the way gymnastics should be taught in schools in order to prevent the renaissance of any military element in education and society.

Gradually, the country's political and economic development became dependent on Nazi Germany. The Versailles Treaty had deprived Germany of its colonies. Consequently it suffered from a chronic shortage of raw materials and turned to Bulgaria to remedy the situation. Nevertheless, politically the advance of Fascism in Bulgaria between 1919 and 1944 did not follow a clear pattern of progression. The first military Fascist coup in 1923 generated a counter movement – the first mass anti-Fascist uprising in the world – in September of the same year. The period between 1927 and 1934 was marked by a process of de-

Fascistization preceded by the restoration of bourgeois parliamentary democracy.

In 1933 when Hitler came to power in Germany he immediately launched a crusade against the Communist and anti-Fascist movements. The Nazis framed the Reichstag fire trial with the intention of subjecting all progressive forces in Germany and elsewhere to terrorist laws. Three Bulgarian Communists (including the leader of the Bulgarian Communist Party – Georgi Dimitrov) were selected as scapegoats.[9] Dimitrov was accused of being a barbarous Communist and fire-raiser. Eventually, Dimitrov was discharged and his trial resulted in the public censure of Hitler. More notably, however, it illustrated perfectly the application of the Nazi doctrine which divides the people of the world into three racial categories: culture-creating races (the Aryans), culture-bearing races (Orientals, Latins and Slavs), and culture-destroying races (Gypsies, Negroes and Jews). These racial prejudices determined the respective superior–inferior attitudes in German–Bulgarian relationships and, despite the close alliance, the German Fascist attitudes to Bulgarian Fascism.

A second military coup in 1935 paved the way for the monarcho-Fascist dictatorship, and established the personal regime of Boris III. From 1935 onwards national governments were formed according to the dictates of the Court and no longer represented any political parties. Tsar Boris III and Adolph Hitler were very close. They met seven times, and always demonstrated great mutual respect for each other's personalities and achievements. Economic integration also grew closer. German capital investment, until 1935 a modest 5.5 per cent of the total foreign investments in the country had increased to 16 per cent in 1939 and reached 29.1 per cent in 1944, the highest of all investing countries. A similar trend characterized foreign trade. In 1933 Bulgarian exports to Germany represented 38.2 per cent, and imports 36 per cent of total trade. By the end of the pre-war period in 1939, these figures were 67.8 per cent and 65.6 per cent respectively. During the war itself Germany established a full monopoly equal to 95–100 per cent of the exports of Bulgarian meat, fruit and vegetables, 85 per cent of the wine and 65 per cent of the tobacco and maintained a negative trade balance with a massive debt of 766,500,000 Reich Mark in 1944, which was in fact a way of subsidising the Nazi military economy.

Bulgaria's economy, state administration, education, literature, sport and language were heavily influenced by Nazi doctrine. The ultimate purpose of the Bulgarian–German alliance, as seen by the monarch and his loyal political élite, was to guarantee the country's aspirations to regain her position as a leader of the Balkans. Despite its officially proclaimed neutrality, Bulgaria's government turned down the USSR proposal in 1940 for a Pact for Friendship and Mutual Assistance,[10] disregarding the signatures of several millions who insisted on the signing of the pact, and in March 1941 the Prime Minister B. Filov signed a treaty joining Bulgaria to the Fascist bloc.[11] Bulgaria thus became totally integrated with Germany, ideologically, politically and economically.

As suggested before, Bulgarian chauvinism, sustained historically by past glory, the might of the first Bulgarian kingdom and the desire for a leading role in the Balkans, has always had national politics as its main preoccupation. Regional dominance has always underpinned most major political decisions, and justified any changes. The underlying principle of Fascist nationalism was that of unity of the nation, revolving around the core idea of the nation as a single public organism. It symbolized Bulgaria's missionary design on the Balkans. In Bulgarian eyes, as the only people with inherited 'state-creative' abilities, Bulgarians were specially chosen to determine the political and cultural development of the other nations in the region.

The Fascist movement in Bulgaria never had a mass social base or the support of the traditional bourgeois parties, since there was no single Fascist organization with its own national Führer and with extensive public influence over society. Such a situation substantiates the claim made by many authors that Bulgaria's Fascism was a military monarchist alliance without a clear ideological framework. In this respect, it was similar to Italian Fascism, where Mussolini fashioned his ideology after taking control, whereas Hitler articulated his ideology before he came to power. But as L. Baradat points out, 'neither theory was developed into a logical whole' which holds true for Bulgaria as well.[12] This is the specific characteristic of Bulgarian Fascism. Its manifestations could be found everywhere, in state policy, in public movements, in political life and, of course, in sport.

The Fascist period in Bulgaria clearly marked a distinctive attitude towards sport as an ideological variable and emphasized its potential for shaping a new type of man capable of fulfilling an historic mission in society. The early 1898 theoretical foundations of Bulgaria's sport, laid by the country's first national organization Unak (Hero), which subscribed to the concept of holism, that is, the balanced development of human physical and intellectual education, was gradually replaced by the vulgarized doctrine of Apollonism (Bulgaria's equivalent of 'athleticism,' after the ancient Greek god of male beauty, Apollo), which was symbolized by the strong male body and its utilitarian purposes.[13] The emergence of the Superman as the epitome of the political athlete and the related body politic reflects the Fascist commitment to power, discipline and virility, in the interests of the restoration of national dignity, and for the construction of a new society. Within their historical and geographical context the Bulgarian Fascists subscribed, and were committed, to the notion of the historic mission of the master race based on the theory of élitism proposed by the guiding philosopher of the Third Reich, Friedrich Nietzsche, who identified leadership with the 'heroic man' who had the will for power and the desire to dominate. As is well known, this Superman (Nietzsche used the word *Übermensch*), he predicted, would emerge and rise to power in order to impose his law and his will on the spineless multitude with its Christian slave morality. Hence, human domination became the highest moral expression in life, a proposition with its emphasis on strength that clearly highlighted the supremacy and exclusivity of the body, and its necessary transformation into a public organ – the body as a 'politicum'. This seductive morality served to restimulate the Bulgarian impulse for regional supremacy.

THE BODY CULT AND THE TALE OF KRALI MARKO

'What celebration of science, or art can compete with this grandiose festival of sport?,' asked Dr N. Sheitanov commenting on the 'most grandiose manifestation' of the modern body cult – the clash between the two human bodies of the American boxers Dempsey and Tunney, in Chicago in 1927, in front of 160,000 spectators, and another 50 million radio listeners from all over the world.[14] This questioning of the primacy of the intellectual – science and art – over the physical – the body – represents, as J. Hoberman argues, 'the core of Nazi political anthropology'.[15] Mussolini and Hitler, who largely ignored the written word, misinterpreted Nietzsche to serve their cause, by asserting that life was a continuous struggle between strength and weakness, in which the stronger had always been victorious. As Hitler declared in his address to the German Gymnastics Festival in 1933, 'life will not be protected by weak philosophers, but by strong men', whereas Mussolini demanding passion and obedience commanded his followers: 'Feel, don't think.'[16]

The rise of the body cult in Bulgaria's post-First World War Fascist movement can be attributed to three main influences: socio-political reality, historical preoccupation (nostalgia for a Great Bulgaria), and ideological dependence (cultural and ideological subordination to outside doctrine). As a process, the rise of the body cult emerged in the 1920s stimulated by the lessons of the war. In an attempt to outline the end of an epoch marked by the subordination of the body, Sheitanov noted that 'the spirit was crushed by grandiose events and horrible experiences…, the war asserted the belief, that the body is the prime feature of man'.[17] Subsequently, the general shift of society from bourgeois democracy to Fascist monarchy, transformed the concept of sport for the first time in Bulgaria's modern history, from being a fashionable endeavour of civilized Europe into a state institution.

The sporting equivalent of the later political and state Superman ideal for the earlier Great Bulgaria was the epic heroic figure of Krali (winged) Marko. For centuries, he had represented one of the most popular characters in Bulgarian folklore, capable of any physical achievement. Krali Marko epitomized the complete athlete, 'throwing like a feather' his 600 kg mace, lifting up the whole earth like 'a beautiful lassie', hitting the opponent always between the eyes, jumping over mountains, flying on his horse, or effortlessly swimming across the Black Sea, and 'relaxing with a faithful lover, while talking to the stars'. The 'Bulgarian muscle man' knew no boundaries as he sought to win recognition in a fight with God himself! Krali Marko honoured exploits and disdained perfidies as the honourable did in sport, where the most valuable thing was achievement, rather than trickery. Markonian values typifying the past now typifyed the present. The notion of power derived from the athletic body and the unrelenting drive to conquer highlighted virility, aggression and strength. These now became the essential attributes of the character of the New Bulgarian Man. These values further justified the introduction of body politics based on military fitness, and its use in assuring the potent unity of the nation.

Bulgarian folklore then proved a vital source of inspiration for the Fascist regime in shaping the modern myth of the Superman. In the search for the national roots and the identity of the New Man, folklore was brutally misinterpreted. In the words of Sheitanov, 'according to national folklore, Bulgarian sport demands from the man, through body exploits, to raise himself up to be a 'godlike man'.[18] The new 'godlike' man, however, was not based on the God of the Bible. The Fascists detested Christianity because it disdained and denied the body and the body cult. Theirs was rather a new god, not bound by Christian laws, whose authority stemmed directly from a powerful, invincible body, and the adulation of those who shared the same values. The rise of the body cult under these specific circumstances was an attempt to make a strong appeal to some of the prominent traits of historical Bulgarian political culture discussed above. Thus, the transfer from the body as representative of a political athlete to the body as representative of the 'politicum', constitutes a natural extension of the Fascist attempt to achieve the subordination of society, and one particularly relevant institution – sport – now to be considered.

Ideologically, Bulgaria's physical culture and Nazi sport as J. Hoberman argues for the latter, 'prefigured in, and in some respects derived from, the doctrine of Friedrich L. Jahn, founder of the gymnastic movement in Germany in 1811. It was Jahn who first seized upon the concept of *Volkstum* to denote a cultural and racial nationalism which would require little improvization on the part of the Nazist.'[19] The three fundamental themes of Jahn's corporal education – racial superiority, the health of the *Volk* and military education, as others have made clear in this volume, constituted the core of Nazi physical culture. The Nazi sports ideology, however, Hoberman continues, 'surpassed Jahn's doctrine in three ways. First, it ascribes a "deeper significance" to Jahn's racial mysticism than even the master himself; second, it has a deeper appreciation for adolescence as an "initiation into manhood"; and third, Nazi doctrine presupposes the "reawakening of the sense for public life" the body as Politicum.'[20]

In Fascist Bulgaria it was Jahn's doctrine which was used for the establishment of the national sport movement. In the search for the country's salvation after the partition imposed by the Berlin treaty, military education in the form of people's gymnastics societies was borrowed directly from Jahn's Turnverein movement by the founders of the first revolutionary committee, Edinstvo (unity), in 1878.[21] These early gymnastics societies emphasized three essential roles of sport: the education of the individual and society, organization and control throughout of society and the dominance of the military character of education. The first gymnastic club in the country was the German *Turnverein*, established in 1883. After a period of expansion of the gymnastic movement, in 1897 the then Ministry of Education issued a directive encouraging all educational authorities to promote the establishment of gymnastic clubs in the country, based on a wide membership of people from all walks of life. Once they had joined the club 'they no longer represented the social strata they belonged to, and became ordinary members like everyone else'.[22] The presentation of sport establishments as places where class distinctions were diminished, suggests that they were seen as specific institutions for social education. This ideological tradition was further developed in the years of the monarcho-Fascist dictatorship.

The acquisition of military skills was ensured through the kind of sports that were stressed, such as shooting, gymnastics, wrestling, fencing, riding and weightlifting. The lessons of the First World War further reinforced the stress on military education. American and English soldiers' fitness and physical skills, particularly their ability to throw hand-grenades, two-thirds further than Bulgarians, was used as a strong argument for improved fitness training. The example of Italian physical culture in educating the young through organizations such as Balila and Avangardisti served as a rationale for the introduction of the first Physical Education of Bulgarian Youth Act in 1931. It was preceded by clear concern for the increased popularity of the Bolshevik's ideas amongst young people, and the need to protect them from Communist visions. The main concerns of the government, however – the poor physical condition of the youth, the lack of activity on the part of voluntary sport organizations, and the need for strengthening state control over physical culture – emphasized three issues which paved the way to a new, uniform and centrally controlled system of sport subordinated to state doctrine. Although, the law was presented as an important regulator for the establishment of harmony in the nation, its latent intent was revealed during parliamentary debate. In a blunt speech in favour of the new sports law, D. Ivanov,[23] chairman of the national umbrella sports governing body – the National Sports Federation – argued that the aim of the corporeal education was:

> to develop youth morally and physically, to teach them how to fight (not to be like a granny), and to speak of eternal peace – although such a peace existed only in the grave. They should recognize that life is a struggle, a fight for existence, and that in any case since life was sport, as in sport, there would be either victory or defeat.[24]

It is worth noting the similarity between the key expressions in Jahn's writings and the official terminology adopted in the Bulgarian Fascist literature on corporal education. It could be claimed that the Fascist sports ideology never seriously developed beyond the limits of corporal education and its utilitarian purposes improving health, or as preparation for war. It was subordinated to the ultimate goal – the achievement of human and state superiority. The strong presence of the Russian school of physical culture in the country, and its contribution particularly towards the diffusion of such English sports as rowing, yachting and tennis (none of them of course of Russian origin) in the pre-war years, did not prevent the assertion of German corporal education. The ideological association (with Germany) was even further consolidated when in 1937 the Bulgarian Ministry of Education invited one of the principal figures of Nazi physical culture, and member of the International Olympic Committee, Carl Diem, to Bulgaria with the purpose of developing a uniform youth organization along the lines of the Hitler Jugend. The outcome was a national youth organization known as the Brannik (Defender).

Despite the clear ideological linkage of Bulgaria's corporal education to the German and Nazi sports doctrine, in a similar way to its political development, it nevertheless showed a degree of inconsistency regarding subscription to Nazi principles and practices. In an attempt to gain full control over the physical education of youth, the Ministry of Education introduced in 1938 a Soviet military fitness campaign 'Ready for Labour and Defence' (GTO), under the name 'Bulgarian Sport Badge'. Given the totalitarian character of Soviet physical culture, and the lack of consistent principles behind the Fascist ideology, it could be argued that Bulgarian Fascism was open to any ideas that contributed to its ultimate goal, regardless of their ideological background. In retrospect, Bulgarian Fascism seems to have surpassed the three fundamental aims of Jahn. Firstly, corporal education was placed at the heart of the educational system as a 'paramount condition for any education', thus it was the chief contributor to 'the creation of the healthiest and the purest Bulgarian view of life'.[25] What is more, it was given a role in the achievement of a long-term objective, the creation of a handsome, healthy and desirable body type.[26] Secondly, sport was seen as a public necessity, and the best guarantee of individual and public health. Thirdly, the military nature of Bulgaria's sport was adopted by the state, and incorporated into the school system and national sport movements.

In order to abolish the submission of brawn to brain sport had to ensure the creation of a Bulgarian national Superman moulded and controlled by the state.

THE FASCIST STATE AND THE BODY AS POLITICUM

The idea of extending the notion of the political athlete to the body politic in the pursuit of the Superman did not depend on the existence of co-operative relationships alone. The assimilation of the strong, healthy body into the public domain, and the introduction of body politics, represent an essential element of the Fascist ambition – the subordination of society. Everything in society – political parties, organizations, religious groups, and individuals –had to be subordinated to the communitarian will, so that the individual and the community become one. As R. Macridis notes, 'Communitarism called for constant participation; it aimed to inculcate a spirit of individual attachment to the whole and a readiness, not only to obey, but also to sacrifice everything for the general interest as defined by the Nazi.'[27]

Because of its utilitarian orientation in the service of the creation of a new man and society, in the main Bulgaria's sports community willingly accepted an inferior position in relation to the superior position of the state. The national sports governing bodies were committed to a co-operative, rational and efficient association, in line with the guidelines established by government. Apart from some brief periods in the 1920s and the 1930s, when the Bulgarian Communist Party criticized the state's attempts to use sport for the Fascist cause, no national sport organization ever opposed openly any decision of the regime. Gradually, the monarcho–Fascist state included sport in the political agenda, imposing three distinct interrelated processes of: creation of an athletic manhood, introduction of state sport policies, and establishment of state political leadership.

The principle of subordination required the construction of massive support for the new role of sport as body politics, by various groups in the population. The state started to promote the ideal of an athletic manhood after the military Fascist coup in 1923, and the first target groups were children and youth. Following Italian and German examples, the Bulgarian Boy Scout organization was established in 1923, heavily supported by the Ministries of Education and Defence. In a directive to all schools in the country, the then Prime Minister A.

Tzankov even ordered that the Scout uniform had to replace the school uniform. The organization was set up in the hope of finally offering something that would fascinate young people, and keep them away from the pernicious influence of the Communists. The Boy Scout was portrayed as one, who 'doesn't want anything from anyone. He needs nothing, and loves everything ... He is a knight ... He serves his cause with Jesuitical obedience, he is polite, industrious, and judicious.'[28] The image of the Scouts, along with their patriotism, physical fitness and nascent virility, was the means of introducing a whole new symbolic system based on the notion of the group fitness and the group mind. However, this organization, which was quite alien to Bulgarian reality, had to face the competing ambitions of other bourgeois organizations, each claiming greater responsibility for reviving the country. This prevented the Scout movement from developing on a wide scale, and from becoming a mass national youth organization.

Another powerful avenue for the promotion of athletic manhood was school physical education. Physical education both derived from and complemented the basic spirit of Bulgarian education from the 1930s to the mid-1940s. It was defined as an attempt to achieve 'love of labour and creativity; passion and discipline; moral will; clearly defined national awareness; profound religious consciousness; heroism; self-optimism, and optimism in the people's future'.[29] The contribution of corporal education to this process was seen as 'education of the whole person through the body, that is, through physical activities, health efforts, and related educational methods'.[30] School physical education was characterized by its clear practical application and, particularly after the Fascist coup of 1934, assumed an increasingly military nature, putting an emphasis on marching and drilling. When the Zveno Fascist-political group[31] gained power, they launched the slogan 'Through sport for the mother country', justifying and giving physical education a clear militaristic direction to follow.

Physical education and sport provided excellent opportunities for the display of communalism and the unity of the nation as basic outcomes of the 'athletic' ideal. The Nazi's victorious symbolism was also put in place, as teams at all levels of competition had to line up in V formation for saluting in the German style. This potential for manifesting 'athletic' manhood was recognized and exploited by the state in a number of ways, including direct financing of spectacles and prestigious events, along with moral and political support.

FIGURE 3.1
NATIONAL GATHERING OF UNION UNAK, 1931

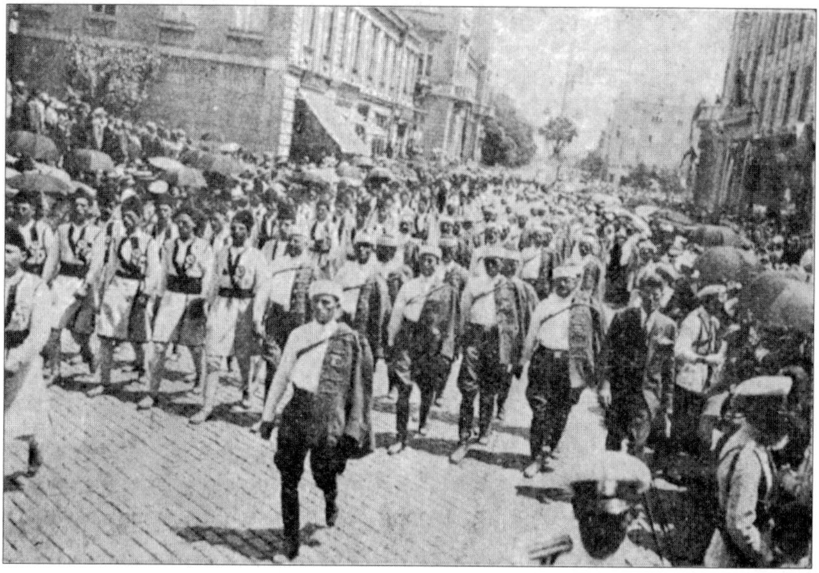

Championed by the always loyal national gymnastics union Unak (Figure 3.1), sport governing bodies developed a sensitive response to the leading political line, and were keen to declare their support in an attempt to secure better political and financial status. Spectacles such as Unak's quadrennial gatherings (similar to the Czech Spartakiades), bilateral matches with German teams, and notably participation in the Balkan and Olympic Games of 1936 were used to promote the cause, and assert the values of Fascist sport. In 1931, the Bulgarian government fully backed the idea of the National Olympic Committee to stage a multi-sport event involving the Balkan countries – the Balkaniades.[32] The first games were held in Sofia the same year, and Bulgarian athletes demonstrated their supremacy over the rest of the region. From then to the present time, Balkaniades have been interpreted by government and sport administrations as a means of asserting national identity. The Olympic torch relay (proposed by Carl Diem) ran throughout the country, in connection with the 1936 Berlin Olympics, as part of the Olympic flame's route from Ancient Olympia to Berlin. All the participating town administrations, including heads of schools, police and the army were involved in the preparation of the event, as it was seen also as a means of strengthening Bulgarian–German relationships.

The new body politic was clearly discernible in the complete state intervention in physical education and sport, based on a concern to improve public health, promote military education, control sport movements, and advance the cause of the state against Communism. Between 1923 and 1941 various military Fascist governments made serious attempts to introduce greater uniformity in physical education and sport, subjecting it to the political will. It became a norm for any new government to establish a new central structure of sport to serve its policy. National public and voluntary sport governing bodies did not emerge as result of a common need initiated by grass-roots level organizations; they were rather imposed as typical state creations to enable the Fascists to secure control over and establish a uniform society. This totalitarian emphasis remained a feature of the Bulgarian national sports movement during its Communist (1945–89) and even post-Communist period (1990 to the present day).

In 1923 the military Fascist government set up the Bulgarian National Sports Federation (BNSF) as a voluntary umbrella governing body, in order to co-ordinate all sports matters and suppress workers' sport clubs. The first workers' sports club, established in 1890 in Sofia, had a mission to oppose a bourgeois club created a year earlier in the same catchment area. The class division of Bulgaria, sport – workers (Communist) and bourgeois (Fascist) – and the use of sport for obtaining political advantage escalated between the 1920s and the end of the 1930s. This tension represented a unique phenomenon in the sense that the Bulgarian Communist Party (BCP) and the Fascist governments perceived sport predominantly as a political battleground, and the issue of who controlled sports establishments was the one that mattered. On the one hand, tension was heightened by Russia's attempts to facilitate the penetration of Communist ideas in the country through the newly established Red Sports International, whose popularity in the 1920s exceeded even the Olympic Games. In a BCP resolution of 1921 sport for young people was seen as a means of 'developing a healthy body and unlimited energy needed for the forthcoming struggle against capitalist slavery'.[33] The angry young man breaking with his bare hands a massive chain girding his naked muscled body on the cover page of the Union of Communist Youth's *Handbook for the Physical Education of Working Youth* (1923) illustrated the point well (Figure 3.2).

FIGURE 3.2

COVER OF THE *HANDBOOK FOR THE PHYSICAL EDUCATION OF WORKING YOUTH* (1923)

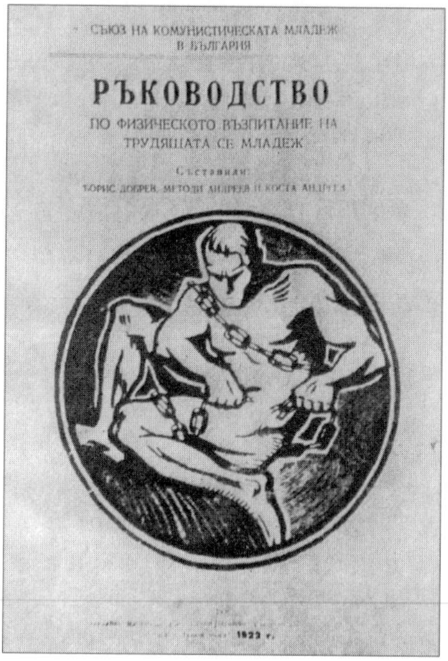

On the other hand, tension was also accentuated by the Nazi doctrine of the corporate state, facilitated by German ideological and cultural influence, and promoted by the state. Thus, in the struggle for power for the triumphant (Fascist) athlete and for the suffering (Communist) hero, the ultimate goal was the elimination of the political opponent and sport was given an essential role to play in this process.

A significant attempt of the Fascist government to strengthen its control over sport, involving for the first time state policy towards physical education and voluntary sport, came in 1926. As before, this move was preceded by a clear ideological concern about the penetration of Bolshevism and the need to preserve young people from the invidious influence of Marxist organizations. A state body for physical education was created with a separate budget and with the specific purpose of introducing a uniform system of physical education in schools. Simultaneously, the government initiated the establishment of a new national umbrella organization – the Confederation for Physical Education – under the authority of the Ministry of Education, which embraced all national sports governing bodies. It took over all important aspects of sporting activities and services previously delivered by voluntary organizations. Unak, for example, was deprived of the right to run staff training courses, a practice it had pioneered and successfully undertaken for more than 30 years.

State control over sport and the physical education of youth was further cemented by the first Sports Act adopted in 1931. There were three important implications for the way sport and physical education were to be developed. First, the idea of the corporate state was manifested in an attempt to establish workers' sport in factories. Second, never before had the Bulgarian state allocated a special budget for sport and, in the context of ideological control over sport, this law provided clear advantages. Third, the allocation of material resources was based on the successful attainment of government criteria. The existing and newly established sport organizations were supposed to meet certain quantitative indicators, such as the number of affiliated members, activities and participants, in order to qualify for a government subsidy. From an organizational point of view, this process marked the beginning of the totalitarian governance of sport and paved the way for a moral totalitarianism that was vulnerable to administrative ambitions and the political commitments of a small élite of sport organizations. From an ideological standpoint this could be understood as approaching the Fascist vision of the leader as an embodiment of the state itself, or in the words of Mussolini as 'the living sum of untold souls striving for the same goal'.[34] But from the point of view of sport, both interpretations represented a move away from its essence as a free, recreational human activity, an approach further reduced in the Communist period.

The Olympic movement had a strong appeal to the body politic since the Olympic Games provided an opportunity for manifesting Fascist superiority. State contributions to allow participation in the 1924 Games equalled 4 per cent of the country's foreign debt, whereas for the 1928 Games it was a negligible 0.02 per cent of the budget. The Bulgarian government, reluctant to support the country's participation in the 1932 Games, was subsequently quick to attach ideological importance to the concept of the Games and declare its support for the 1936 Nazi Olympics. Germany's response was in the spirit of true partnership. Hitler became personally involved and presented a grant of 200,000 Reich Marks to the sport representative of Bulgaria's region of Varna for the construction of a new stadium. An impressive Bulgarian national

FIGURE 3.3
BULGARIAN KING BORIS III AS A GUEST OF HONOUR AT THE BERLIN OLYMPIC GAMES

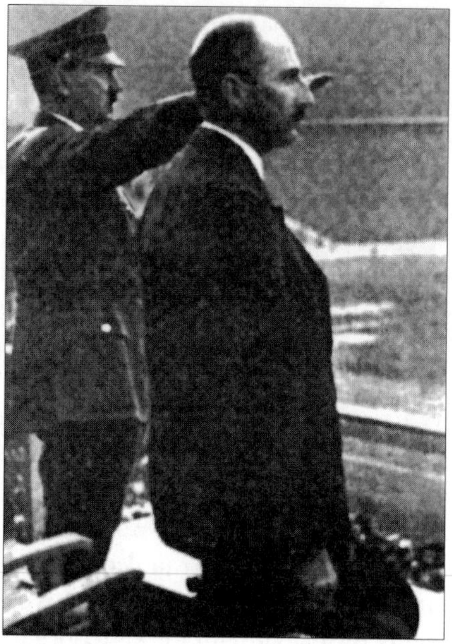

delegation of 94 athletes and officials took part in this highly effective Nazi display, which was otherwise boycotted by various progressive movements and governments around the world. Bulgarian athletes participated in six out of 18 sports in the Olympic programme – athletics, cycling, gymnastics, riding, fencing and shooting – since participation was a significant gesture of support for the character of national physical education, one that favoured the military training of youth, at the expense of other sports. The presence of Boris III next to Hitler during the opening ceremony of the Games is indicative of the political closeness of the two countries and their sport policies (Figure 3.3).

The glamour of the 1936 Olympics did not prevent preparation for the Second World War. Rather it provoked a more effective organization of youth and the use of physical education to military ends. A joint secret decree of the Ministries of Education and War in 1935 entitled 'for the total (corporeal, moral and public) education of Bulgarian youth, and for the organizations for corporal education and sport' envisaged stricter control over the education of young people, and more specifically, their pre-military training in accordance with the plans of the Ministry of War. The idea for the creation of a state youth organization was proposed, heavily supported by Germany, and in due course realized.

Harsh state intervention marked another escalation in 1937, with the amendment of the Physical Education of Bulgarian Youth Act (1937). This gave the Minister of Education greater powers, enabling him to intervene directly and demand full accountability of all sport governing bodies. Furthermore, the minister enjoyed unrestricted rights to appoint a delegate to the executive boards of sports organizations, to dismiss these boards, and to appoint a new leadership at the discretion of his representative. These developments preceded what could be called the pinnacle of the Fascist body politic – the law for the Organization of Bulgarian Youth (1941), and the establishment of the Brannik state organization with compulsory membership – individual or collective – of all young people between the ages of ten and twenty-one. The aims of the organization summed up the Fascist doctrine of the state – 'Believe, Obey, Work, Fight'. Eventually, it was meant to provide the 'only liberty that can be taken seriously, the liberty of the state', and paid tribute to what Mussolini had prophesied for the Fascist state as a 'synthesis of all values which interprets, develops, and gives power to every aspect of the life of the people'.[35] The common purpose of the organization was to 'educate and train Bulgarian youth for a faithful service to the Tsar, country, state and people's aspirations'.[36] Moreover, it was called upon to 'strengthen youth's consciousness of the supreme duty to the state', to create 'unanimity and the Bulgarian view of life', to teach youth 'to lead a modest and Spartan life', and 'to be brave in defending its supreme duty' and to provide pre-military training prior to military service.[37]

Brannik was given the supreme authority to control all aspects of sports movements – the authorization and control of sports establishments, the nature of activities and their international relations, the appointment of executives. Sports organizations became totally dependent on the state reflecting the subordination of physical education and sport in a true Fascist totalitarian manner. Voluntary sports governing bodies did not question the situation, and attempted to demonstrate obedience and endorsement. Unak ordered that all Communists should be expelled from the organization, and the Cyclists Union readily assisted the government in printing posters which spoke out against resistance. When eventually youth had to be pressed into military service in March 1944, the Chairman of the Bulgarian National Sport Federation, Batembergski, issued an appeal addressed to all sport establishments, stating that 'the Bulgarian state authority calls on people to defend the state... we evoke the energy, the future warriors, and if necessary the exploits of real young men – Bulgarian athletes... Athletes, on guard for the defence of the state!'[38]

The state body politic, and its plan for the subordination of physical education and sport, inevitably demanded the development of a cohort of loyal and obedient leaders of all national sports governing bodies. Communitarian values manifested themselves in the Fascist principle of leadership and the institution that best combined authority and control with representation. All key appointments were considered a matter of political priority, yet another strategy further developed in the Communist period. The chairmen of national umbrella governing bodies (being party officials), were members of Parliament, top military officials, or, in the case of the Bulgarian Olympic Committee – St Tchaprashikov, Chairman of the Bulgarian–German Chamber of Commerce.[39] The close relationships between the three fundamental elements – 'athletic' manhood, state totalitarian intervention in sports movement and the loyal political leadership formed the core of the body politicum, initiated and promoted by the Fascist sports policy in Bulgaria.

EPILOGUE

The shaping of the Superman in Bulgaria's Fascist period was a complex and controversial phenomenon, as it did not arise as a distinct expression of the national character; rather it was inspired and imposed by outside influence. Despite the striking common theoretical, social, political and economic roots of Italian Fascism, German Nazism and Bulgarian monarcho-Fascism, the Bulgarian variant due to its imported nature, from the very beginning of its emergence after the First World War, was doomed to be only a replica of what was supposed to be 'mainstream Fascism'. According to Nazi racial doctrine, Bulgarians as a Slav nation were given the role of culture-bearer nation. Therefore, they had to follow, and optimally to fully interpret the real Nazi model. Germany's political, economic and cultural policy towards Bulgaria between the two World Wars clearly illustrates these attitudes.

One distinguishing feature of the Bulgarian variant of Fascism was the inconsistency between ideology and practice. Bulgaria never matched the German scale of uniformity and blindness although, as Stanley Payne[40] writes in *A History of Fascism* 'its militant and expansionist policy earned it the nickname "Prussia of the Balkans"'. There was no exclusive Fascist party or sports governing body with a national leader. This partly explains a public dissonance with Fascist totalitarism, for example, how it became possible to turn the visit of the Moscow Spartak football team in 1940 into a massive pro-Soviet manifestation in the heart of Sofia, which forced the Foreign Office to send a special note to Germany in order to assert the country's loyalty to the German–Bulgarian pact. Even more dramatic evidence of dissonance, was the fact that Bulgaria did not submit its Jews to the Holocaust, which encouraged the participation of Jewish teams in the world Makabiades Games. However, Bulgaria's Fascist sports ideology and practice clearly embraced nationalism and chauvinism, violence in pursuit of policies and anti-Communism.

In its various manifestations, Bulgaria's Fascist 'doctrine of sport' followed a path of ideological evolution and military escalation. National folklore, together with the ideological heritage of Friedrich Jahn's gymnastics movement, was wilfully misinterpreted to provide the popular characteristics of the Fascist political athlete and body politics. Politically, the country was preoccupied with the notion of the Great Bulgaria and the desire for national self-assertion by gaining back its position as a leader of the Balkans. This was reflected in the endorsement of the body in political life. From an historical point of view, it is worth noting that many of the practices originating in the Fascist period were given different ideological interpretations, and continued during the Communist rule of the country.

NOTES

1. Bulgarian King (1918–43), born 1894, died 1943, son of Tsar Ferdinand, from the German Royal family.
2. Bulgaria during the reign of Kings Simeon, Samuil and Ioan Asen II before and after 1230.
3. Prince Alexander of Battenberg, a nephew of the Russian Tsarina, imposed as the first Bulgarian Prince (1879–86) by decision of the Great Powers: Tsar Alexander II (Russia), Chancellor Bismark (Germany) and Queen Victoria (Great Britain).
4. N. Genchev, Nuzhni sa Seriozni Izsledvanija za Fashisma v Balgarija (Serious Studies of Fascism in Bulgaria are Needed), *Historical Review*, 4 (1968).
5. The Military League and Organisation Kubrat known for their military grouping, discipline and unity, formed after the First World War by General Lukov, one of King Boris' closest friends.
6. Bulgarian Prime Minister, leader of the political coalition Popular Entente –Sgovor, 1923–31.
7. The Treaty of Neuilly-sur-Seine imposed on Bulgaria by the Great Powers and signed on the 27 November 1919 by the Prime Minister Al. Stambolijski.

8. Z. Natan (ed.), *Ikonomikata na Balgarija do Sochialisticheskata Revoljuchija* (Bulgarian Economy before the Socialist Revolution) (Sofia, 1969), p.476.
9. Georgi Dimitrov (1882–1949), political leader of the Bulgarian Communist Party, General Secretary of the Comintern and Prime Minister after 9 September 1944.
10. After long political discussions and deliberations, eventually the Government and Tsar Boris turned down the USSR proposal (so called Sobolev's action) on the grounds of the neutrality proclaimed in 1939 fearing that it would jeopardize the country's strategic relations with Germany.
11. Prof. Alexander Tzankov, Bulgarian Prime Minister (1923–26) who came to power after a military coup organized by the Military League.
12. L. Baradat, *Political Ideologies: Their Origin and Impact* (London, 1994), p.238 (hereafter *Political Ideologies).*
13. Union of Gymnastics Societies – Unak (Hero) was established in 1898 with 15 founding societies as the first national umbrella sport governing body. It aimed to provide overall physical education and training for the population. Unak represented Bulgaria in the major international sport federations – FIFA or the International Gymnastic Federation.
14. N. Sheitanov, *Kult na Tjaloto* (Body Cult), Physical Education (Sofia, 1928), p.13 (hereafter *Physical Education*).
15. J. Hoberman, *Sport and Political Ideology* (London, 1984), p.162 (hereafter *Political Ideology*).
16. lbid: p.165.
17. N. Sheitanov, *Physical Education*, p.7.
18. Ibid., p.24.
19. J. Hoberman, *Political Ideology*, p.163.
20. Ibid., p.163.
21. Inspired by the Russian Military Command committees Edinstvo emerged as an organized reaction against the decisions of the Berlin Treaty of 1878 with the aim to provide military training to the entire male population.
22. N. Petrova, *100 Godini Obshtestveni Fizkulturni Organizacii v Balgarija* (100 Years of Voluntary Sport Organisations in Bulgaria) (Sofia, 1978), p.47 (hereafter *Voluntary Sport*).
23. lbid., p.81.
24. Bulgarian National Sports Federation established in 1923 as an umbrella sport governing body incorporating all clubs, leagues and organizations.
25. B. Filov, *Pismo ot M-r Predsedatelja B. Filov do MNP* (A Letter from the Prime Minister B. Filov to the Ministry of Education) (Sofia, 1941).
26. A. Minchev, 'Sportat e Zdravno–Obshtestvena Neobhodimost' (Sport is a Health and Public Necessity), *Kultura, Zdrave, Krasota* (Sofia, 1938), 17.
27. R. Macridis, *Contemporary Political Ideologies – Movements and Regimes*, 4th edition (Glenview, Illinois, 1989), p.207 (hereafter – *Movements and Regimes).*
28. N. Petrova, *Voluntary Sport*, p.89.
29. N. Petrova, 'Sashtnost i Funkcii na Fizicheskata Kultura prez Epohata na Kapitalizma' (Nature and Functions of Physical Culture in Bulgaria during the Capitalist Epoch), in A. Solakov (ed.), *Fizicheskata Kultura i Sportat prez Vekovete* (Physical Culture and Sport throughout Ages) (Sofia, 1982), p.162.
30. lbid., p.162.
31. Political group Zveno (Link) is the political organization of the Military League which took over power after a military coup in 1934. It abolished all political parties, confiscated their properties and funds and eventually disbanded itself. The leaders of the coup – K. Georgiev and D. Velchev were later used by Moscow for the Communist coup in 1944.
32. The Balkaniades was a Bulgarian initiative to offer a multi-sporting event for all countries in the region and to serve as a means of promoting peace, which first materialized in 1931. Although the Balkaniades today enjoy the recognition and support of the International Olympic Committee they never achieved the status of a major international sporting event.
33. N. Petrova, *Voluntary Sport*, p.71.
34. L. Baradat, *Political Ideologies*, p.251.
35. R. Macridis, *Movements and Regimes*, p.215.

36. *Zakon za Organizirane na Balgarskata Mladezh* (Law for the Organization of Bulgarian Youth) (Gazette No.18, 25 January 1941).
37. Ibid.
38. N. Petrova, *Voluntary Sport*, p.97.
39. Stefan Tchaprashikov, a rich businessman, tobacco tycoon and Bulgaria's ambassador in Berlin, IOC member for Bulgaria since 1929, and Chairman of the Bulgarian Olympic Committee.
40. Stanley G. Payne, *A History of Fascism 1914–1945* (London, 1995), p.133.

The Iconic Symbolism of Niels Bukh: Aryan Body Culture, Danish Gymnastics and Nordic Tradition

HANS BONDE

Niels Bukh (1880–1950) was an internationally recognized Danish gymnastics teacher, one of those Danes of the 1930s who did not feel they were represented in the Danish party system and on the whole rejected the parliamentary system.[1] He also dissociated himself from the Danish Nazi party, which he considered a laughable imitation of the German parent party which he greatly admired.

In the course of the 1930s Bukh probably became the best known living Dane. From 1912 on he participated in all the Olympic Games – except Los Angeles in 1932 and London in 1948 – and was a permanent fixture at the world fairs. In the 1920s he had promoted Denmark by travelling every summer to various European countries, and in 1923 and 1926 to the United States. Throughout the remainder of the 1930s he continued his travels unabated, including tours to the two 'new' continents – South America in 1938 and South Africa in 1939.

Bukh was seen as both the outward and inward face of Denmark. He demonstrated his version of the western, civilized body to many thousands of young people all over the world at a time when the new mass medium – film – had not yet become the central vehicle for this project.

Bukh created images of 'Danishness' which stuck in the memory regardless of whether they were 'six men on the plinth' or rural lads executing formal perfectly synchronize movements. His value in terms of national symbolism was strengthened by the fact that his gymnasts, unlike for example the Denmark football team, became known as an original product – Danish Design bodies. The King of Denmark appeared as early as 1923 at the inauguration of Bukh's stadium and decorated him several times personally – the last time in 1935.

The main purpose of this essay is to explain how and why Niels Bukh and his gymnastics first became a symbol of *folkelighed*, then later, for large sections of the Danish public, came to represent right-wing extremist attitudes.[2] It also seeks to contribute to our understanding of the relationship between sport and politics.[3] In historical research we sometimes operate with an unfruitful distinction between political and cultural history. Niels Bukh recognized no such distinction; for him, the ability to form and stage-direct the bodies of young people justified access to political power; indeed, it was a political act of national importance. This is why we can turn the focus on the level of political awareness in a man who was in principle known essentially for his gymnastics.

Bukh's gymnastics is an example of how strong a role sport can play in the cultivation of national identity. The importance of Bukh and gymnastics for national identity in Denmark can be compared with the importance of Fridtjof Nansen and skiing in Norway.[4] The British cultural historian J.A. Mangan has listed at least three examples of sports and athletics promoting: national solidarity, international confrontation, and international co-operation and understanding.[5] Bukh's gymnastics acted at all three levels and, as we shall see, not least at the second: as an arena for national confrontation.

How far was the political and ideological significance of Bukh's gymnastics established by the actual expressive forms of the movements, and how far by shifting interpretations of signs that depended on time, place and context? I have no background in the linguistic theory of semiotics: I use the theory of signs exclusively as inspiration for a better understanding of the changing meanings that were assigned to gymnastics. Thus I follow a strong tendency in modern semiotics to emphasize concrete analyses of meaning in terms of broader cultural semiotics rather than for the sake of abstract theory. The slogan is 'semiotics in practice'.[6] If gymnastics is an appropriate subject for semiotic analysis it is because it involves a display of aesthetically appealing movements.[7]

My own initial view – which I probably share with most Danes today – was that the gymnastic forms themselves expressed discipline, mental rigidity and the typical reactionary spirit of the 1930s, in line with the young men with spades over their shoulders from the German *Arbeitsfront*. This is undoubtedly an association that arises because our modern knowledge of the Holocaust colours our view of the inter-war years so strongly that phenomena from that period are interpreted either as contributing to or counteracting Nazism. It is also related to the feeling that Bukh himself was profoundly reactionary, which is then transferred to his gymnastics. To balance this 'wisdom of hindsight' we have to try to understand the framework within which the people of the period thought. Although the connection between Bukh's gymnastics and the German *Arbeitsfront* would have been logical for Bukh, the same is not necessarily true of his pupils and contemporary observers of gymnastics.

While working on a biography of Niels Bukh I have come to the conclusion that Bukh's gymnastics, considered in isolation, only involved a few meanings, such as the cultivation of a certain degree of authority and collectivism. Whether these meanings were interpreted in terms of a Grundtvigian agrarian ideology with an emphasis on the power of the household patriarch and the cultivation of a national sense of community, or of a Nazi cult of the Führer and the Aryan race as one organism, depends on the time, place, context and interpreter.[8]

Bukh's gymnastics team rarely performed alone. As a rule Bukh himself featured either in the presentation of the team, standing erect in the demonstration area, or by directly 'conducting' the gymnasts. It was therefore natural to interpret the symbolism of the gymnastics in terms of his personality, to let 'the author' interpret the work; and there is no doubt that much of the political profile that has been attributed to Bukh has also been transferred to his gymnastics.

Two examples will serve to illustrate the relatively arbitrary relationship between sign and meaning. Niels Bukh's gymnastics gradually replaced the so-called Swedish gymnastics which had been widespread in the countryside in Denmark around the turn of the century, and also in schools in many other countries. Swedish gymnastics had been created by the Swede Per Henrik Ling (1776–1839) and had become very widespread in rural high schools[9] and village community halls[10] as part of the Danish farming community's political and cultural resurgence in the 1880s. At the rural high schools gymnastics instructors were trained so they could go into the community halls and teach this rather awkward, physiologically-based type of team gymnastics, where the leader of the team commanded every single movement.[11] Although Swedish gymnastics was far more like military drill and partly shaped from movements that initially were preliminaries to fencing, they were interpreted in Denmark as a democratic form of expression, since they were used in the gymnastics and shooting movements' popular front against an undemocratic government – the right-wing Estrup regime. Another example was the so-called 'German gymnastics', which was a Nazi attempt to create a culture of the body in keeping with the German 'national character'. After the war this kind of gymnastics spread through democratic Denmark, incidentally resisted by a recently politically converted Niels Bukh, who paradoxically rejected the German systems as 'un-Danish'.

A MASCULINE REVOLT

The analysis of Niels Bukh's career in this essay is viewed as the history of the struggle over the interpretation of his gymnastics. Whilst democratic forces often tried to steer the gymnastic movement in a democratic direction as protection against the virus from the south, the Nazis saw his gymnastics as symbolizing 'the Nordic race', a view which, as we shall see, was not alien to Bukh.

In the period 1920–26 Bukh created a gigantic sports ground which was completely at odds with the proportions of the small South Funen village in which it stood. In 1920 he founded Denmark's first gymnastics high school. His construction projects of the 1920s culminated in the inauguration of Denmark's first indoor swimming baths in 1926. In keeping with his Greek inspiration, everything was built in neoclassical style.

As a teacher, Bukh was an innovator. In Ling's Swedish gymnastics, 'the command' was absolutely central. The pupils must not move without being given the order to do so, and this led to pauses between the exercises. Niels Bukh dictated a new exercise while the previous one was still in progress, so that no time was wasted. Thus he replaced the compartmentalized Swedish gymnastics with 'serial gymnastics'.[12] The idea was that the pupils, after a few months of 'primitive' gymnastics, would have become so supple that they would be qualified to practise the so-called 'athletic gymnastics', which were aesthetically appealing exercises developed with displays in mind. Athletic gymnastics was inspired by Swedish gymnastics, but Niels Bukh developed a number of new exercises, including the so-called 'double work' where the men held on to and carried one another.

At the school, Bukh's birthday was the big annual event, whilst Constitution Day played no role. If one visited Bukh at the Gymnastics

High School one first had to climb a long staircase, go through an imposing entrance portal, on through rooms and past statues, reliefs and large paintings, to end up in Bukh's private suite, at Bukh's enormous desk. Bukh's megalomaniac urge to cultivate the large and pompous was evident from the giant sports hall with room for 8,000 people, built with a very high balcony from which he could conduct events. Bukh had his strongest appeal when he 'conducted' his large gymnastics teams. The spectators could get the impression that team and leader had merged, and that Bukh had a special electrifying power over his gymnasts.

Throughout the 1930s Bukh might have been inspired by his great example Hitler. He would greet people with a 'characterful' handshake and strong eye contact, and would be accompanied by two large Great Danes. Like Hitler he had no children, but he liked to appear with children in pictures. Although he had an unusual ability to make a strong impression on other people, the charisma attributed to him must be said to have been created to a great extent by his talent for the *mise-en-scène*.

Niels Bukh's gymnastics was developed by a man for men. His aim was to make the young men 'straight, strong and dexterous', as 'their ideal of a man is'.[13] Rallying to Bukh's gymnastics was a kind of rebellion among young men, who rejected the more static and physically weaker male ideal of the older Ling-style gymnastics instructors. Bukh's supporters claimed that hard, primitive gymnastics were justified by the difference between the two sexes. Bukh's gymnastics were 'at all events decidedly male gymnastics'. They were unsuitable for 'women and weaklings'.[14]

Physically, Bukh's male gymnasts were greatly masculinized by their training – this could be measured physically. A medical examination of one third of the team from 1917/18 showed that most of them had, during the course, achieved 'strong physical development'. Despite the hard training their weight had risen by between a minimum of half a kilo to a maximum of 8 kg owing to the increase in muscle mass. The thorax had expanded substantially in most of them, as shown by the increase in the lung capacity of 14 out of 16 pupils. One had achieved an expansion of 5 cm.

The incredible tempo set by Bukh, especially in men's gymnastics, gave the young men the potential to demonstrate dynamic physical development and thus their affinity with dynamic modern life. Bukh's fluent serial gymnastics expressed and embodied the fact that many rural dwellers were now moving from an external discipline to internal constraints where self-control was 'in the backbone' and the movements 'came by themselves'. In many parts of the world Bukh's gymnastics fascinated people with its pace, which gave an impression of modernity.

But besides the masculine element, there was also unusual rhythm, elegance and roundedness in Bukh's male gymnastics. If the feminine element also made an impact in wide circles, it was because it was balanced by the strongly masculine image. His gymnastics for men, through striving for extremes, was at once more masculine and more feminine than previous gymnastics.

THE NAZI AWAKENING

Bukh's demanding gymnastics were developed during the First World War alongside his praise of a strong national defence capability and national service, but in the course of the 1920s, with his very aesthetically oriented gymnastics, he helped to detach national gymnastics from the 'spirit of 1868', a term for the national revival which had permeated the country, especially the rural population, after defeat by Germany and the loss of the three duchies Schleswig, Holstein and Lauenburg. As early as the national rally at Dybbøl in 1928, well nigh all male gymnasts were influenced by his gymnastics. It was precisely this emancipation of gymnastics from the idea of defence against the Germans that laid Bukh's gymnastics open to shifting interpretations in the course of the 1930s. Bukh first had to free gymnastics from the conventional meaning in order – as we shall see – to give it new meaning later.

Bukh's liberal upbringing in a Grundtvigian school environment did not prevent him, throughout the 1920s, from developing a strong animosity to the parliamentary system and proposing measures to centralize and politicize the life of Danish youth. At the end of July 1933, amidst the international crisis which had hit Danish agriculture very hard, Bukh was able to inaugurate his new sports hall and an outdoor swimming pool. He had now created a complex with proportions that would have seemed large even in the capital. In the words of the newspaper *Aftenbladet*: 'Niels Bukh has built a cathedral of athletics, but he has built it in a village.'[15] He was at a high point in his life; a national hero, the owner and creator of an enormous privately owned sportsground and internationally famous, as was clearly marked by a visit from the Prince of Wales on the occasion of the topping-out ceremony on 1 October 1932. Incidentally he built on such a large scale because he intended to make the Ollerup Gymnastics High School an international centre of physical culture. As a crucial sign of this he worked to hold an international gymnastics festival of unprecedented dimensions which was to outdo the Olympic Games – a plan he had already begun to develop after the Olympics in Paris in 1924.[16]

At the ceremony inaugurating Bukh's new sports hall in 1933 the Social Democrat Minister of Education, Borgbjerg, was the principal speaker. In his speech Borgbjerg offered the government's congratulations. He was clearly concerned about the advance of German Nazism, and more specifically about how the notoriously reactionary Niels Bukh and his large crowd of pupils would react to this challenge. He though that Bukh's gymnastics had a positive democratic significance: 'I believe that in this country we have the conditions necessary to take the lead – not least at a time when spiritual darkness, mental coercion, violence and dictatorship, regimentation and slavery, are rearing their heads in countries where we least expected them. In this country we have a free, unconstrained and humane mentality, and in this area we still have what is necessary to take the lead and show the world what we mean by these things.' Niels Bukh then appeared on the balcony of the hall and was greeted with 'minute-long applause'. After this the 'Japan' team gave a demonstration followed by the 275 female pupils of the summer school.

Borgbjerg's hopeful attempt to interpret Bukh and his gymnastics as a bulwark against the waves from the south was ill-judged. Even before the Nazis came into power, Bukh had felt that his authoritarian and corporative ideas were highly compatible with German National Socialism and its cult of the Führer. A German teacher called Lange,[17] who had worked on the Gymnastics High School project for about a year, as well as other German friends of Bukh, had given him 'true information' about the state of affairs in Germany and had thus boosted the confidence he 'had had from the outset in Adolf Hitler'.[18] Among Austrian and German gymnasts, long before the seizure of power, a strong foundation for Nazi ideals had developed, and it was precisely these people who had supported Hitler before his takeover with whom Niels Bukh cooperated and communicated through letters and visits to the Gymnastics High School.[19] In Hitler Bukh felt that a man had now finally come to power who was able to implement on a large scale what Bukh had tried to realize, in his own little kingdom of Ollerup, long before the Nazi seizure of power.[20]

THE JOURNEY TO BERLIN

Bukh was clearly deeply interested in experiencing Nazi Germany at first hand. In October 1933 he was invited on a tour to Hungary and Austria, and he took advantage of the opportunity to visit Berlin both on the way out and on the way back. On its way home from Hungary the team was invited to give a demonstration. For the new German regime it was important to establish normal relations quickly with the outside world, including sporting relations, not least with the Nordic countries and the international sports and athletics leaders who were friendly to them.

Before the display, rumours had circulated that 'Niels Bukh has been told that Hitler wishes to attend our demonstration.'[21] This did not happen, however. Before the grand entry Bukh was afraid that the troupe would not be permitted to bring on the Danish flag and impressed on the gymnasts how important this was;[22] but his fears proved unfounded. The German organizers must have had a good idea of Bukh's political preferences, for when the team, with the Danish flag at its head, entered the hall, it had an enthusiastic reception from about 3,000 uniformed, Nazi-saluting spectators, most of whom came from the Nazi teachers' union.[23] The display took place in the middle of the hall on a large platform surrounded by 'young brown-shirted Nazis and swastika banners'.[24] The troupe demonstrated both gymnastics and folk dancing, and the whole demonstration was 'rewarded with the loudest possible applause'.

After the show the chairman of the Union of National Socialist Teachers, the *Gauleiter* Abs, who had been on a course at Ollerup,[25] made a speech in which he referred to Niels Bukh as an admirer of Adolf Hitler and quoted him as saying that 'he would like to have been Denmark's Hitler, if only he had been 20 years younger'. Abs led the crowd with a triple 'Heil!' for the Danish King[26] and for Denmark, and the orchestra played the Danish Royal Anthem *Kong Christian*, which the German audience listened to with arms outstretched in the Nazi salute. Abs then presented Bukh with a swastika flag and Bukh thanked him, with Abs as interpreter, by praising 'the beauty and order that prevailed in the new Germany created by Hitler', and assured all present that he would 'inform the Danish people of the true situation in Germany'. Bukh expressed his 'admiration of the German leader Adolf Hitler', for whom he and his troupe 'called for three cheers',[27] and this was followed by the German National Anthem, to which Niels Bukh offered the Nazi salute and his gymnasts followed suit. The 'head of the Berlin gymnastics authority' stated that 'German youth could learn from the hard, firm method that Niels Bukh used in his gymnastics'[28] and another of the Germans praised Denmark for being a 'happy, sublime country…with the pure, unmixed Aryan type that they have'.[29] For his display team Bukh had picked out blonde pupils with blue eyes because they symbolized 'Nordicness' Finally, the SA battle song *Horst Wessel* was sung.

BUKH AND THE REICHSSPORTFÜHRER

The comment about the 'Aryan type' was, according to Niels Bukh, made by 'Hitler's representative'.[30] He can only mean Reichssportführer Hans von Tschammer und Osten, who was a member of the Stab des Stellvertreters des Führers.[31] Von Tschammer had been appointed Reichssportführer on 19 July 1933, and became Niels Bukh's most important political partner in the Third Reich. When Bukh met von Tschammer, he was busy with the elimination of the large Social Democrat, Communist and Christian athletics organizations and regimenting the whole of the German voluntary sports sector into one huge Nazi sports association. The Reichssportführer became a popular figure in Nazi Germany and a well-known personality in the international athletics world. However, he had no great effect on the history of the Third Reich, and the influence he did have was mainly limited to 'voluntary' sport, company sport and the training of sports instructors. The last of these roles undoubtedly explained the invitation the Nazi gave to Bukh's demonstration.

The collaboration between Bukh and von Tschammer was of course mainly due to their common support for the Nazi project. In addition, for his part Tschammer could use Bukh as a voluntary Danish contributor to the Nazi mythologizing of the Nordic race, while Bukh could use von Tschammer to spread his own gymnastics system throughout the Third Reich. There was also strong common ground in Niels Bukh's and von Tschammer's view of athletics, especially with regard to the rejection of individual achievement and the struggle to break records.

However, there were also considerable differences between Bukh and von Tschammer. For the Nazis, sport and athletics, like all other areas of life, were politically defined and von Tschammer was more loyal Nazi than sportsman. For Bukh, on the other hand, as a zealous gymnastics instructor, Nazism was a temptation because of the high priority given to physical culture in the Third Reich. In both Germany[32] and Austria the gymnastics federations were among the first to rally to Nazism. It was natural for many German gymnasts to link the cultivation of the body and its achievement with the Nazi cult of beauty and homage to the young, racially pure, perfect body. This association attracted Bukh.

And then there were resemblances, at least in the rhetoric, between the Danish Grundtuigian and Nazi sporting terminology, especially in the Danish term *folkelig* and in German *völkisch*, and the Danish term *fører* (leader) and the German *Führer*. What then really was the difference between a Nazi *Jugendführer* and a Danish *delingsfører*?[33] Historically, there was a world of difference, since the *delingsfører* had been part of a revanchiste front for the recovery of southern Jutland (Schleswig–Holstein) from the Prussians. Nevertheless in Bukh's correspondence with leading German Nazis he played on the *delingsfører* concept when he said that he trained Danish '*Führer*'.[34] There were further resemblances. The *folkelig* Danish rural gymnastics was profoundly alien to the individual self-assertion and the cultivation of record-breaking for its own sake inherent in modern sport. Instead, broad-based sport was to be given a higher priority, and organizations were established to ensure that everyone, young and old, and of both sexes, could engage in sport and athletics. Under Nazism, individuals were not to engage in sport for their own benefit, but for the sake of the nation. The body was political and belonged to the state, so sport and athletics, especially for the young, were not a matter of choice, they involved a demand that one idealistically 'gave oneself' – and in the extreme case with young men – gave one's life for the nation.[35]

THE STORM IN THE PRESS

On arriving back in Denmark the team gave a demonstration in the city of Vordingborg, where Bukh started making strong pro-Nazi statements at the coffee table. One journalist, apparently Jewish, remonstrated with Bukh.[36] Then a correspondent from the very conservative newspaper *Nationaltidende*, who had been present at the demonstration in Berlin, made himself felt. On 20 October 1933, the newspaper ran a front-page article on Bukh's recent visit to Germany headlined 'Niels Bukh is

Denmark's Hitler – but he was born 20 years too soon'.[37] The article attracted huge public attention, not least because Bukh was able to provide information on what was actually going on in Germany. Interest in Germany was intense; rumours abounded about the repercussions of the Nazi seizure of power – there were discussions about the cause of the Reichstag fire, the concentration camps, Germany's withdrawal from the League of Nations, the formation of a Danish committee in support of intellectuals, such as Einstein, fleeing from the Nazis, the pressure on the Austrian Chancellor Dolfuss, and the forthcoming 'election' in Germany (on 12 November 1933). In addition, in the course of the spring and summer, in the so-called 'Easter wind' there had been a strong rhetorical assault on the Dano–German border from North German Nazis, who had been fired by the power takeover. Although the authorities in Berlin had no intention of ruining their good relations with an Aryan neighbour, the furore led to great anxiety and watchfulness – not least in South Jutland, where Denmark shared a border with Germany and the Nazi regime.[38]

Bukh did not deny the assertion made in *Nationaltidende*. In an interview with the newspaper *Berlingske Tidende* he continued to maintain that if he had been 20 years younger he would have 'taken up the problem Hitler has dealt with in Germany'. He would transfer 'the best' of Hitler's principles to Denmark. 'We need to put our house in order. We have got used to having too much of a good thing in this country. I think we are very much in need of a man with strong, pure ideals, instead of the barren, cold form of government we have now.' He rejected foreign 'denigration' of Hitler and claimed that Hitler let the Jews live in peace 'as long as they will work', but Hitler would 'drive them out of speculation and administration, in other words prevent them from exploiting the productive workers'. Referring to Hitler's recent speech on radio, Bukh concluded, 'you won't find a cleaner and more honest foreign policy than Hitler's in Europe. There is no falsity in him. Nothing in the press will ever shake my faith in him again.'

Bukh's visions ran in the direction of a youth revolution under his leadership, and this was quite in keeping with German Nazism's idea of a youth movement:

> Youth is what we need, and the day is perhaps not so far off – at least I don't think so – when the young will take a hand. I won't say here what I would do, I only say that it is what we need. Oh, you

> should see how satisfied, happy and enthusiastic the Germans are under their new form of government.

When the storm in the press raged, Bukh embarked on a tour of Denmark. Everywhere he took the opportunity to air his views at meetings following the displays. Large sections of right-of-centre opinion argued for Bukh's right to spread Nazi propaganda, although his anti-Semitic diatribes could be too much to swallow. In the rural press the general attitude was that Bukh had overreached himself and abandoned essential cultural values like intellectual freedom and the human dignity of the Jews. The Social Democrats did not dwell on Bukh's anti-Semitism, but were angry at his defence of a state that had crushed the biggest European worker's movement.

Bukh remained unrepentent. The very strong criticism in the press provoked a typical reaction from him. He tried to take the offensive by further radicalizing his views. At the end of October he sent an account of 'my view of the new Germany' to between 12 and 14 newspapers and periodicals.[39] Here he repeated all his views on Nazism, even exacerbating his harshly anti-Semitic tone. He considered it was 'hard for the many noble and valuable forces in the Jewish people who had to suffer innocently', but if 'such a giant task as the new leaders of Germany must fulfil at a fast pace' was to succeed, 'distinguishing between good and less good alien elements may be impossible, and regrettable violence may therefore be difficult to wholly avoid'.

CONCLUSION

Bukh's encounter with German Nazism was akin to a religious awakening. Nazism meant that at last a man had come to power who fought for the same ideals as he felt he had already begun to realize 13 years before at Ollerup – a charismatically-led cult based on the physical culture of the young. We must remember here that the Nazis attempted, in George Mosse's words, to establish a 'new religion with elements of mysticism and liturgical rites'.[40] The Nazi cult of 'primal forces' and the primal instincts in mankind and in the race[41] harmonized well with Bukh's 'primitive' gymnastics, in which the debased body of civilized man was to be taken 'back' to its original, 'natural' form.

Bukh is an example of the way the Nazi movement created nothing new, but built on existing German and more broadly European cultural currents, including Bukh's 'Nordic' gymnastics. Around 1920 Bukh had already fully developed his neoclassicism, his extreme cult of physical beauty, his cultivation of the Nordic look and the cult of youth and the body, his contempt for democracy and a highly developed cult of personality – all items of ideological heritage that were also to form part of Nazism. For Bukh there was no doubt that these ideological components were compatible with Nazism's cult of the Führer and anti-Semitism. And for the Nazis there was no doubt that Bukh's aesthetics and physical culture could be part of the development of the new Aryan culture.

In the judicial repercussions after the war, the story of Niels Bukh turned into a struggle over what he and his iconic gymnastics had symbolized. Was it the gymnastics of the Aryan race or an expression of Danish agrarian society's 'emancipative nationalism'?[42] Arguably, in the final analysis, for Bukh it was not enough to be internationally acknowledged. His restless striving for ever greater fame ensured that he also wanted to be a great man in the Nazi New Order in Europe. Who knows? With the defeat of the Germans in 1945 his wings could no longer bear him and he plunged to the ground. Although he survived as a Danish youth leader, he worked himself to death unsuccessfully to regain his former position. He died a broken man in 1950.

Bukh illustrates quite clearly the association between the male body as a political icon and Fascist idealism. For Bukh the strong body was a political metaphor representing the health of both the male body and the political state.

NOTES

1. This essay is part of my work on a biography of the political, ideological and national impact of Niels Bukh on Danish society which will appear in Danish.
2. The concept of *folkelighed*, translated here as 'democratic national sentiment' is central to the understanding of the thinking of the Danish rural population. *Folkelighed* has a range of meanings (the democratic spirit, the common touch, broad popular appeal) which contrast with 'élitism' and the concept involves a vision that all citizens of a society can come together in a national community. In this vision the farmers are the backbone of the nation, since they feed the rest of the population, and in Denmark they played a central role in the realization of democracy. The Danish historian Lorenz Reerup has suggested the translation 'emancipative nationalism'.
3. For a broad introduction to this theme see G. Redmond, *Sport and Politics* (Champaign, Illinois, 1984).
4. M. Goksøyr *et al.*, *Winter Games, Warm Traditions* (Oslo, 1996).
5. J.A. Mangan (ed.), *Tribal Identities: Nationalism, Europe, Sport* (London and Portland, OR, 1995), p.1.

6. K. Gall Jørgensen, *Semiotik – En introduktion* (Copenhagen, 1993); J. Johansen and S.E. Larsen, *Tegn i brug* (Odense, 1994).
7. I see the gymnastics displays, including Bukh's leadership of them, as consisting of an expressive side (*signifiant*) and a content side (*signifié*), and the question is how they determine one another; cf. my heuristic approach in the article 'Farmers' Gymnastics in Denmark in the Late Nineteenth and Early Twentieth Centuries: A Semiotic Analysis of Exercise in Moral Action', *International Journal of the History of Sport*, 10, 2 (1993), 198ff.
8. The common denominator in, and the main source of inspiration for, the Danish farmers' movement was the Danish poet and pastor N.F.S. Grundtvig (1783–1872), who argued against the 'dead and weary' knowledge produced by the Danish school system and tried to revive the mythological heritage of Scandinavia.
9. The Danish *folkehøjskole* (rural high school) tradition is based on the idea that people, especially the young, can meet at rural schools where the aim is not to take examinations but to develop in the company of other young people.
10. In the *forsamlingshus* (community hall) farmers could gather to listen to lectures which could range thematically from 'technological innovations in agriculture' to 'the importance of the religious spirit in the age of materialism'.
11. O Korsgaard, *Kampen om kroppen* (Copenhagen, 1982), pp.82ff, and Trangbæk, *Mellem leg og disciplin* (Åbybro, Denmark, 1987), *passim*. By Swedish gymnastics I mean here the gymnastics inspired by the Swede Ling as cultivated at the Danish rural high schools and in the community halls.
12. This is Bukh's own term, in the September issue of *Gymnastisk Tidsskrift*, 1917.
13. *Ungdom og Idræt*, 15 June 1917.
14. P. Maigaard, *Ungdom og Idræt*, 28 January 1916. See also 'J.R.', ibid., 4 February 1916.
15. 31 July 1933. This section is based on the article 'Ollerup – Danmarks og Nordens Olympia', *Fyns Tidende*, 31 August 1933, unless otherwise stated.
16. R. Nielsen, *Niels Bukh* (Copenhagen, 1950), p.162.
17. K. Krogshede in *Årsskrift for Gymnastikhøjskolen* (1936), p.35.
18. *Berlingske Aftenavis*, 28 October 1933.
19. R. Nielsen, *Niels Bukh*, p.150.
20. Interview with A. Mortensen.
21. M. Gudiksen in *Vejle Amts Folkeblad* (12 October 1933).
22. Interview with H. Lykke and H. Mortensen.
23. H. Lykke, ibid.
24. Krogshede in *Årsskrift for Gymnastikhøjskolen* (1933), pp.47–9.
25. Ibid. (1936), p.17.
26. According to Bukh's account in *Berlingske Aftenavis*, 28 October 1933.
27. Ibid.
28. *Nationaltidende*, 20 October 1933.
29. *Berlingske Aftenavis*, 20 October 1933.
30. Ibid., 28 October 1933.
31. D. Steinhöfer, *Hans von Tschammer und Osten* (Berlin, 1973), p.146. The whole of the following passage on the Reichssportführer is based on Steinhöfer's biography. Incidentally Bukh is not named in this book.
32. H. Bernett, *Sportpolitik im Dritten Reich* (Schorndorff, 1971), and Steinhöfer, ibid.
33. Literally divisional leader or platoon commander, the army-inspired term for a Danish gymnastics instructor in the countryside.
34. In a letter to von Tschammer of 12 March 1938 Bukh referred to the courses at the Gymnastics High School as having been established 'für Führer'.
35. W. Joch, *Politische Leibeserziehung und ihre Theorie im Nationalsozialistischen Deutschland* (Frankfurt, 1976), pp.49ff.
36. Interview with Hanne Lykke.
37. *Nationaltidende*, 20 October 1933.

38. H.S. Nissen, 'Folkelighed og frihed – Grundtvigianernes reaktion på modernisering, krise og nazisme', in O. Feldbæk (ed.), *Dansk identitetshistorie* Vol.3 – *Folkets Danmark* 1848–1940 (Copenhagen, 1992), pp.587–673.
39. *Gymnastikhøjskolens årsskrift*, 1933, p.112.
40. G.L. Mosse, *The Crisis of German Ideology* (London, 1966), pp.312ff.
41. Ibid., p.316.
42. See also H. Bonde, 'National Identity and the Body, The Nordic Olympiad in Denmark in 1935', *Scandinavian Journal of History*, 20 (1995), 295–313.

5

Fascists *and* Christians! In the Spanish Martial Tradition of the Soldier-Monk

TERESA GONZALEZ AJA

Spain is a country in which Fascist politics survived longer than in any other part of the world, but where, curiously, categorical Fascism took its time to develop and, what is more, did so in a very watered down fashion for many years. Religion played an extremely important role in Spanish culture and traditions, 'creating a climate of national Catholicism which would resist modern secularization for a long time'.[1]

The study of Spanish Fascism cannot be considered to be an exclusive search for similarities with Italy or Germany. After all, in spite of their common characteristics, the majority of Fascist movements, except those which were created after the German occupation, were responses to national crises and fed on national traditions. There are very significant differences. For example, in Spain there were no First World War veterans to fill the ranks of paramilitary organizations, since this country had taken no part in the war. Moreover, in Spain the civil war produced enormous social and economic upheaval in an already strife-torn country. The consequent revolutionary ferment in the industrial north and the rural south profoundly shocked the Spanish ruling classes. In many aspects, the 1917–23 Spanish crisis was analogous to the 1917–22 Italian crisis, a crisis which was simply anaesthetized by the dictatorship of Primo de Rivera and re-emerged with greater force in the conditions of economic depression during the 1930s. In Spain the common belief arose, as previously in Italy and Germany, that the existing political order could no longer adequately guarantee the economic interests of the middle and upper classes. It was then that the search began for an extraordinary means of defending such interests.

The first official manifestation of Spanish nationalism in the twentieth century was Primo de Rivera's *coup d'état* in 1923. Miguel

FIGURE 5.1

JOSE ANTONIO PRIMO DE RIVERA

Oil painting by Antón Sáenz De Heredia, Palace of the Senate, Madrid

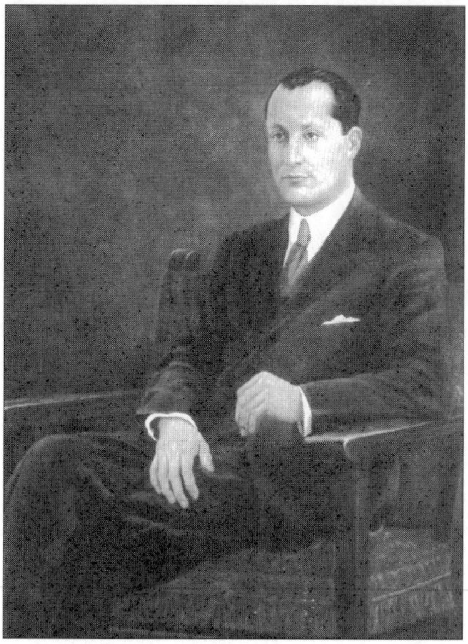

Primo de Rivera was neither intellectual nor politician, but just simply a slightly out-of-date Andalusian general who felt profound admiration for Mussolini's regime. The dictator, accompanying King Alphonse XIII who called him 'my Mussolini',[2] visited Rome during the first months of his government, and in 1926 signed a treaty of 'friendship and arbitration' with Italy. 'But Primo de Rivera could go no further because the political and ideological structures of Italian Fascism were too complex for a mentality as shrewd but as simple as his.'[3]

Furthermore, Fascism also found its echo not only in the political classes but also in the Spanish intelligentsia. Precisely one of the foremost adversaries of the politics followed by the Directorate under the leadership of Primo de Rivera, Francesc Cambó, would be among the first intellectuals of some standing, to become intensely interested in the Fascist phenomenon. Cambó edited one of the pioneering Spanish works on the origins of the nature of Fascism, *Entorn del feixisme italià* (About Italian Fascism).[4] In this context special mention should be made of Giménez Caballero, founder and director of *La Gaceta Literaria*

(1927–32), a magazine which began its life as a forerunner of the avant-garde movement in literature and art to end up being the organ of Fascism in Spain. About 1930 Caballero became totally captivated by 'Roman' Fascism. He was much less interested in National Socialism, although part of the initial Nazi propaganda in Spain, drawn up by party members resident in Madrid, was printed at the same printers where he produced his own *La Gaceta Literaria*.[5] His book *Hercules Playing Dice* was a collection of essays in which he developed the pure and extreme avant-garde attitude of exaltation of sport and the machine as the defining elements of the idiosyncrasy of the current times: athletics, boxing, football, motoring, swimming, and the cinema.[6] What Caballero does in this book is develop the ideas proclaimed by Ortega y Gasset on the existence of 'two different castes of Men', the common men of the masses and the illustrious men of the select minority.[7] Caballero claimed the new European Caesarist regimes, together with the new art movement, were examples of phenomena of his era. 'Over the uncontrollable, turbulent, and voracious tumult of the masses: these rulers, these guides: the Heraklidan Fist.'[8] Here we have a political interpretation of the élitist sociological philosophy of Ortega y Gasset, and the philosophy of Nietzsche.[9] However, it should be borne in mind that for Caballero Fascism was a Spanish invention which pre-dated the politics of Mussolini, in fact which dated from the Catholic monarchs.

> For Spain the *fascio* existed before any Italo Balbo stuck it in his hat. Our Catholic Monarchs put it on their shield: their *haz* (bundle) of arrows, instead of the *fasces* and *lictoria*. We do not need borrowed symbols. We have been a nation since slightly before the new and proud Italy and the pre-potent Germany. A mere difference of four centuries![10]

La Gaceta Literaria, reflected the cultural environment of the moment, each day more politicized. The intellectuals, who initially had collaborated on this project of a plural and renovating reality, abandoned Caballero 1931 (some even earlier, as early as 1928, when his predilection for Fascism became evident). This was the result of the adoption of clearly partisan political attitudes by Spanish intellectuals with the advent of the Republic.[11] They said goodbye to pure and dehumanized art to embrace a more realist, humane and political position. It is for this reason that it is not surprising that, with the passing of time, Caballero boasted that from *La Gaceta Literaria* 'sprang the two spiritual youth movements which would decide the future of Spain':[12] Communism and Fascism.[13] Spanish 'Fascism' could not prosper under the authoritarian provincialism of Primo de Rivera's regime. At the beginning of 1930 he was forced to resign, but what followed was not much better. Two brief semi-dictatorial governments, presided over in succession by a general and an admiral, were unable to re-establish political peace, and in addition, they came up against the great world economic depression. In the midst of great confusion, Alphonse XIII left Spain in 1931 and the Republic was declared.

That same year Onésimo Redondo Ortega, who had worked as a lecturer in the Catholic School of Mannheim in Germany, and had had the opportunity to become familiar with Nazi ideology,[14] founded a political group called the Castilian Juntas of Hispanic Action. Redondo wanted a revolutionary national youth movement which was politically radical and nationalist from an economic point of view, conservative from a religious point of view, but violent in its style and tactics. He exhorted the young to prepare themselves for the fight. 'Youth should take exercise in physical struggle, should love violence as a matter of course. National violence is just, is necessary, is convenient. One of our permanent watchwords is that of cultivating the spirit of violence, of military conflict.'[15] Redondo would join Ramiro Ledesma Ramos, a great connoisseur of German culture and admirer of the progress of Adolf Hitler and National Socialism, and together they would constitute the National Syndicalist Offensive Juntas (JONS). The members of the JONS formed the first official political organization which existed in Spain with the national syndicalist label. As their emblem they adopted the arrows and the yoke of the Catholic monarchs, and Ledesma would coin various slogans like 'arriba!' (upwards) and 'Spain, one, great and free!', which later on would become clichés in national syndicalist propaganda.

During the Republic, and especially after 1933, the most marked 'Fascistization' would occur in the JAP which was the militia of the youth movement organized by the Spanish Confederation of Autonomous Right-wing Parties (CEDA).[16] However, the symbol of their ambivalence and that of the CEDA in general, was shown in the semi-Fascist salute which they officially adopted, i.e. raising the right hand to the right shoulder, palm facing forward, arm bent, elbow down alongside the body.

Precisely this same year, 1933, José Antonio Primo de Rivera, son of the military dictator of the 1920s, founded the Falange. José Antonio was an enthusiastic admirer of Ortega y Gasset and of other theoreticians who preached the need for an élite. This belief in the mission of what was later called a 'creative minority' was combined with the simplistic political notions on which his father's dictatorship had been founded. A small group of reformers with a nationalistic mentality had, with authoritarian procedures, swept away the political chaos in which the country was submerged in 1923. The same solution, he thought, could be applied to the problems of 1933, provided that it was supported by a real political movement which was powerful and well organized. The ideology of his party took many concepts from Fascist Italy: the defence of Christian values against the dangers of Marxism, a totalitarian state which would create a classless society promoting the interests of the workers, and the manifestation of imperialism at the expense of the weaker races.

The Falange was a small entity until the outbreak of the civil war, but during the conflict the number of its members increased – in the same way as did the Spanish Communist Party – to about two million, many of whom fought against 'the reds' in the different Falangist militias. José Antonio managed to agglutinate, in time, the diverse Fascist currents which existed during the republic. But the rise of the Falange was hindered by two fundamental blows which would be the origin of its eternal political frustration: the execution of José Antonio Primo de Rivera in the Alicante prison in November 1936 and the incorporation of the party, by Franco, into the ambiguous 'Movement' in 1937, when the so-called Unification was carried out, in which the right-wing pre-war groups were subsumed into the Spanish Traditionalist Falange (FET) and National Syndicalist Offensive Juntas. From this moment on, the Falange would evolve in the shade of the Caudillo.

Some scholars have argued, explicitly or implicitly, that the study of Fascism in Spain should be limited to the Spanish Falange and not include the Francoist epoch, an approach, which as P. Preston[17] maintains, is a little unfortunate, but which is due on the one hand to the development, which had little to do with Fascism, of Spain from 1957 onwards and, on the other, to the continual efforts made by Franco, after 1943, to dissociate himself from the Axis. Even so, the Fascist nature of the style, ideology and myths of the Falange are unquestionable.[18]

It is true that from the moment of Franco's ascent to power, an era began which was marked by the personality of this man who was until his death in 1975, 'Caudillo of Spain by the Grace of God' and, as stated in article XI of the statutes of the party 'The Chief (who only) answers to God and to History'. It should be borne in mind, of course, that the phenomenon of Francoism lasted for nearly 40 years, which is why it was far from being a homogenous whole, and was enormously affected not only by the changes produced because of internal conditions, but also, and not least importantly, by international conjunctures. However, until 1943, the identification of Francoism with Fascism was undoubtable.[19] In Spain it was firmly believed, while Hitler and Mussolini were giving help to the rebels, that the future world order would be Fascist, and the common feature of all the Spanish right-wing organizations was their sympathy for Fascism. They did not hesitate to shower coarse praise on the German and Italian regimes, and juvenile militarized branches proliferated, considered indiscriminately by the Spanish left as Fascist. It is even less surprising that Franco's war effort, supported by the powers of the Axis and with a Falangist façade, was seen by his contemporaries, both inside and outside the country, as a Fascist endeavour.

Thus if Nazism and Fascism, with due account taken of their differences, can be considered as the German and Italian Fascist responses to the crises in their respective societies, in the same way it can be claimed that the right-wing groups which supported the rebels in the civil war should be considered, at least potentially, as the Spanish Fascist response to the crisis in Spanish society.

In 1939 Spanish foreign policy was directed towards Italy and Germany. Both had given the first examples of new authoritarian states, and constituted a new diplomatic and military area with which to be aligned, one whose power was rapidly increasing. This does not mean that the Spanish regime was simply a satellite of one of the Axis powers (although Italy considered it as such), rather that Franco's politics, from beginning to end, were based on pragmatism and the idea of what was best for Spain. Thus, for example, as well as signing a friendship pact with Germany at the end of March 1939, Franco's government also signed a treaty of mutual friendship for ten years with Portugal, which maintained a traditional Anglo-Portuguese alliance.

It is important to point out that Spanish sympathies leaned towards Rome, rather than Berlin. Serrano Suñer made a state visit to Rome immediately after the civil war, with the aim, in part, of expressing the desire of the Spanish regime for a closer identification with Italy than with Germany, in response, to an extent, to the fact that Italy had

FIGURE 5.2

RAMÓN SERRANO SUÑER (Oil painting by Ignacio De Zuloaga, 1940)

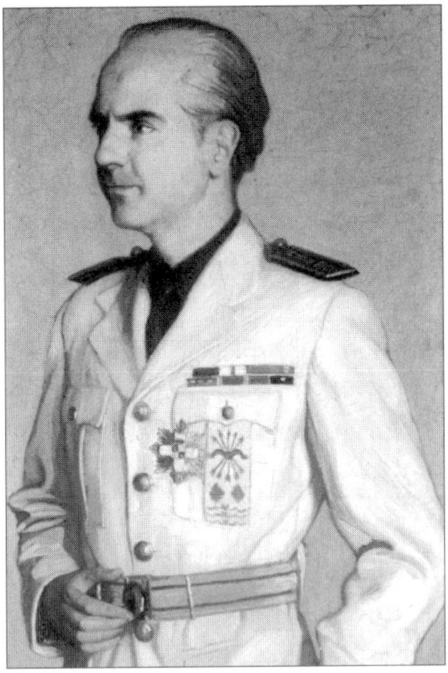

FIGURE 5.3

FRANCO MEETS HITLER, HENDAYA, OCTOBER 1940

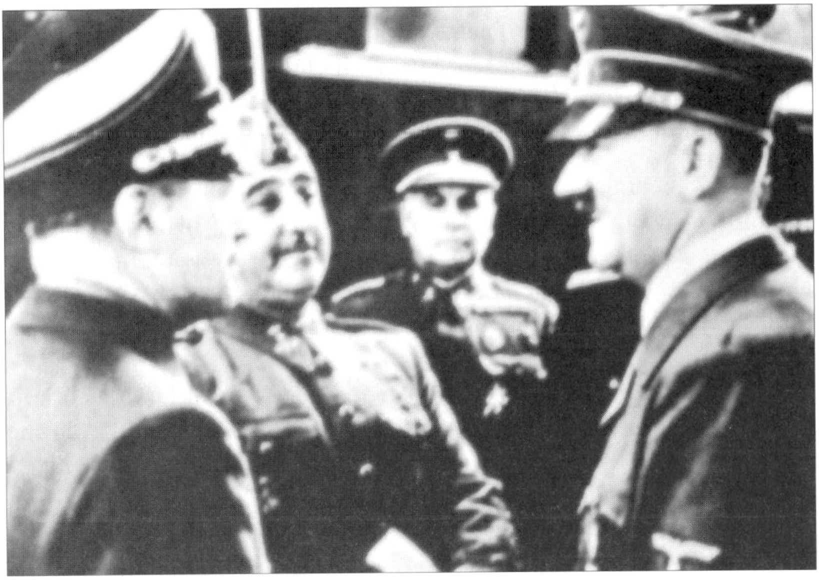

contributed more than Germany to the Nationalist victory.[20] The new Spanish regime looked much more to Rome than to Berlin, seeing in Fascist Italy the nearest thing to a model to imitate. However, after the swift conquest of France by Germany, Spanish foreign policy changed completely. In June 1940 the greater part of political and military opinion in Madrid had rapidly turned towards Germany. On 17 July of this same year, during the celebrations for the fourth anniversary of the national uprising, Franco's speech to the National Council of the FET y de las JONS, had a clearly anti-Semitic and aggressively imperialistic tone:

> We have spilt the blood of our dead to make a Nation and to forge an empire ... And even in the last moments when that most holy of queens put her hand to her will, she signed a political will for her people: the mandate of Gibraltar, the vision of Africa, political unity, political expression, political mandates which even after four centuries survive as an eternal lesson.

In a burst of Fascist existentialism, he declared:

> We do not want life to be easy and comfortable. We want life to be hard, life to be difficult, we want the life of virile peoples...Five hundred thousand dead were offered in the first European battle for the new order, for the salvation and the unity of Spain. We are not alien to the problems of the world. Our rights and our ambitions have not lapsed; Spain which wove and gave its life to a continent now has regained its strength and virility. It has two million warriors ready to fight to defend its rights.

He sang the praises of discipline and unity as the key to Spanish ambitions, and the magic of the 'fantastic victories' of Hitler 'on the European battlefields'.[21] The day after the speech, it was announced that Hitler had awarded Franco the highest decoration that the Third Reich could confer on a foreigner: the Great Golden Cross of the German Order of the Eagle.[22]

This surge of Spanish enthusiasm reached its zenith with Hitler's invasion of the USSR in June 1941, which gave rise to a strong emotional response on the part of many people in Madrid, particularly among the Falangists. Barely 48 hours after the invasion, the Spanish government asked to be allowed the possibility of having some form of Spanish participation without it seeming to be an official entry into the war. Before the huge mass of people concentrated in front of the Falangist headquarters, on 24 June Serrano Suñer launched his famous phrase 'Russia is guilty' during his speech, referring to the Soviet responsibilities in the Spanish war and to the loss of lives, and declared that 'history and the future of Europe demand the extermination of Russia'. The anti-Soviet struggle in the East was declared to be an extension of the Spanish crusade in the civil war, and Spain to be a 'moral fighter' in the new conflict. Spanish participation would take the form of a corps of 20,000 volunteers which would be known as the Blue Division (the colour of the Falangists' shirts), and which would fight alongside the German troops in the Soviet Union. These troops began to depart from Spain on 17 July and arrived at their positions on the Soviet front on 4 October.

It cannot be denied that the enthusiasm in the nation was genuine, and the summer of 1941 was the culmination of the warlike feeling in favour of Germany, as can be seen in the news stories which appeared in the press of the time, where the most pro-German of Franco's speeches is cited: 'Not even the American continent can dream of an intervention in Europe without embracing a catastrophe … In this situation, to say that the outcome of the war can be changed by the entry into action of a third country is criminal madness … The war has been badly planned and the allies have lost.' And he concluded by stating that Germany was heading the 'battle that Europe and Christianity has been waiting for, for so many years, and in which the blood of our youth will be joined to that of our comrades of the Axis, in an expression of total solidarity'.[23]

However, Franco's pro-Axis declarations were not so frequent nor so extreme as those of Serrano Suñer, the Minister who had the greatest influence and freedom of action as, although they tended to agree with regard to foreign policy, it is true that the latter advocated a political system which was more coherent and integrated, and in this sense more completely Fascist, than Franco wished to accept.[24]

The leaders of the new Spanish state firmly believed that the European order was moving towards the implantation of 'organic' authoritarian regimes. Although Spanish post-war society and its institutions were in no way totalitarian, in the sense of complete control by the government, the new government was a more direct personal dictatorship than those of the USSR, Italy or Germany. During the first four years after the civil war, Franco led the government as if it were an army. There was a clear predominance of the Fascist style in its attitudes, as for example in the ritual invocations of 'Franco, Franco, Franco'. The name of the Caudillo was painted on the façades of many public buildings throughout Spain, and his photograph was placed in all public offices, as well as on the new postage stamps and new Spanish coins. A telling image:

> On a hot Sunday afternoon, 25 June 1939, Seville and Racing from El Ferrol played the first final of the Generalissimo's Cup in the Montjuich stadium in Barcelona. Three months had passed since the end of the civil war, and less than five since the surrender of Barcelona to General Yagüe. The two teams lined up before the start of the match and raised their right arms to give the Fascist salute. A few seconds later, over the stadium loudspeakers came the Falangist battle hymn 'Cara al sol' (Facing the sun). The players began to sing enthusiastically, and the crowd which filled the stadium – in which there were many soldiers – quickly followed suit, standing, arms raised and singing with one voice.[25]

As we can see, sport also suffered 'Fascistization', as a series of 'external signs' were adopted, among which could be found for example the Fascist salute, which had to be given before each match, or the use by the National team of blue shirts, instead of their usual red shirts. It was the period defined by the word 'blue', introduced by General Moscardó, who was the head of the National Sports Delegation (DND),[26] and was at the same time president of the Spanish Olympic Committee (clearly contravening the rules of the International Olympic Committe which stated that the different national committees should be strictly non-political) and responsible for the sections of Sports Medicine, Legal Affairs, Transport, Press and Propaganda, the department of military sports and sports in the Movement. He was also head of the department of national federations, and his control over the different federations was total. The DND not only nominated the presidents and vice-presidents of the different Spanish federations, but also the members of the their boards of directors and, in addition, the presidents and vice-presidents of all their regional branches. And, as if this were not enough, Article 4 of the Decree confirmed the right of the DND to veto any decision of any federation which was not to its liking. With all this the whole of Spanish sport was covered. As stated by Cazorla Prieto: 'All social organization of sport was subject if not to absolute state or parastate control, certainly to a rigid discipline on the part of the public authorities, whereby any hint of social protagonism was practically stifled.'[27]

The new organism was to be a delegation or agency of the General Secretariat of the National Movement, the only political party permitted and an uneasy alliance of Falangists, monarchists and Carlists. Its mission was to use the international sports arena to exhibit Spanish virility and 'fury', the way the German and Italian regimes had done in the decade from 1930 to 1940. Thus from the very beginning any possibility of sport having some degree of independence with regard to the new political power was put firmly aside.

Furthermore, with regard to sport, there was an attempt in Spain to follow the model of Nazi Germany, but Franco was never willing to invest a great deal in this activity, as Hitler or Mussolini did. However, the Falange considered football an excellent means of mobilizing the masses under their banner, of reflecting traditional Hispanic 'virile and impetuous' masculine values, and, above all, of showing the world the impressive power and potential of its 'new Spain'. Its aim was to create a Spain in which everyone would practise one sport or another, while the best sportsmen of the race would exhibit their high level of ability in international competitions, especially in the Olympic Games, and would gain the admiration of the world. Sport should be where the Hispanic masculine values about which the Falange talked so much and so often – virility, impetuosity and 'fury' – would be incarnate. The last of these three values was the easiest to apply to football because the myth of 'Spanish fury' had existed in the world of football since the 1920 Olympic Games. However, in hungry Spain, all these aspirations were destined to fail.[28]

During the first years, football was an important element in the hands of the recently founded regime, becoming a vehicle for Fascist attitudes and propaganda, although the national team, due to the ostracism which Spain suffered during the 1940s, found hardly any countries to play against. If we analyse the international matches which were played with other countries in the first years of the dicatorship, we can see that during the 1940s exhibition matches were played against teams from Nazi Germany and Fascist Italy and, for identical reasons, against Portugal, with whom the RFEF (Royal Spanish Football Federation) arranged, in the period from 1941 to 1950, no fewer than ten matches, which naturally contributed to maintaining a highly cordial atmosphere between Franco's dictatorship and that of Salazar. However, the

FIGURE 5.4
SOCCER MATCH, MALAGA, 1940

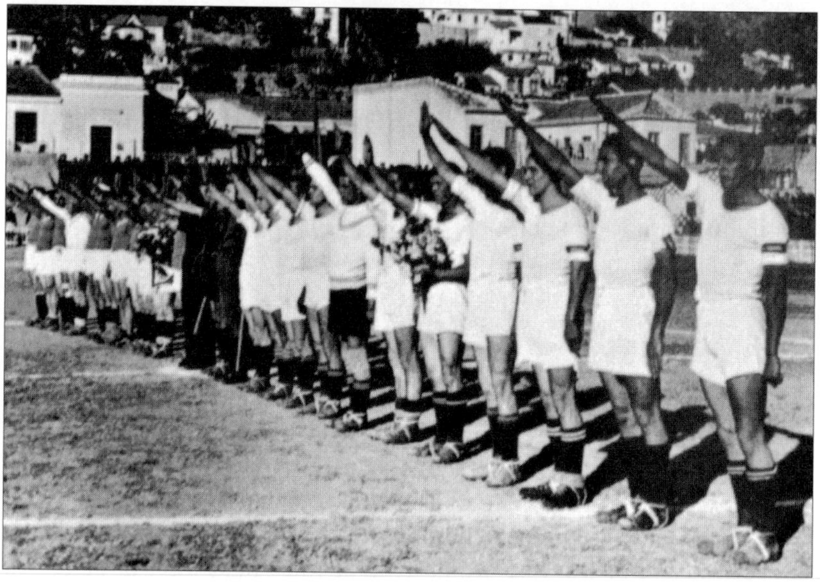

FIGURE 5.5
FRANCISCO FRANCO
Oil painting by J.A. Aguiar, *c.* 1939, Salamanca Town Hall

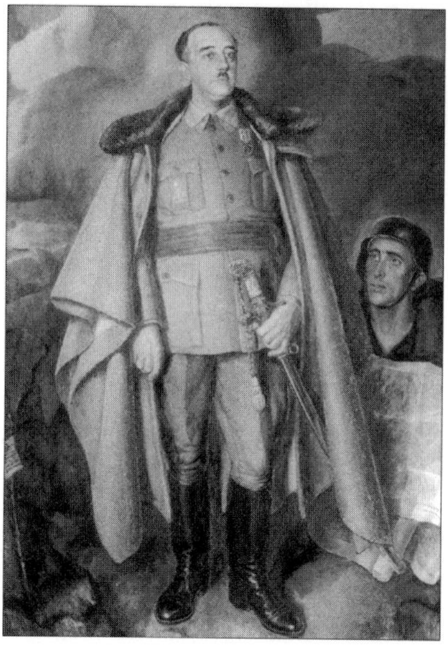

attempts by the RFEF to organize friendly matches with England from 1945 onwards were destined to fail.

That same year, some 'cosmetic' measures were taken to detach the regime from its Fascist image. In the Cabinet meeting of 7 September 1945, the official use of the Fascist salute was repealed to the dismay of the Falangist ministers.[29] The new political order tried to use all the means at its disposal to create an image which would give it a certain amount of prestige with national and international public opinion. Intellectuals, writers, artists, sportsmen, whether through their own convictions, in exchange for a position or recognition, or because of the pressure of events, would put their name and their work to the service of a concrete political cause. However, the greatest problem which arose, was the absence of a doctrine. Francoism was a situation and a changing correlation of forces, and it was basically the trajectory of one person passing through different moments with the aim of surviving them.

Within the image that Francoism wished to project, an important part was played, as in all totalitarian regimes, by the idealized image of man. It was a case of making physical and moral violence not only tolerable, but agreeable, endowing them with a mask which was attractive to the senses. However, the lack of a concrete theory makes a scientific study of this theme impossible. Francoism did not possess a concrete aesthetic. It is true that it fed on images which came from Fascism and Nazism, but it did not possess a specific theory. It is thus a vain endeavour to try to study the masculine image as an objective reality in the cultural tide of the epoch. Consequently, to talk of the cult of the body, means to talk of the adaptation of different models to different stages and to the needs of a very concrete personality.

In this sense, the defence of the physical appearance of Franco himself, comparing him with Hitler and Mussolini, which Caballero made in 1938, in the middle of the civil war, and which he entitled 'Franco's smile', is emblematic. It is worth quoting in full.

> FRANCO is a smile. His deepest secret. We do not agree with the portraits which paint FRANCO: serious, with knitted brows, grave, doctoral. As if to give him the air of a Mussolini or Hitler.
>
> Little by little we must eliminate hallucinatory mimicry which is already in danger of taking away the Spanishness from such a Spanish Movement as ours, even though our Movement has accepted certain general historical lines.

It is, above all, unfair to search for this mimicry in the figure of the Caudillo which is so very Spanish.

MUSSOLINI's secret is his look and the way he sticks out his jaw.

He is the Duce of a people like the Italians who know how to gather together in magnificent parades and aduntas in the sun and in the open air and they need the Condotiere with his eyes like the sun and the gestures of a tribune – standing on a balcony or leaning on a balustrade – to be understood and led.

HITLER is, in a vivid sense – his trimmed moustache and his sideways combed hair, which, under his military cap, give him an air somewhere between martial and popular, doctoral and solemn – which goes very well with a people like the Germans who are so disciplined and ordered.

But FRANCO is a smile. FRANCO's smile has conquered Spain. And has conquered all of its people.

It is the sign that the people of Spain and the combatants of Spain needed to reach their triumph and consolidate their victory.

Because a people, which is so rebellious, quarrelsome, fierce, tribal, and given to civil war as ours when fighting breaks out, could only be pacified by a Caudillo with a smile. This is the great secret of why FRANCO is neither envied nor envious in a country which is as rancorous and envious as ours.

Here where passions have exploded into blood, where every Spaniard fights his own shadow, where the soul of the people was and is convulsed and everything is wrath, war and combat, only this supreme smile of love and peace, which is FRANCO, could calm it, bring it peace, and close its wounds.

FRANCO's smile has something of the Virgin's mantle laid over the sinners. It has both paternal and maternal tenderness.

In his smile we see that the most powerful man in Spain, the man who can strike down the destinies of all others, knows how to forgive, knows how to understand, knows how to embrace.

It is true that FRANCO has moments of infinite gravity, of pain, of bitter solemnity. But this is always our fault. And making FRANCO serious should be severely punished. Because one thing that all combatants, and now all Spaniards, know is that the best decoration, the best prize that can be awarded in our Cause is none other than this: to deserve a smile from FRANCO. FRANCO's smile.[30]

FIGURE 5.6

'THEY WON'T GET THROUGH! 1936 WE WILL GET THROUGH! 1937'

Poster by Puyol (Library of Catalonia, Barcelona)

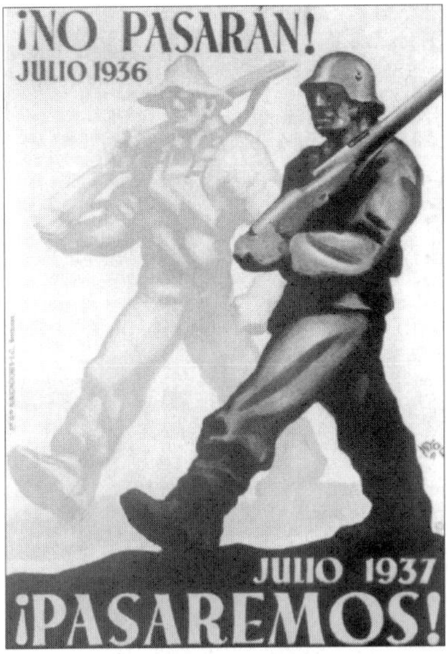

FIGURE 5.7

'SPAIN, ONE, GREAT, AND FREE'. POSTER OF THE FALANGE, 1937

(J.M. Armero Collection)

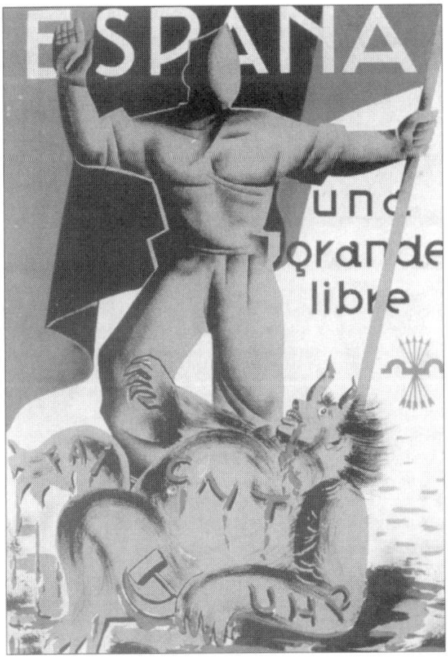

FIGURE 5.8

MAN WILL BE FREE THROUGH SOCIALISM. POSTER OF THE VALENCIAN SOCIALIST FEDERATION

by J. Barrera, 1937 (National Historical Archive, Salamanca)

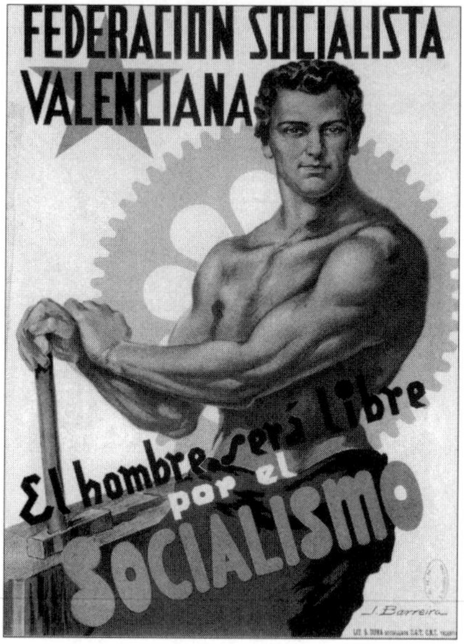

FIGURE 5.9

POSTER FOR THE PEOPLE'S OLYMPICS, BARCELONA

by Arteche, July 1936 (National Historical Archive, Salamanca)

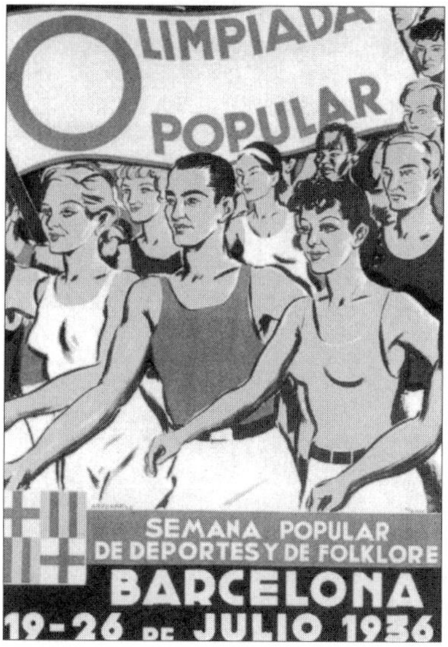

FIGURE 5.10

'THE FIRST GALLOPS'

by Carlos Sáez de Tejada, 1938. Published in the magazine *Vértigo*, San Sebastian

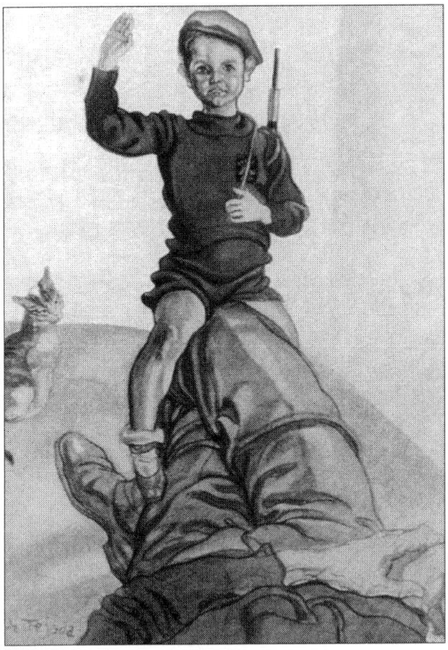

FIGURE 5.11

'ALLEGORY OF THE FALANGE'

Watercolour by Teodoro Delgado, 1937 (Private Collection)

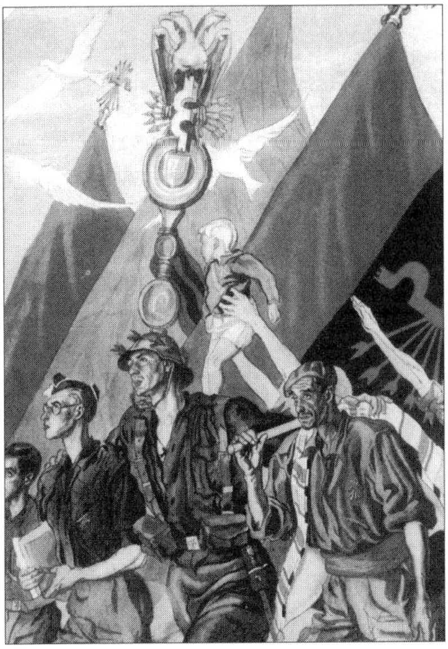

FIGURE 5.12

'ALLEGORY OF THE "REQUETÉ" [CARLIST VOLUNTEER]'

by Carlos Sáez de Tejada, 1937 (Private Collection)

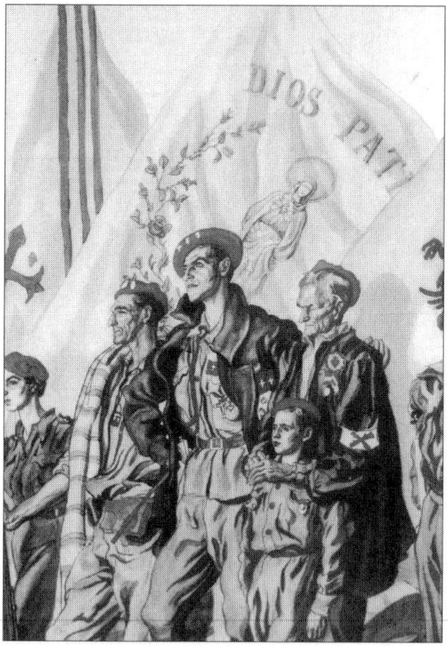

FIGURE 5.13

'SPAIN HAS ARRIVED'

Poster from the National Propaganda Service (Private Collection)

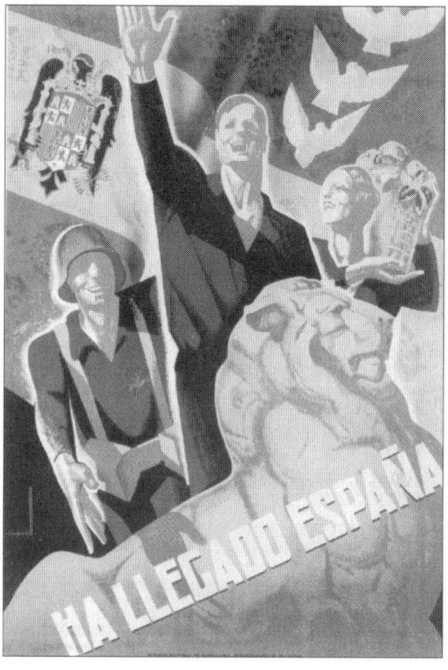

FIGURE 5.14

NATIONALIST PROPAGANDA, 1937

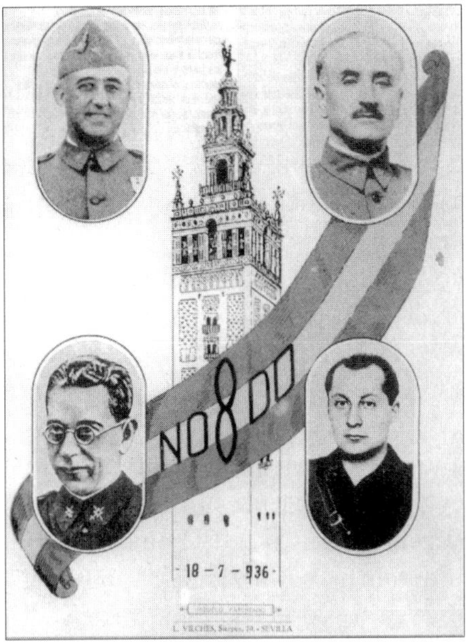

FIGURE 5.15

CARTOON BY ROBERTO ALCAZAR, 1940

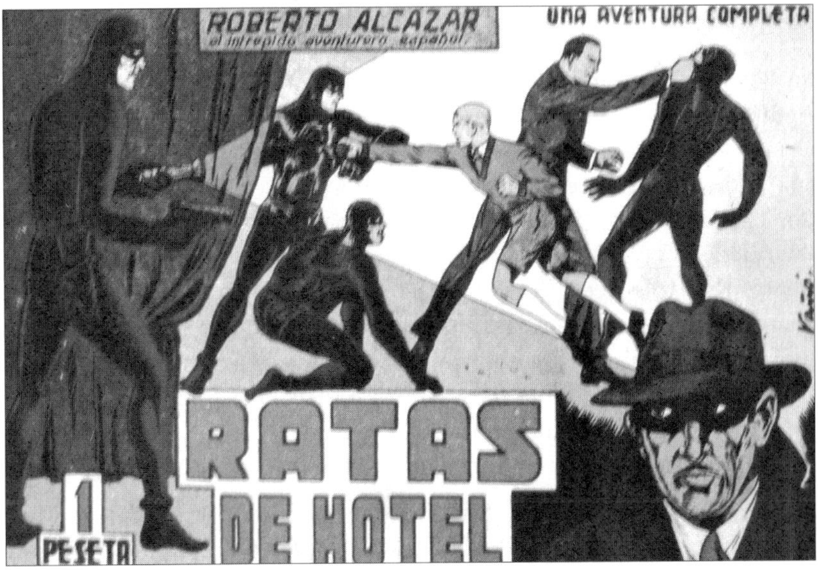

Obviously, given the physical build of Franco, Caballero paints a 'style', and not an image. He rejects an athletic appearance, which Franco totally lacked.

Nevertheless, in Spain as elsewhere, in the Fascist period there was a defence of the myth of the perfect man, which included his physical appearance, although it would always be nearer the image of the perfect gentleman, of the 'soldier-monk', a compound of austerity, spirit of sacrifice, and impassiveness when faced with bloodshed. Thus, although there is no hesitation about including certain athletic aspects, and on occasion the Francoist soldiers are represented as valiant athletic heroes, there is a certain preoccupation with the slimness of the characters, and in a slightly mannered fashion the figures are elongated in the style of El Greco and at times even the hero athletes are endowed with a certain feminine halo.

Francoism took up the inheritance of national Catholicism allied to a certain affection for the magnificence of the monarchy. Caballero, Rafael Sánchez Mazas, Eugenio Montes and Dionisio Ridruejo presided over the development of dominant cultural inclinations, which coexisted with the very typical José María de Pemán, and managed to leave room for Eugenio d'Ors, a master of the aesthetics of the war generation, and for a certain number of ideas which came from Ortega y Gasset, and were transmitted via José Antonio.

M. Bertuchi produced a series of paintings which were very successful in 1939, and which depict symbolic scenes like that of soldiers in shadow who, arms raised, salute the luminous apparition of their commander, and that of the troops on the beach facing the sea, also with arms raised, saluting the vision of the Crucifixion of Jesus which appears above the clouds. A series of plates which were used to make picture cards for children, were produced by Carlos Sáenz de Tejada with the title 'Artifices of Victory'. They figured the Legion, the Youth Organization, the Carlist volunteer, the Navy, the Regular Army, the Army brought from Morocco, the Falange, the Medical Corps and the Air Force. They were publications with a political purpose and helped to diffuse widely the new Fascist ideals, but naturally with their Hispanic peculiarities. In this sense, special mention should be made of the comics aimed at educating children, which were conceived as instruments of propaganda.

> One of the characteristics of the heroes of that time was the adoption of two complementary characteristics. On the one hand,

> they copied from the American heroes of the Batman or Superman type, their extreme athletic character, their giant proportions, their enormous muscularity, their apparent virility, their total courage, as if born of faith in their own invulnerability. But, on the other hand, they presented a markedly homosexual aspect. Moral censorship, which in those sanctimonious times, made consummated sexual relationships to appear sinful, dictated that when a hero was in love with a woman, their love should never be fulfilled. They were always, chaste, distant fiancées, with no direct contact with the hero, as happened with the Masked Warrior's Ana Maria or Fernando's Sarita. In contrast, the need to capture the interest of the young readers meant that they had to incorporate young men or boys, with whom they could identify, to participate in the heroic deeds. This produced the famous pairs of an older hero accompanied by a little boy hero, almost always handsome and blond.'[31]

Physical appearance was used as a means of propaganda. It was an attempt to create an emotive mythology for the middle classes, to act as a screen to hide conflict and transform reality into an image of Unity, Order and Hierarchy. The family was *the* institution *par excellence*, and as a means of tying individuals (men, women, and children) to it, there would be enormous sexual inhibition which would regard the body as the 'abominable garb of the soul' as Gregory the Great called it. This meant that it would never stop being considered somewhat sinful. It is a well-known fact that official chastity made it obligatory not only to wear a swimming costume on the beach, but also a bathrobe.

Emphasis was placed above all on 'style', as noted in the case of Franco's appearance. Style permitted the plebeian to become an aristocrat, anyone to belong to the ruling sphere. From this was born the great preoccupation with elegance, which tended to make society a people of lords, as they said in Germany, or gentlemen or nobles, as was claimed in Spain. The uniform was one of the fundamental elements of this task. Following the model of Fascist Italy and Nazi Germany, the shirt was emphasized. In Spain the blue of the workers of the era was adopted, as the intention was to have roots in the popular, but an instrument of elegance was also required, as in the case of the white bush jackets of the Falangists. Moreover, the Blue Shirts were given a military appearance with pockets, accordion pleats, shoulder pads, leather straps, and gaiters, to which were added aggressive symbols like skulls or cross-bones and a knife in the belt.

Another essential element was monumentalism, dear to totalitarian regimes, although naturally with the characteristic features of each of the areas. This search for style and a colossal vocation explains the great importance of ceremonials, concentrations, parades with banners or torches, incense burners, musical accompaniment or displays by youths where pre-military, gymnastic and sports exercises were performed by masses of members from all the provinces. The National Manifestation organized in the summer of 1938 by the Youth Front, unfailingly recalls the showy demonstrations of the Fascist youth or the resounding Reichjugendtag der NSDAP of 1934 in Potsdam. Of the Youth Front, Franco said:

> The State, which maintains and re-establishes the effectiveness of Church and family rights in education, hopefully founds its own work to politically and militarily forge the men who will inherit the sacrifices of our generation. All the means that the State has should be applied to watch, keep and support the Youth Front, the truly favourite work of the regime. I say that it will be a useless and dangerous task for those who try to hinder it.[32]

It was the institution which monopolized the responsibility for planning and executing youth policy during the first half of Franco's regime. The Youth Front was included, initially, in the group of organizations and systems which practised or were agencies of a 'pro' youth policy. And this assignment was clearly reinforced if it is borne in mind that the beginnings of its functioning coincided with those of 'national Spain', a connotation, as a political model, located in the orbit of authoritarian regimes. In terms of a youth policy, this institution coincided fully with the other Fascist models until the end of the Second World War. From then on, during the second half of the 1940s, motivated by the international blockade, it not only conserved these features, but even reinforced them more clearly, if that were possible, cultivating them intensively as a differential factor, at least from the point of view of external appearances.[33]

This organization had, as well as a series of Commands, three Advisers: the Central Adviser for Physical Education, in agreement with the Ministry of Education, the Central Adviser for Pre-military Education, in agreement with the Ministry of the Army, and the

Religious Adviser of the National Delegation, 'who will be nominated in the manner provided'. In order to be able to carry out its educational mission with Spanish youth, from the 'political, physical and pre-military point of view', the National Service of Instructors was created, for whose training the José Antonio National Academy of Officers and Instructors was founded in 1941,[34] and the Isabel la Católica School for women.[35] Their objective was to train young 'members' to be Party militants and to undertake the 'political initiation' and 'physical education' of non-members, as well as 'to safeguard the fulfilment of the orders of the Movement, with regard to youth, in the school and workplace'.[36] They organized programmes of extracurricular education in which, in addition to what was taught in the school or the workplace, there were complementary classes in political indoctrination and pre-military education was initiated, in a cyclical plan which culminated in compulsory military service and incorporation into the Party militia.

Furthermore, the old summer camps were replaced by camps or hostels organized by the Youth Front, the Feminine Section and the Unions Organization for Education and Rest. The ideology of these camps was far removed from the hygienic postulates from which the summer camps were born. The accommodation in tents, use of the Falange uniform, the military style of the activities, the hierarchization, use of the familiar form of address when talking to the 'officers', use of standards and so on, made them more similar to the activities of the Hitler Youth, emphasizing their marked Fascist characteristics. The National School, Syndicalist, Labour and University Games were created, which was, according to J.M. Cagigal, 'the most important, and socially most transcendent task carried out by the organisms of the Movement in the fulfilment of the function with which it was charged – that of promoting physical education and sport among young Spanish people'.[37]

As coeducation disappeared, physical instruction of the two sexes became totally different. Boys performed exercises of a marked military nature, martial and virile. Girls practised Swedish and rhythmic gymnastics and characteristic popular dances from various Spanish regions. For a long time female participation in sports was limited to the less violent ones: basketball, volleyball and gymnastics, and for a long time, athletics were forbidden to women. The educational system as a whole was used to inculcate ideas and values which would ensure acceptance of the new regime. The only values tolerated were religious and patriotic. To inculcate them efficiently into the new generation, the Church and the Falange were incorporated into the educational system.

Within the educational programme, sport was affected by the same problems as education in general. The attitude of the regime was marked by total rejection of secularism and of any innovative or Europeanizing tendency, and the assertion of what was most traditional and Catholic in Spain. An exhaustive set of regulations on the characteristics which those persons charged with teaching should possess inspired the enthusiasm of the provincial committees charged with purging all the teaching staff in primary, secondary and university education and from special schools that did not conform. These committees had been formed as a result of the publication of a Decree on 8 May 1936. The school, like sport, stayed in the hands of those who were sympathizers of the regime, and who in many instances lacked qualifications. In this way, their services were not only rewarded but, given their proven loyalty on the battlefield, they would also be guaranteed to inculcate the values for which they had fought in the new generations. The Ministry of Education, which previously had been called Public Instruction and Fine Arts, was entrusted to Pedro Sáinz Rodríguez, who brought out a study plan in 1938,[38] which followed the model implemented in Italy by Gentile,[39] although it gave greater importance to religious topics.

To conclude, it should be pointed out that the religious aspect is probably the one which symbolizes the fundamental difference between German Nazism, Italian Fascism and the Fascism which developed in Spain. In contrast to Italy and Germany, where historical circumstances made Fascism fashionable, its promoters in Spain could not build a large party of the masses nor have an important electoral pact. The ideology of the middle classes was not embodied in a party but in the Spanish Church and the mental attitude which surrounded it, while the position which was nearest to Fascism, that of the Falange, was isolated in a small area with no hope of growing.

On the day of his investiture, Franco stated that Spain would be reorganized within a 'totalitarian' concept, through its 'natural institutions' and by means of a 'hierarchical' regime which would base the expression of the national will on the 'technical organisms' and the 'corporations'. There is no doubt that all these ideas were contained in the abundant Fascist propaganda, but the most solid supports for Franco's thought are not to be found there, but in the two robust pillars of Spanish nationalism and the Church as the stabilizing elements of state unity; both aspects were viewed by Franco from the perspective of his special world, the Army of his time, in which he had lived since his childhood.

Perhaps a fitting way to sum up all that has been said, is to refer to Franco's fundamental artistic work and the one which constitutes his pantheon: the Valley of the Fallen, because it is basically the personal achievement of Francisco Franco. Nothing better, then, than to conclude with the words of Franco himself who stated:

> The Escorial is the monument to our past glories, and the Basilica and annexes of the Valley of the Fallen the milestone and starting point of our future. Our monument is of greater importance today, especially for those abroad, because they are so little used to witnessing these great works of the spirit. Neither are the people who experience these achievements the best placed to understand them. When the Escorial was built many Spaniards murmured, as history records, about the expenses which Philip II incurred in his fight against nature to raise his great stone building. In our time, some will also undoubtedly murmur against what this great and grandiose monument has cost. However, if they just thought about how it is destined to offer honour, prayers and a grave to all our fallen for God and for Spain, the monument has cost less than if a thousand pesetas had been given for each of the fallen for a modest grave.[40]

In the Valley of the Fallen the bodies of the self-sacrificial warriors of Fascism *and* Church were enshrined and celebrated.

NOTES

1. S.G. Payne, *Historia del Fascismo* (Barcelona, 1995), p.323.
2. V. Peña Sánchez, *Intelectuales y Fascismo* (Granada, 1995), p.120 (hereafter *Intelectuales*).
3. S.G. Payne, *Falange, Historia del Fascismo Español* (Paris, 1965), p.6 (hereafter *Fascismo Español*).
4. Barcelona, 1925. The Castilian translation was published at the same time. *En Torno del Fascismo Italiano* (Barcelona, 1925).
5. F. Guillén Salaya, *Los que Nacimos con el Siglo (Biografía de una Juventud)* (Madrid, 1953), p.121.
6. E. Giménez Caballero, *Hércules Jugando a los Dados* (Madrid, 1928) (hereafter *Hércules*). In this book we can read such revealing sentences as: 'Because our epoque is this: athletics, cinema, the dice cup … gambling, speed, light, dice cup, and geometry', p.13.
7. J. Ortega y Gasset, *La Deshumanización del Arte* (Madrid, 1960), pp.4–5.
8. Caballero, *Hércules*, p.213.
9. V. Peña Sánchez, *Intelectuales*, p.183.
10. *Genio de España. Exaltaciones a una Resurrección Nacional y del Mundo* (Madrid, 1939), p.226.

11. In 1931 Ledesma Ramos published the first issue of *The Conquest of the State*, based on Fascist ideology, and for their part, José Díaz Fernández and Antonio Espina founded *Nueva España*, a rigorously left-wing publication. Many other collaborators dispersed to political publications with different leanings.
12. J.C. Mainer, *Falange y Literatura* (Barcelona, 1971), p.89.
13. See Payne, *Fascismo Español*, p.13.
14. Following the habitual attitude of clerical Fascism of those years, he declared that Adolf Hitler represented 'Christianity versus Marxism', *El Estado Nacional*, 19, 20 March 1933.
15. Cited by Payne, *Fascismo Español*, p.14.
16. The CEDA, theoretically advocated legal and non-violent parliamentary practices, but in practice, the constitutional revision which it so desired, seemed to tend towards a more authoritarian and corporative Catholic republic. Its objectives were never clearly defined.
17. P. Preston, *Las Derechas Españolas en el Siglo XX: Autoritarismo, Fascismo y Golpismo* (Madrid, 1986), p.19 (hereafter *Derechas Españolas*).
18. A complete analysis of the Falange is presented by Payne in *Fascismo Español*.
19. On the controversy which has arisen with respect to the similarities and dissimilarities between Francoism and Fascism see Preston, *Derechas Españolas*, pp.18–41.
20. See S.G. Payne, *Franco, el Perfil de la Historia* (Madrid, 1992), p.93.
21. *Arriba*, 18 July 1940; *La Vanguardia Española*, 18 July 1940; *The Times*, 18 July 1940.
22. *La Vanguardia Española*, 19 July 1940; *The Times*, 19 July 1940.
23. *Arriba*, 18 July 1941.
24. R. Serrano Suñer, *Entre Hendaya y Gibraltar* (Madrid, 1947) pp.123–32.
25. D. Shaw, *Fútbol y Franquismo* (Madrid, 1987), p.17.
26. It was created on 22 February 1941.
27. Luis Ma Cazorla Prieto, *Deporte y Estado* (Barcelona, 1979), p.198.
28. Spain had been playing for about 20 years and had never played abroad. With regard to the Norwegian, Swedish, Danish and Belgian teams which participated, it did not seem to have a chance, but it won its first match against Denmark and played the semi-finals against Holland. It won, and the press began to talk of the great success of the Spanish footballers and of their 'fury', a term which served to define the characteristics of Hispanic play for many years, even after the civil war.
29. J. Tussel, *Franco y los Católicos: la Política Interior Española entre 1945 y 1957* (Madrid, 1984), pp.102–6; L. Suárez Fernández, *Franco: la Historia y sus Documentos* (Madrid, 1986), IV, pp.52–3.
30. A. Cirici, *La Estética del Franquismo* (Barcelona, 1977), pp.77–8.
31. Ibid., pp.164–5.
32. Francisco Franco, 6 December 1940.
33. The model would come into open crisis from the beginning of the 1950s, along with the death throws of autarchic politics.
34. Decree of 2 September 1941.
35. For an analysis of the evolution of these schools and their different syllabi, see S. Fernández Nares, *La educación física en el sistema educativo español* (Granada 1993), pp.140–94.
36. J. Sáez Marín, op. cit., p.79.
37. J.M. Cagigal, *El deporte en la sociedad actual* (Madrid, 1975) pp.122–3.
38. The Law of 20 September 1938, on the Reform of Secondary Education. Spanish Official Bulletin 23 September.
39. S.G. Payne, *El régimen de Franco 1936–1975* (Madrid, 1988), p.280.
40. *Pueblo*, 1 May 1959, Interview given by Franco to the editor of the newspaper.

Return to Manhood: The Cult of Masculinity and the British Union of Fascists

TONY COLLINS

'This century is ours! And we shall live it in the full beauty of our manhood.' So proclaimed British Union of Fascists (BUF) member Theo Lang in February 1935.[1] Fortunately his prediction did not come to pass, yet his declaration of the centrality of manhood to Fascist politics was undeniably correct. Both Hitler's Nazis and Mussolini's Fascists were consciously and aggressively masculine (as were others across the world as this volume makes clear), and the British Fascists were no different.

The BUF was a self-defined masculine organization whose politics aimed at establishing a self-proclaimed 'virile form of government' which would appeal 'to the spirit of British manhood'.[2] The centrality of manliness to the organization was demonstrated both in its philosophy – 'Fascism believes in manhood, in courage, in determination, in selflessness, in the essence of life' – and in its immediate political programme – 'Manliness, courage, thought and discipline are weapons with which security, peace and comfort can be obtained.'[3]

The manliness it espoused was the militaristic masculinity of the late Victorian and Edwardian age, as described extensively by J.A. Mangan,[4] which was put to the service of an organization which was prepared to use violence against its opponents in the socialist and Jewish movements. Indeed, it would not be stretching the point too far to suggest that the BUF's politics could be described as the ethos of public school masculinity as a political programme.[5] While this ethos has been extensively considered, and despite useful explorations of the BUF's attitude to women and the activities of Fascist women, little has been written about the relationship between British Fascism and masculinity.[6] This is curious since it was the BUF's commitment to manliness and its construction of a distinct masculine identity which provided a crucial element in the underpinning of its paramilitary politics.

For the BUF Fascism and masculinity were one and the same. A.K. Chesterton, cousin of G.K. Chesterton and one of the BUF's senior propagandists, believed that 'in Fascism there appears once again on the world scene, vigorously contending for world masterdom, the great creative urge of the masculine spirit which through the ages has sped man forward to the heights of his achievement … It is the spirit of action, the conquerors, the law givers.' Indeed, he argued, this was what Fascism's enemies found so disturbing: 'the democrats who fear Fascism rationalise that fear to disguise the fact that it is the masculine approach before which their spirits shrink … what frightens them is the masculine principle that bids males among them to be men and the females women'.[7] And at the heart of this masculine spirit was a belief in the centrality to life of the body and physicality

> When the masculine principle struggles through to its epic victory there is no longer that contempt for the body which exists when those are in command who feel themselves able to grace only an armchair civilisation that has no need of muscle or of limb. That is life's first requirement – an adequate adaptation to its physical needs; a capacity to rejoice in sheer living.[8]

Consequently, the BUF believed that the future Fascist state was the healthy human body writ large: 'just as in the human body every limb and every organ is attuned to serve the whole of the body, so in society every section and interest must be subordinated to the general interest of the State as a whole. This is the corporate conception of society… what is called Fascism or National Socialism.'[9] Conversely, the Fascists portrayed their enemies in pathological terms, as undermining the health of the body/state – for example, Chesterton wrote of 'the cancer of Jewish culture'.

'Hardness' was therefore a crucial component of the BUF conception of masculine fitness. In this it followed lock-step in the British public school tradition of character building. As Philip Mason has pointed out, the public school system aimed at hardening those boys who passed through it, not least because it was felt that the downfall of the imperial ruling classes of the Classical period was due to their succumbing to softness and effeminacy.[10] The Mosleyites felt this danger more keenly than most and their belief was that inculcating physical and mental 'hardness' was justified as a reaction against what they saw as the softness and decadence of liberal democratic society. More importantly, it was also viewed as an essential quality which would enable the party to take power. 'Physically, mentally, spiritually, [the Fascists] must follow the fixed purpose of the dedicated life. Such men and such lives in the end must triumph because steel endures and cuts clean and cuts through,' proclaimed BUF leader Sir Oswald Mosley in 1937.[11] The imagery of steel and metal was a recurrent metaphor in describing the hardness expected of the ideal Fascist: indeed, in one speech Mosley declared Fascism as the 'steel creed of an iron age', and extended the analogy by describing how Fascism 'comes to power through the fiery ordeal of sacrifice and struggle, in challenge to all existing things'.[12] In the hands of Leigh Vaughan-Henry, the metaphor was turned into a programme of action: 'a new hardness of character, a new hardness of mind, is the demand of the age … We need the quality of iron in our spirits and our minds. We need harder, more metallic thought. We need more concrete hardness in our building of ourselves and of the ways in which we express ourselves.'[13] Visually, the theme was upheld by the drawings and illustrations used in the BUF press, in which male bodies were idealized into angular, sharp figures with exaggerated muscular development, staring determinedly into the distance.

The implication of violence in this definition of maleness was brought to the fore in the practical organization of BUF. The Mosleyites described themselves as 'the warriors of the new age' and in his 1932 political manifesto *The Greater Britain*, Mosley had stated that 'in our ordered athleticism of life we seek, in fact, a morality of the Spartan pattern'.[14] Consequently the BUF was organized on strict military lines with a chain of unquestioning command stretching down from Mosley through district leaders to local branch officers. In the BUF press, members were referred to in military fashion by their rank in the organization, with the lowest rank and file members having the prefix 'Fascist' attached to their names. At the Mosleyites' national headquarters in London, 'Black House', a former teacher training college in Chelsea, life was also organized on military lines. As well as housing administrative offices, the building also served as a barracks for the BUF's 'defence force', who would be woken by reveille, undergo inspection by their commanding officer, undertake drill and prepare for activities at meetings and newspaper sales.[15] The pervasive sense of violence was at the heart of the BUF. Even in his sympathetic biography of Mosley, Robert Skidelsky acknowledges that 'the military atmosphere was deliberate. Mosley wanted to create an efficient instrument of action'.[16]

It is difficult to overestimate the importance which the BUF attached to the question of masculinity. 'National Socialism, of whatever expression, stands or falls by the virility of its manhood and the perfection of its womanhood,' declared *The Blackshirt* in 1937.[17] Although Martin Durham has argued that there was a degree of ambiguity, at least on paper, in the BUF's stated policies on women, in everyday discourse there were few greater insults in the Fascist lexicon than to accuse a man of effeminacy or to charge society with succumbing to femininity. Politicians from the traditional parties were scorned as being 'old women'; there were no 'real men' in parliament, only 'political mothers' and A.K. Chesterton mocked parliamentary leaders as 'Mrs Baldwin, Mrs MacDonald and Miss Eden ... the nation swirls and faints amidst these oppressive feminine vapours'.[18]

Indeed, one of the problems of the age which the British Fascists sought to rectify was the fact that 'today, probably for the first time in history, "men" are ashamed to be men. The full-blooded virility of the warrior is traced to the machinations of Satan. It is a blasphemy!'[19] In a major front-page article for *Action*, Chesterton argued that many of Britain's ills were due to the 'masculine spirit' being submerged in the modern age by the 'matriarchal principle'. Democratic idealism was 'a mother's lullaby' which had allowed problems to be avoided because liberal democracy encouraged people to 'fly for comfort to their mother's lap', instead of confronting problems in a manly fashion. Matriarchy was a 'regression to the womb' which had created 'a world of mental weaklings'. He went on to polemicize against the traditional imperial view of Britain as the Mother Country, arguing instead that it should be called the Fatherland and that too little attention was being paid to the great men of British history: 'there have been men in these islands, as well as cackling demented hens. Let us smash the matriarchal principle.'[20]

The spectre of gender confusion haunted much of the BUF's writings, whether by men or women. Dinah Parkinson outlined her ideal of womanhood by arguing that under Fascism 'women will be encouraged to be true women, not the pitiful copies of masculinity so prevalent today. Men will be truly men, unlike the specimens to be found in spurious "intellectual" circles'.[21] The perceived lack of masculinity of the intellectual was a constant target for vituperation. An article entitled 'The She-Men Of Letters' pilloried the work of James Joyce and, quoting an extract from *Finnegan's Wake*, declared that it was 'difficult to conceive that the passage quoted here could be the work of a masculine mind...'[22] In a fit of indiscriminate condemnation, the article also went on to lambast T.S. Eliot, Wyndham Lewis and D.H. Lawrence, all of whom had some sympathies with elements of the philosophy of Fascism, if not the BUF's politics. Beverley Nichols was similarly scorned, being mockingly referred to as 'she' in one article – although this did not stop him from becoming a contributor to Mosley's press later in the 1930s.

In particular, left-wing inclined intellectuals had opprobium poured upon them for their alleged effeminacy. Oxford University was held to be populated by 'innumerable specimens of the Bloomsbury variety, from the long haired apparition with the multicoloured umbrella to the less common tinted lips and eyebrows'.[23] Student participants in a 1936 May Day demonstration were characterized as 'pale, weak, bespectacled youths across whose foreheads droops a lank, poetic cow lick...'[24] Although the word 'homosexual' was never used explicitly, the BUF press constantly tried to draw a link between ostensible Marxists and homosexuality: 'the Pink and the Pansy' being the most common epithet used to equate Communists and homosexuals. And, as ever, behind the rhetoric lay the desire for violence: describing 'Bloomsbury socialists' as a 'motley crew of middle-aged softies' a 1933 article bemoaned the fact that British explorers and adventurers were 'too hard to stay in England and be jailed for laying hands on such as you, you squinting sycophants of decadence'.[25]

In fact, the BUF was violently opposed not only to intellectuals, but to intellectual activity itself. In 1934 *Fascist Week* declared that 'man was not born to preserve present civilisation' and that 'it can only be ended by the Fascist axe'. Later that year *The Blackshirt* proclaimed, 'Our first duty to "culture" is to destroy it.'[26] The author of the article, G. de Burgh Wilmot, stated that 'when art becomes a purpose in itself, it ceases to have any value. Its function is essentially as a relaxation for man', arguing that 'the disease of "culture" in the twentieth century is more dangerous than the Black Plague of the Middle Ages', before concluding that 'if we have to choose between barbarism and decadence, I choose barbarism without hesitation'. For those readers who had failed to get the message, he ended by reasserting that the BUF 'assert[s] our belief in a barbaric attitude to life'.[27]

As well as being a weapon in the struggle for a Fascist future, the BUF's cult of masculinity was underpinned by a desire to return to a mythical golden age, part 'Merrie England' Elizabethan feudalism, part Nazi-style 'blood and soil' past. While embracing technological advances and glorying, like the Italian Futurists, in the steel and iron of the mechanical age, the BUF contradictorily also managed to embrace a vision of history in which the natural state of manhood was to commune with nature. 'Throughout history, the man's place has been the battlefield, or the backwoods, or with the hunters in the jungle … on the track or in the arena, fighting, struggling, proud of his virility in the unceasing battle against evil and disorder,' wrote de Burgh Wilmot.[28] The abandonment of such a way of life and the rise of urban living had helped to undermine the means by which men could preserve their masculinity: 'The grime and smoke and the rumble of traffic [in cities] kill the senses and rhythm of manhood. There can be no healthy life in such an environment.'[29] What was necessary to restore manhood was a return to a rural, more natural way of life, which would help destroy the 'softness' which had been created by the decadent culture of the cities and recreate the environment in which manly virtues could be embraced: 'Anyone who knows the earth and the countryside accepts its hardening yet stimulating influences, its healthy discomforts with appreciation … a natural foundation for a man's life is the daily round of the farmer.'[30] This desire to get back to nature was practically demonstrated by the popularity among BUF members of hiking, youth hostelling and other similar activities based on exploring the countryside.

This opposition to urban living was the stock in trade of many Edwardian commentators writing about the state of Britain in the years leading up to the First World War. Writing in 1903, George Shee had blamed the deterioration in the physical fitness of army recruits on an abandonment of 'English pastoral life' for towns and cities.[31] Most notably Robert Baden-Powell, the founder of the Boy Scout movement, held that the outdoor life, whether of the British countryside or on the Imperial frontiers, was vital for fitness and health, while frowning upon the deleterious effects of city living. It is therefore not surprising that the Boy Scouts was one of the few movements which the BUF viewed with sympathy. This was an affinity shared by all British Fascist organizations: the first British Fascist grouping, the British Fascists, 'viewed Fascism as the adult growth of the Scout movement', according to Robert Benewick, while the Imperial Fascist League, a rabidly anti-Semitic sect opposed to Mosley, also thought that 'the ideals of the Scouts are very near to those of Fascism'.[32] The BUF saw itself as continuing and generalizing the Scout tradition and argued for the creation of a new youth movement comprising the Scouts and its own young members which would put Scout law into 'everyday practical application'.[33] This was not merely opportunism – the BUF was entirely prepared to accept Baden-Powell's teachings as its own: 'Lord Baden-Powell was probably the first national socialist England had, though he has never realised it; at least, he was imbued with the spirit of Fascism.'[34]

Although it would be exaggeration to characterize the Boy Scouts as a Fascist organization, there was more than a grain of truth in the identification of the Scout movement with many of the principles of the BUF. For Baden-Powell, like the BUF, true manliness was inseparable from British nationalism and physical, militaristic training. *Scouting For Boys*, his 1908 book which launched the Scouting movement, laid the utmost importance on a boy becoming a 'real man' in the tradition of Ralegh, Drake and other British heroes. The movement was dedicated to the preservation of the British Empire, strongly racist and, on paper at least, committed to every scout learning how to shoot in order to be ready for war. If the battle for manliness was not pursued, there were ominous consequences for the British race: 'God made men to be men ... We badly need some training for our lads if we are to keep up manliness in our race instead of lapsing into a nation of soft, sloppy cigarette suckers,' Baden-Powell wrote in 1922, in a style and sentiment which was to be echoed throughout the 1930s by countless BUF propagandists.[35]

Baden-Powell and the BUF also shared an abhorrence of the practice of spectating at football matches, especially when it was done by young people, accusing spectators of squandering their energies. 'Be players, not spectators,' exhorted sports columnist James Larrant in *Action*, going on to proclaim that 'it is the determination of Fascism that they [young people] shall not be condemned to be eternally spectators, that they shall know the joy of playing the games which will make them happier and fitter citizens'.[36] A.K. Chesterton, while similarly condemnatory of spectating as an activity, argued that the 'hero-worshipper' of soccer players and teams could be utilized to good effect under Fascism: 'much of the devotion of his generous nature will be lifted clear from its present objectives and placed unreservedly at the disposal of the man destined to lead the nation to the conquest of all the perilous problems of the age'.[37]

The alleged passivity of football spectators was linked by the BUF, as it had been by pre-World War One commentators, to the supposed decline in the standard of male national fitness. This was a constant source of concern to the BUF and its press made regular references to Britain being a 'C3 [i.e. unfit for military service] nation' and the demand that 'Britain Must Be A1 Again' figured prominently in Fascist propaganda.[38] For the BUF, little had changed since the turn of the century when bodies such as the 1904 Inter-Departmental Committee on Physical Deterioration reported on the alarming apparent lack of physical fitness among the urban working classes. 'At the present time the average Briton is a weak specimen, undersized and underdeveloped', argued F.G. Hargreaves, spelling out the ominous consequences: 'The physique of the nation is of paramount importance for the future of our race. Nothing is more certain of the fact that Britain, as a great power, even as a race, is doomed within a few generations, unless we recover our national and natural fitness.'[39] As can be seen from the views of Shee and Baden-Powell, there was nothing new or unusual about such a view, which had been common currency in the decades before the First World War. Nor was there anything original, other than the Fascist rhetoric, about the Mosleyites solution to the problem – a large increase in the level of physical training undertaken in schools.

Under Fascism, the educational system would be reshaped and huge emphasis placed on physical fitness. Up to seven years, children would engage in 'nothing but play and amusements'. The years between seven and 14 would 'mainly be devoted to physique building and medical supervision'.[40] Mosley, who himself had spent most of his schooldays as a keen sportsman or 'blood' showing little interest in intellectual pursuits, elaborated on the policy, explaining that 'much of this training will be done in the open air, in the body-building process of PT and manual labour. Right up to the age of 18 the duty of building a child's body will be as great a preoccupation of the nation as the building of its mind'.[41] Only after the age of 14 did the BUF envisage any academic work taking place. Indeed, as we saw earlier, intellectual activity was viewed as being strictly subordinate to the glorification of the body. As A.K. Chesterton put it, the BUF had an 'absolute conviction that spiritual and mental health largely depend on physical health'.[42] Because of this, a British Fascist regime would make physical training compulsory for all young people, 'as the duty of keeping fit in National Socialist eyes is the first of all duties which men and women owe to their own posterity'.[43] As J.A. Mangan's work on the cult of athleticism in the Victorian and Edwardian British public schools highlights, this exaltation of physical fitness over intellect and intelligence, or 'the antithesis of life to intellect' was deeply rooted in the public school ethos. Far from importing German and Italian ideas which were alien to British society, as is often argued, Mosley and his organization echoed views which were common currency in pre-First World War Britain.[44]

THE CULT OF MOSLEY

As with its spiritual forefathers at the start of the century, hero-worship was an important aspect of the BUF's definition of the masculine ideal. Its pantheon of heroes was predicated on the perceived manliness of those British historical figures it sought to emulate. Sir Francis Drake was hailed for being 'the Elizabethan man of action'; Clive of India for possessing 'those virtues which Fascism inculcates, courage, leadership and responsibility', and even the unlikely Edward VIII for being a 'warrior king'. William Morris was held up as a 'pioneer of Fascism', not least because 'he was a MAN' (emphasis in original).[45] But the 'very embodiment of British manhood' and the BUF's masculine ideal was its leader Sir Oswald Mosley.[46] A baronet, he was successively a Conservative, Independent and Labour MP and founder of the New Party in 1931 before finally abandoning parliamentary politics completely and forming the BUF in 1932. From his schooldays at Winchester, physical activity and sports had always played a crucial role in Mosley's life. He excelled at boxing and was the youngest ever winner of the public schools' fencing championship. Even as BUF leader he remained a keen fencer, being a runner-up in British epée championships in the 1930s and a member of the British fencing team at the 1935 Empire Games.

For the BUF, Mosley was the Fascist superman. In the words of de Burgh Wilmot: 'we can put our faith in Mosley [because] he is a man of war against the evils of economic depression ... He is a man who is not ashamed of physical fitness, of health and vitality. He is a man in the tradition of manhood.'[47] His leadership of the BUF was based on unquestioning loyalty and obsequious fawning. Invariably the Fascist press referred to him as 'The Leader'; phrases such as 'The Brilliant

Leadership of Oswald Mosley' peppered articles and *Action* treated its readers to a weekly biographical series on Mosley which ran to over 20 instalments.[48] William Joyce, later to be hanged by the Allies for his role as Nazi propagandist Lord Haw-Haw during the Second World War, described him as 'the greatest Englishman I have ever known'.[49] At times, he was held to have almost supernatural powers: 'it is in him … that the inspiration for greatness can be found and by his example physical fitness can and will be attained'.[50] His physical prowess in particular was a source of great satisfaction for his followers: 'we justly admire our Leader's magnificent physique', wrote one in 1934.[51] When an enterprising anti-Fascist managed to score a direct hit on The Leader's head with a brick during a Liverpool rally in 1937, rendering him unconscious, *The Blackshirt* printed a photograph the following week of a bandaged Mosley with the caption 'The Leader's superb constitution is enabling him to make a rapid recovery.'[52]

Few articles talked about Mosley without mentioning his 'greatest virtue – courage'.[53] While this sometimes referred to his political career, particularly his leaving the mainstream British parliamentary parties and starting his own movement, much of this admiration for Mosley's ostensible bravery was based on his capacity for violence. *Action* approvingly quoted playwright George Bernard Shaw's praise of their leader as 'a man bound to be disliked because he looks like a man with some physical courage and is going to do something, and that is a terrible thing'.[54] In the New Party and the early days of the BUF, Mosley was well known for joining in fights at meetings between his supporters and anti-Fascist demonstrators – indeed, this willingness to 'get stuck in' made Mosley a more appealing figure to those attracted to the violent solutions offered by the Fascists. For example, one of the key factors in persuading Arthur Beavan, later to become a leading Fascist organizer in south-east England, to join the BUF was seeing Mosley leap from the speakers' platform at a public meeting to take part in a skirmish which had broken out.[55]

If Mosley was the epitome of manhood, his lieutenants also sought to advertise their masculine virtues. In a series of profiles of BUF leaders beginning in 1936, *Action*'s greatest concern was to demonstrate how each individual measured up to the warrior ideal. The Mosleyite conception of courage was especially valued. The portly Neil Francis-Hawkins, Mosley's head of organization, was euphemistically described as 'a well-built young man', who was 'much admired for his physical bravery'. John Beckett, former Independent Labour Party MP and one of the more anti-Semitic of Mosley's entourage, despite his mother being Jewish, had 'inexhaustible energy ... [an] adventurous recklessness ... almost savage courage'.[56] Compliments about the physique of those profiled were especially common: one had a 'robust ... fine powerful figure'; another had 'an upright carriage [which] makes an immediate impression'; Major General J.F.C. Fuller, Mosley's military expert, had the 'power of commanding attention'. Even Anne Brock Griggs, who organized Fascist women's activities in southern England, had 'an attractive physique' although this was tempered by the fact of her 'motherhood of two charming children'.[57]

THE BUF AND THE ATHLETIC BODY

Physical fitness was not only an ideal to strive for, it was an everyday obligation of the BUF member. Mosley exhorted his supporters to 'live like athletes', and *Fascist Week* declared in the early days of the movement that 'physical training is an essential part of Fascist activity'.[58] To this end, a wide range of activities was organized by branches, including keep fit classes, to ensure that their members met this requirement. *Action* ran a weekly 'How to Keep Fit' column which outlined a daily plan for fitness: 'rub yourself down with a rough towel. A quick and tepid bath is to be recommended,' it advised in the best traditions of British public school spartanism. In a tinpot version of the Nazi 'Strength Through Joy' movement, regular summer camps were organized on the English south coast where physical training and outdoor pursuits were undertaken. Of the participants at the 1934 West Wittering camp, it was noted that 'their bodies are formed, their muscles are supple and their minds are in tune. The Blackshirt spirit prevails.'[59] Mosley's personal prescription for fitness was simple: 'Eat Less, Drink Less, Talk Less' – although clearly he did not believe that the latter injunction applied to himself.[60]

Sport was a crucial component of this athletic regime. At one stage or another in its history, the BUF had boxing, rugby union, soccer, cricket, tennis, golf, swimming, rowing, cycling, motor cycling and hiking sections. Its Hackney branch soccer team played in a local league. As in other countries, Fascism and its cult of masculine heroic adventure exerted a particular attraction for aviators – Mosley himself had been in the Royal Flying Corps during the First World War – and in May 1934 the BUF was able to stage its first air rally, consisting of five planes.

Motor sport was another area in which Fascism found fascination, and the BUF included among its supporters two motor cycle record holders, the captain of the Crystal Palace speedway team and Malcolm Campbell, who carried the BUF's pennant on his car *Bluebird* when he broke the world land speed record in 1934.

Rugby union also held a prominent position in the BUF's pantheon of sports. Peter Howard, Oxford University and England rugby union captain, had been the secretary of Mosley's New Youth Movement and had played a key role in assembling the 'defence force' at Mosley's meetings in the early 1930s, receiving a lacerated temple for his efforts during a New Party rally in Birmingham in 1931. The BUF encouraged branches to organize teams, *Action* carried instructions on playing the game and, echoing Victorian rugby advocates such as Loretto school headmaster H.H. Almond, the sport itself was held up as the epitome of manly physical recreation: 'it is a real Fascist game, for a man who plays Rugger must be determined to "get there" by co-operation with the rest of the team'. It fitted perfectly the culture of physicality, violence and manliness which the BUF sought to encourage: 'To be able to crash into an opponent and bring him down, to push and sweat in the scrum, to race down the touchline with the ball, to give and take hard knocks, and after the game to fraternise with your opponents, is one of those joys which has to be experienced to be appreciated.'[61] The 1936 Hospitals Cup Final contested between two teams of medical students was praised for its 'traditional rigour and vitality'. Coincidentally or not, Douglas Jerrold and G. Ward Price, two sympathetic observers, favourably compared the BUF's treatment of protesters at the infamous 1934 Olympia Rally to the violence to be seen on the field at an average rugby union match.[62]

But it was boxing which was exalted as a sport above all others. This was not only because of its innate masculinity but also because, like the ju-jitsu classes the BUF organized, it had a practical relevance to the organization's daily activities. Mosley himself had been a schoolboy boxing champion and one of the most famous, if short-lived, supporters of the New Party was Ted 'Kid' Lewis, the Jewish boxer from London's East End who was world welterweight boxing champion. Joe Beckett, a former British heavyweight boxing champion, and Len Harvey, who at one time or another held the British heavyweight, light-heavyweight and middleweight titles, were well-known BUF supporters, while the BUF's Welsh Organizer, Tommy Moran, had been the Royal Navy's light heavyweight boxing champion.

The importance of boxing to the nascent Fascist movement had been highlighted in mid-1931 when the New Party had attempted to set up athletics clubs and an 'active force' to steward its meetings, under the leadership of Kid Lewis. 'The only methods we shall employ will be English ones. We shall rely on the good old fist', Mosley told the press in May 1931.[63] In January 1934, Defence Force Control, the military arm of the BUF, ordered all branches to form boxing teams. The stated aim of this command was to enable inter-branch tournaments to be staged, which they were, but in reality the objective was to ensure that the BUF was physically prepared to strike at its opponents.[64] That this was the case was proved beyond doubt at the June 1934 Olympia rally, when, illuminated by searchlights, Fascist thugs tore into protesters.

Moran himself wrote regularly on boxing in *Action* giving advice and hints on how to fight: 'to counter a left swing, wait until the swing commences, then raise your right arm to the position of the half Fascist salute', being one such tip.[65] Boxing tournaments between branches became regular events, especially among those in London's East End – the winners of one tournament receiving flights over the capital in the aeroplane of a member of the BUF's flying corps.[66] More than any other, the sport was seen as a means of asserting the superiority of British manhood: A.G. Findlay, another regular writer on boxing, claimed to be interested only in 'the betterment of British boxing. It is placed before anything else because I'm British and my pride makes me want to see my country at the top of the world – particularly sport.'[67] However, the fact that many of the best British boxers also happened to be Jewish, and in the eyes of the BUF not 'British', gave those believers in the innate physical superiority of Anglo-Saxons obvious problems. The BUF's explanation for Jewish boxing success was simple – the boxing business was a 'racket' controlled by Jewish promoters who fixed fights against non-Jews. At one point *Action* went so far as to claim that British heavyweight Tommy Farr was being prevented from fighting Joe Louis because Jewish interests supported Louis.

This crazed view of the world reached its most vicious with the advent of a regular column, 'The Sporting Jew', purporting to expose Jewish machinations in sporting life. Not only boxing but also all-in wrestling was held to be under Jewish control. In early 1937 the column hailed the Nazi government's banning of Jews from German golf courses, expressing the hope that similar measures would be adopted in Britain, while at the same time acknowledging that a widespread informal bar to Jewish membership of British golf clubs already existed: 'I do not know of any courses in Britain where a ban on Jews exists, but at many clubs the administration merely fails to elect them without giving reason.' The following year the BUF called on the Jockey Club, the controlling body of British horse-racing, to ban Jewish 'thugs and tricksters' from the country's race courses.[68]

This hatred of Jews was rationalized by reference back to the masculine 'fair play' ethos of British public schools' games.

> We look upon our games as something to enjoy, to keep bodily fit and treat them as just games. In the other way, they are treated partly as a business with 'heads I win, tails you lose' motto. It does not matter how much time and money we Britishers spend in trying to make others adopt our mentality to athletics and games of any description, we cannot alter their racial characteristics. They [the Jews] cannot understand the meaning of 'a good loser' … Their mentality is exactly the same in business as in sport – to win at any price and to hell with the other fellow.[69]

This argument was but an echo of the debate on amateur and professional sport which took place in Britain at the end of the nineteenth century. Although Jews were now the target, the same arguments had originally been directed against working class sportsmen, whom the supporters of amateurism accused of playing sport purely for monetary gain and undermining the pursuit of games as body and character-building pastimes. Jews were also denounced for their 'unsportsmanlike' behaviour as spectators, for being partisan, jeering the referee and barracking the opposing team, again exactly the same charge which was commonly used against the working-class crowds when they began to attend soccer and rugby matches *en masse* towards the end of the Victorian era. In fact, although the BUF accepted professional sport, its ideal was that of Victorian public school amateurism – as one of the organizers of its boxing tournaments explained, the ethics of amateur sport was the same as 'the spirit which activated Fascists. Under these rules and within Fascism one must play the game for the game's sake, play for one's side and not for one's self, accept decisions graciously and be chivalrous towards a defeated opponent.'[70]

CONCLUSION

The reassertion of masculinity and the violent rooting out of all vestiges of effeminacy was at the heart of British Fascist politics in the 1930s. This was true both for the programme of the Fascist state of the future that the Mosleyites sought to establish and for the day-to-day political activities through which they hoped to achieve it. In this, it consciously based itself on the ideals of the masculine warrior patriot which the Victorian and Edwardian public schools sought to create. Its insistence on the primacy of the male, of the necessity of physical hardness, on the importance of violent militarism and the assertion of the physical over the intellectual all came from the philosophy which dominated British middle class education in the decades before 1914. One can also trace elements of political practice back to the mass parades, rallies and uniforms of pro-imperial organizations such as the Boy Scouts, the Primrose League, the National Service League and others, all of whom shared the BUF's desire to defend the Empire through the propagation of manly virtues.[71]

Yet, unlike the Fascist movements in Germany and Italy, there was a serious contradiction at the heart of the BUF's violent appeal to masculinity – their opposition to war in Europe. The Mosleyites carried out a continuous campaign against a European war throughout their existence, even denouncing conscription into the British army in 1938.[72] Although many commentators have ascribed this to Mosley's revulsion at the horror of the First World War, the two major reasons were that the BUF's programme for Britain was based on maintaining the intactness of the British Empire, for which world peace was a prerequisite, and, more obviously, that they had no stomach for a war with their Fascist cousins in Germany or Italy. But this ostensible pacificism clearly jarrred with the centrality of the masculine warrior ideal to their politics, leaving them unable to capitalize on simple jingoistic British patriotism from the mid-1930s or to consistently pursue their claims of being the best defenders of British national interests. Indeed, as Linehan points out, many rank and file members joined the British forces to fight Germany as war began to approach in earnest.[73]

In one sense, the BUF's opposition to the Second World War was its most important, and arguably its only, break from the British public school masculine ideal of the pre-First World War era. For while it embraced the cult of the manly warrior, its Fascist ideology prevented it from embracing the forthcoming war in the same way as the outbreak of war in 1914 was welcomed with open arms by those who were educated into what Mangan has described as a 'martial, moralistic manhood'.[74] It can therefore be argued that British Fascism in the inter-war years was actually less warlike than the propagandists of imperial manhood in Victorian and Edwardian times. For the BUF, the outlet for the violence inherent in its concept of masculinity was not on the frontiers of the British Empire or the fields of Northern France but on the streets of London, Manchester, Leeds, Liverpool and many other British cities – where its enemies in the socialist, trade union and Jewish movements dealt it a series of defeats with which the British warrior-patriots of an earlier generation would be unfamiliar.

NOTES

1. *The Blackshirt*, 8 Feb. 1935, 8.
2. *The Blackshirt*, 5 Dec. 1936, 4, and 5–11 Jan. 1934, 2.
3. *The Blackshirt*, 8 June 1934, 6. *Fascist Week*, 2–8 March 1934, 2.
4. For a detailed discussion of this. see J.A. Mangan, 'Play Up and Play the Game: The Rhetoric of Cohesion, Identity, Patriotism and Morality', in *Athleticism in the Victorian and Edwardian Public School* (Cambridge, 1981), pp.179–203, J.A. Mangan, 'Concepts of Duty and Prospects of Adventure: Images of Empire for Public Schoolboys', in J.A. Mangan, *The Games Ethic and Imperialism* (London, 1988). pp.44–70, J.A. Mangan, 'Moralists, Metaphysicians and Mythologists: The 'Signifiers' of a Victorian and Edwardian sub-culture' in Susan J. Bandy (ed.), *Coreobus Triumphs: The Alliance of Sport and the Arts* (San Diego, 1988), pp.141–62, J.A. Mangan, 'Duty unto Death: English Masculinity and Militarism in the Age of the New Imperialism' in J.A. Mangan (ed.), *Tribal Identities: Nationalism, Europe, Sport* (London, 1996), pp.10–38, and J.A. Mangan, 'Gamesfield and Battlefield: A Romantic Alliance in Verse and the Creation of Militaristic Masculinity', in J. Nauright and T. Chandler (eds.), *Making Men* (London, 1997), pp.141–57. For a discussion of the debate associated with the presence or absence of late Victorian and Edwardian militarism, see J.A. Mangan, 'The Nordic World and Other Worlds' (ch.9) in H. Meinander and J.A. Mangan, *The Nordic World: Sport in Society* (London and Portland, OR, 1998), pp.173–97, and the New Introduction to *Athleticism* to be reissued by Frank Cass in 2000.
6. See Martin Durham, 'Women and the British Union of Fascists' and David Mayall, 'Rescued from the Shadows of Exile: Nellie Driver, Autobiography and the British Union of Fascists', in T. Kushner and K. Lunn (eds.), *The Politics of Marginality* (London, 1990) and Martin Durham, 'Gender and the British Union of Fascists', *Journal of Contemporary History*, 27, 3 (July 1992). For a broader discussion, see George L. Mosse, *Nationalism and Sexuality* (London, 1985) and Claudia Koonz, *Mothers in the Fatherland: Women, the Family and Nazi Politics* (London, 1987).
7. *Action*, 9 July 1936, 9. For more information on A.K. Chesterton, see David Baker, *Ideology of Obsession, A.K. Chesterton and British Fascism* (London, 1996)
8. *Action*, 9 July 1936, 9.
9. *Action*, 10 April 1937, 11.
10. Philip Mason, *The English Gentleman* (London, 1982), pp.70–1.
11. *Action*, 26 June 1937, 9. See also E.C. Mack, *Public Schools and British Opinion* (London, 1939), and J.A. Mangan, 'Social Darwinism and Upper-Class Education in late Victorian and Edwardian England' (ch.7), in J.A. Mangan and James Walvin, *Manliness and Morality: Middle-Class Masculinity in Britain and America 1800–1940* (Manchester, 1987), pp.142–3.

12. *Fascist Week*, 17–23 Nov. 1933, 5.
13. *The Blackshirt*, 18 Jan. 1935, 6.
14. *The Blackshirt*, 5 June 1934, 6. Oswald Mosley, *The Greater Britain* (London, 1932), p.38.
15. See Robert Benewick, *Political Violence and Public Order – a Study of British Fascism* (London, 1969), p.96.
16. Robert Skidelsky, *Oswald Mosley* (London, 1975), p.318. For the debate on the violence carried out by the BUF, see Stephen Cullen, 'Political Violence: the Case of the British Union of Fascists', *Journal of Contemporary History*, 28, 2 (April 1993), 115–36, D.S. Lewis, *Illusions of Grandeur* (Manchester, 1987), and Joe Jacobs, *Out Of The Ghetto* (London, 1978).
17. *The Blackshirt*, 23 Jan. 1937, 8.
18. *The Blackshirt*, 28 Nov. 1936, 3, *Action*, 29 Oct. 1938, 5, and *Action*, 9 July 1936, 9.
19. *The Blackshirt*, 8 June 1934, 6.
20. *Action*, 9 July 1936, 9.
21. *Action*, 19 March 1938, 14.
22. *Fascist Week*, 9–15 March 1934, 4.
23. *Action*, 26 March 1938, 7.
24. *The Blackshirt*, 2 May 1936, 1.
25. *Fascist Week*, 17–23 Nov. 1933, 7.
26. *Fascist Week*, 13–19 April 1934, 1.
27. *The Blackshirt*, 3 Aug. 1934, 6.
28. *The Blackshirt*, 5 June 1934, 6.
29. *The Blackshirt*, 3 Aug. 1934, 6.
30. Ibid.
31. George F. Shee, 'The Deterioration in the National Physique', *The Nineteenth Century*, May 1903.
32. Robert Benewick, *Political Violence and Public Order – A Study of British Fascism* (London 1969), p.27. *Fascist News*, Sept. 1929, 1.
33. *The Blackshirt*, 11 Jan. 1935, 10.
34. *Action*, 25 Nov. 1937, 9.
35. Quoted in Allen Warren, 'Popular Manliness: Baden-Powell, scouting and the development of manly character', in *Manliness and Morality, Middle Class Masculinity in Britain and America, 1800–1940* (Manchester, 1987), p203. See also J.O. Springhall, 'The Boy Scouts, Class and Militarism in Relation to British Youth Movements, 1908–1930', *International Review of Social History*, 16 (1971), 125–8.
36. *Action*, 21 May 1936, 15.
37. *The Blackshirt*, 4 Jan. 1935, 6.
38. *Fascist Week*, 15–21 Dec. 1933, 1.
39. *The Blackshirt*, 13 March 1937, 2.
40. *The Blackshirt*, 11 Sept. 1937, 5.
41. *Action*, 15 Oct. 1938. For more on the public school 'blood', see J.A. Mangan, 'Muscular, Militaristic and Manly: The British Middle-Class Hero as Moral Messenger', *International Journal of the History of Sport*, 13, 1 (March 1996), 28–47. See also Mangan, *Athleticism*, Introduction and ch.7.
42. *The Blackshirt*, 11 July 1936, 1.
43. *Action*, 8 May 1937, 3.
44. J.A. Mangan, *Athleticism*, p.44. For a recent exposition of the argument that Fascism was antithetical to British traditions, see Roger Eatwell, *Fascism, A History* (London, 1995).
45. *The Blackshirt*, 22 Aug. 1936, 4, *The Blackshirt*, 5 Sept. 1936, 4, *Action*, 12 Dec. 1936, 4, and *Fascist Week*, 30 March–5 April 1934, 7.
46. *Action*, 9 Dec. 1937, 7.
47. *The Blackshirt*, 5 June 1934, 6.
48. *Fascist Week*, 16–22 Feb. 1934, 2.
49. *Fascist Week*, 9–15 March 1934, 7.
50. *Action*, 9 Dec. 1937, 7.
51. *The Blackshirt*, 31 Aug. 1934, 4.
52. *The Blackshirt*, 23 Oct. 1937, 1.

53. *The Blackshirt*, 1 June 1934, 1.
54. *Action*, 13 Aug. 1936, 7.
55. For Beavan's reminiscences, see Thomas P. Linehan, *East End For Mosley, The British Union Of Fascists in East London and South West Essex* 1933–40 (London 1996), p.281.
56. For Francis-Hawkins, see *Action,* 7 Nov. 1936, 8. For Beckett, see *Action*, 14 Nov. 1936, 8.
57. *Action*, 23 Jan. 1937, 8; 28 Nov. 1936, 8; 12 Dec. 1936, 8; and 21 Nov. 1936, 8.
58. *Action*, 26 June 1937. *Fascist Week*, 17–23 Nov. 1933. The links between British Fascism and cricket in the early 1920s are explored in Andrew Moore, 'The 'Fascist' Cricket Tour of 1924–25', *Sporting Traditions*, 7, 2 (May 1991), 164–74.
59. *The Blackshirt*, 20 July 1934, 6.
60. *Action*, 26 June 1937, 9.
61. *Action*, 24 Sept. 1936, 15. To compare Almond's views on the importance of rugby to developing a 'manly' character, see his 'Football as a Moral Agent', *The Nineteenth Century* (December 1893), and 'Rugby Football in Scottish Schools', in Reverend Frank Marshall (ed.), *Football – The Rugby Union Game* (London, 1893). For a further discussion on Almond, 'Manliness' and 'Manly' character, see Mangan, *Athleticism*, ch.3 and J.A. Mangan, 'Almond of Loretto: Scottish Educational Visionary and Reformer', *Scottish Educational Review*, 11, 2 (November 1979), 97–106.
62. For G. Ward Price, see Colin Cross, *The Fascists in Britain* (London, 1961), p.114. For Douglas Jerrold, see Robert Skidelsky, *Oswald Mosley* (London, 1975), p.377.
63. Quoted in Skidelsky, p.257.
64. *The Blackshirt*, 11 Jan. 1934, 3.
65. *Action*, 20 Aug. 1936, 15.
66. *The Blackshirt*, 25 Nov. 1935
67. *Action*, 6 March 1936, 15.
68. For golf, see *Action*, 6 Feb. 1937, 7. For horse-racing, see *Action*, 4 June 1938, 5.
69. *Action*, 19 March 1936, 8.
70. *The Blackshirt*, 7 June 1935. A typical example of the attitude of many the supporters of nineteenth century amateurism to the working classes can be found in 'Football' by 'Creston' in *The Fortnightly Review*, 55 (1894), 25–38.
71. See John M. MacKenzie, *Propaganda and Empire* (Manchester, 1984), ch.6.
72. *Action*, 15 Oct. 1938, 7.
73. See Linehan, *East End for Mosley*, ch.5.
74. J.A. Mangan, 'Duty Unto Death ', in Mangan (ed.), *Tribal Identities*, p.12.

Bodies from Brazil: Fascist Aesthetics in a South American Setting

LAMARTINE P. DA COSTA and PLINIO LABRIOLA

In a celebrated documentary film *The Architecture of Doom*, produced in 1991, Peter Cohen stated that the profound purpose of the present century's German Fascist experience was the beautification of the world. This startling thesis from the Swedish cinema director was set in a historical perspective embracing culturally endorsed ideals from the Romanticism of Schiller and Wagner to Hitler's Darwinism, explicit in his proclamations of a 'stronger and more beautiful Germany'.[1]

For good measure, Cohen also added to a succession of Fascist images, Fascist elements allowing an understanding of the Nazi ethos: nationalism, ethnic superiority, eugenics, health as a principle of beauty, rejection of modern degenerative art, the cult of the strong body, Ancient Greece and the Renaissance as the aesthetic models for masculinity (*mutatis mutandis*). Brazilian Fascism equally reveals aesthetic foundations, despite a less than total devotion to German Fascist models and principles.

Brazil, irrespective of those who believe in the self-indulgent myth of a non-aggressive nation, is traditionally an authoritarian society often legitimized by aesthetic considerations of social relationships. As Roberto Da Matta, one of most distinguished Brazilian scholars of present times, once emphasized, the biggest country of Latin America and now with the world's eighth largest Gross National Product 'is a scandalous combination of feudalism, Thomism, capitalism, liberalism, hierarchy, favours, corporatism, class domination, bureaucratic insulation and dualistic reason'.[2] Not surprisingly, this confused and confusing combination commonly rejects moral judgements and embraces aesthetic experiences as guidelines for daily life.[3]

Euphoria and 'carnivalesque' are synonymous for this affirmative form of sociability in their strong assertion of 'the politics of the body, pleasure, risk, self-assertion, the individual's right to expect to be happy and to find joy and pleasure in life'.[4] What Michel Maffesoli – French sociologist and post-modern Brazilianist – claims is an 'ethic of aesthetics'.[5]

This distinctive aesthetic determination of social relations, however, has unique historical origins. In contrast to all the other countries in Latin America and the Caribbean, Brazil became, after political independence in 1822, an empire as an extension initially of Portuguese ambition and later of decadent colonial reality. The Brazilian 'empire' was from the beginning a cultural construct joining together colonizers and colonized in a common purpose. Behind this unusual association stood a gigantic and unexplored territory which legitimized the ideas of grandeur soon asserted by the new nation's leaders and intellectuals.[6]

As occurred with Germany in the late eighteenth century, Romanticism paved the way for building the cultural identity of the new empire. Visionary interpretations in Brazilian intellectual and élite romanticist outpourings in literature and the arts created a mythological nation. So the native Indians became heroes and 'pure' racial models in a 'magnificent' expanse of nature which could 'feed the world'. Prior to this arrogance, however, there was a real sense of inferiority in a country sparsely populated by Black African slaves, White Portuguese landlords, and isolated Indian minorities.

In the early nineteenth century the imperial government promoted the settlement of German immigrants in the southern regions of Brazil. Waves of Italian, Portuguese, Spanish, Polish and other ethnic groups followed. By the turn of the century, more than half of the ten million inhabitants of the country were white, concentrated in the major urban areas of Rio de Janeiro (the capital at that time) and São Paulo, the new commercial and industrial centre of Brazil.[7]

Towards the beginning of the twentieth century, the imperial government's project, equally endorsed by a new Republican regime after 1889, to transform Brazil into a white supremacist society, appears to have been successful. Notwithstanding, there was an unexpected increase in miscegenation, obscuring the triumph of Brazilian racism. Since then the racial debate embedded in the so-called doctrine of 'whiteness' ('embraquecimento' in Portuguese) for making the blacks and the Indians whiter, has repeatedly come to the fore. In many respects to 'whiten' the population was associated not only with the expansion of white groups and miscegenation but also with eugenic ambitions to strengthen the body and promote its well-being.[8] As a consequence the medical profession had a high reputation during imperial times, and shared with politicians and artists a romantic vision of Brazil as the second biggest nation of the Americas on account of its many similarities with the United States. Between 1834 and 1845, Eduardo Ferreira Franca published several scientific works on eugenics advocating those prophylactic moral values necessary to ensure a healthy population.[9] Exercise received emphasis and endorsement of sport was explicit and extant until the late 1930s.[10] Alberto Reppold in 1995, analysing what he termed the Biological Model (BM) of Brazilian physical education, concluded that the BM emerged and was implemented in the nineteenth century.

> The republican ideals based on positivist philosophy brought together a naturalistic conception of the society offering a fertile ground for the development of BM ideas. The broad acceptance of physical education in Brazilian society and its inclusion in the school curriculum resulted from the efforts of the medical profession who were then the main supporters of BM. The consolidation of the BM took place from 1930 onwards. Based on the BM, physical education became part of the Brazilian Constitution and was incorporated into several government policies.[11]

Revisiting previous racial assumptions, in 1996, 16 Brazilian scholars in connection with the most prestigious public health institution in the country, published *Race, Science and Society*.[12] It emphasized the strong influence of Joseph-Arthur de Gobineau's racist conceptions of imperial politics, society and science. This proto-Fascist French thinker visited Brazil in the mid-nineteenth century as a friend of the Emperor Pedro II, who was himself both a scientist and dilettante.[13] In all, the contributors confirmed the romanticist and positivist-based cultural construct of the country in the last century, which was followed by a 'reinvention' of the Brazilian racial mixture during the 1930s and 1940s. In this last phase, the so-called Vargas era (1930–45), Brazil became a dictatorship combining authoritarian political traditions, alive since colonial times, with Italian and German Fascism.

Despite the fact that the Vargas dictatorship explicitly assumed a corporatist aspect, similar to Spain of the same period under Franco, Brazilian intellectuals with various ideological inclinations massively supported the dictatorship. This paradox is often explained by their strong belief in nationalism, a phenomenon expertly manipulated by Vargas' despotic regime. This manipulation was especially effective in cultural matters and particularly in sport.[14] The corporatist sport organizations of the country established by Vargas survived under different democratic governments from 1945–64 and were reinforced once again by the military dictatorship that ruled from 1964 to 1985.

One outcome of this weird combination of old and new authoritarian trends in combination with political manipulation was the Choral Movement promoted by Vargas. Like early nineteenth-century Germany, many schools in Brazil established groups of singers in the 1930s and 1940s. The singers usually participated in mass demonstrations both to support and legitimize the national government and its charismatic leader.[15] In one of these demonstrations, held in a sports stadium, 44,000 children performed.[16] Such events united the nation in celebration of the glorification of the grandiose beauty of Brazil.

Thus, the Fascism of Vargas was closely connected with the national promotion of symbolism and ritual with the explicit purpose of promoting national pride conveniently rationalized by the principal of beautification. The usual categories of a Fascist ethos outlined earlier were recognized by the authoritarian and populist government from 1930 to 1945, with the exceptions of neoclassical emulation and rejection of modern art. In short, some features, characteristic of Hitler's regime in Europe, were rejected in favour of a modernist aesthetic, which had remained rooted in Brazilian regional values since the 1920s. The outcome then was unique: under Vargas the country experienced both a Fascist rationale and leadership as a syncretism, involving an acceptance of European Fascist influences but only in association with local and cultural traditions and innovations carefully selected and emphasized by leading intellectuals.[17]

To give one significant example of this pragmatic eclecticism, the avant garde architecture of the Ministry of Education building of the late 1930s (an Oscar Niemeyer and Licio Costa modernist project) is symbolically located just a few hundred metres from the neoclassical building of the Ministry of Finance that was constructed in Rio de Janeiro in response to an Italian Fascist inspiration of the early 1930s.[18] The selective response to foreign influences became even more clear in 1937 when Nazi Germany denounced modern art as a 'degenerate art'. Brazil did not follow suit!

In sport and physical education the Fascist principles of the beautiful and healthy body and aesthetic eugenics produced one of the most successful political consensuses of the Vargas government.[19] Adoption of these principles, as already mentioned, seems to have provided an impetus to the 'reinvention' of Brazilian social unity by disguising cultural contradictions and prejudices in mass physical activity. These physical education propaganda demonstrations developed simultaneously with mass singing events and worker's parades in the city's stadiums, main streets and squares. A strong symbolic emphasis was given to these gatherings by Vargas' prestigious National Department of Press and Propaganda (DIP). In its hands they became gigantic visual lies about a clean, strong and organized society which the populist dictator pretended to have created, but which in reality had never existed.[20] Thus Fascist spectacles during Vargas' rule did not reflect the realities of a typical developing country, but rather an idealistic self-image carried forward from the past and 'framed' by film, photography, radio, parades and monuments.

Misleading propaganda as an explanation of massive patriotic support, however, has only limited validity. For as far back and forward as one can see, Vargas' authoritarianism was as popular as the pleasure of shared partisanship provided by sport and physical education. The powerful images of a crowded stadium with ritual and stylized demonstrations remain as testimonies to the full acceptance of the dictatorship (Figure 7.1).

Clear evidence of Fascist image modelling is provided by the photographs distributed by the DIP in the 1930s and 1940s: collective displays of physical education depicting bodybuilding (Figure 7.2). Any analysis of this aesthetic propaganda device should point out the expressive effect of the anthropomorphic grasp, or even the seduction and self-sufficiency of the body as the focus of our perception.[21]

For reasons of space the story of aesthetic control in its full complexity cannot be told here, but it is worth mentioning Umberto Eco's interpretation of what he called 'Ur-Fascism', or eternal Fascism. This is a basic concept for understanding the Vargas era. The cult of action for action's sake, according to Eco, is one of the features of eternal Fascism, 'action being beautiful in itself, it must be taken before, or without, any reflection'.[22] This was the essence of Vargas' power, joining together and celebrating bodies, music and banners.

The social reality, then, was complicated, yet the basic ideals and actions of Brazilian Fascism were not. However, this primordial Fascism,

FIGURE 7.1

FASCIST CELEBRATION OF BODIES, MUSIC AND BANNERS IN VASCO DA GAMA STADIUM, RIO DE JANEIRO, SEPTEMBER 1941 (Gustava Capanema Collection)

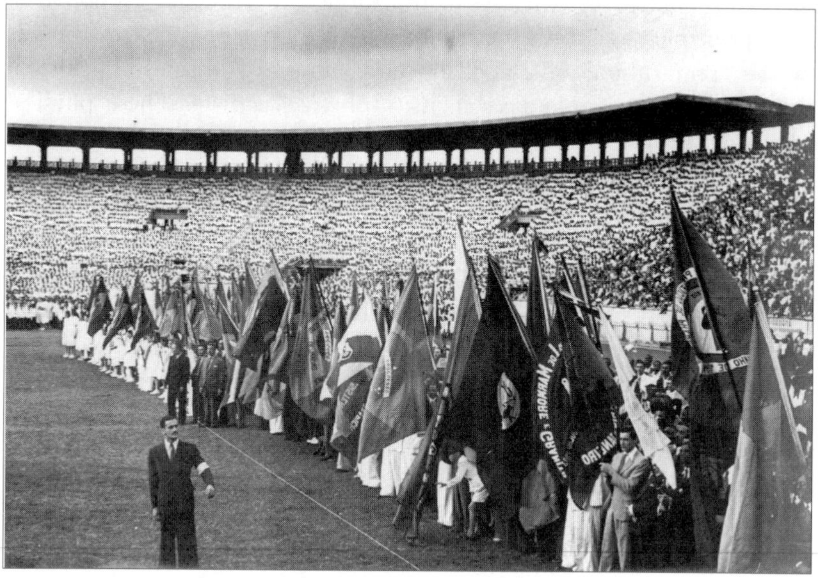

FIGURE 7.2

PROPAGANDA PHOTOGRAPH OF IDEAL PHYSICAL EDUCATION FOR YOUNG MALES DURING VARGAS' FASCIST REGIME (Gustavo Capanema Collection)

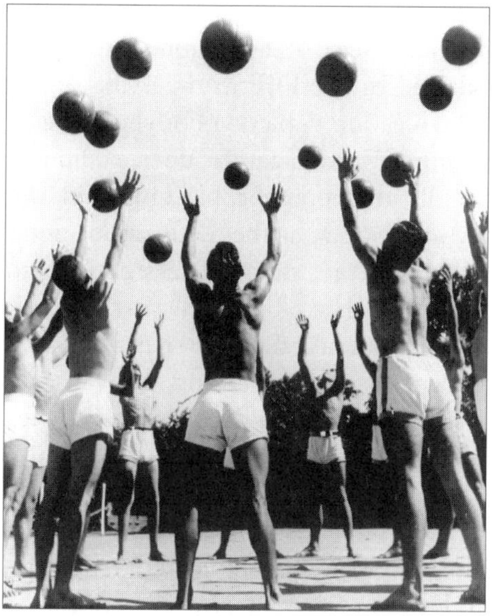

coinciding with a traditional authoritarian mentality, had diverse origins. These were related both to historical community aspirations and recent political indoctrination. While German and Italian ethnic groups living in Brazil developed Fascism as a reflection of their local roots, the Nazi-like party's leaders and affiliates imitated Hitler's and Mussolini's stage managed inculcation.

Fascism was localized in the southern regions of Brazil with extensions in São Paulo and Rio de Janeiro. Even today this area roughly equivalent to one quarter of the continental United States presents visible German and Italian influences, since in a total population of 150 million inhabitants in all the Brazilian States, 6.5 million belongs to the former and 21 million to the latter. In turn, the population evolved in three segments: the Nazi-German, the Fascist-Italian and the 'Integralista' (integral nationalism), a Brazilian version of Fascism, initially inspired by Marinetti's futurist conceptions,[23] then reformed by nationalistic intellectuals and military supporters. Each specific segment had a symbolic identity, rituals and actions. The Vargas government acted as an overall puppet-master manipulating each one according to national or international priorities, in what may be called 'syncretic' Fascism.[24]

Unsurprisingly all factions gave physical activities a favourable reception. Celebrations promoted by Vargas' propaganda machinery – the Race Day, the Fatherland Week, the Flag Day – attracted Fascist congregations and were testaments to the body's imperative in mass politics.[25] Nevertheless the aesthetic and eugenic visions of Brazilian Fascism had their foundation in *local* tradition and were far from being simply reproductions of European initiatives. A brief consideration of German physical activity from the nineteenth century onwards in Brazil, may well throw light on sport as a mechanism of community cohesion prior to the political manipulations of the Vargas era.[26]

The enthusiasm of German immigrants for sport was mostly a matter of self-esteem, a condition not compatible with the modernization theory of sport as proposed by Allen Guttmann.[27] This interpretation focuses on the increasingly systematic organization of modern sport and its dissociation from ritualistic practices. The isolation of those pioneers in rural areas and the need to preserve their cultural traditions by all and any means, and not merely religious and educational, ensured traditional games gatherings and the creation of sport clubs, respectively rituals and symbols of ethnic cohesion.[28] By the end of the nineteenth century, nearly 300 German recreation and sport clubs were located in Rio Grande do Sul, the southern state of the Brazilian Federation[29] – a number only matched very much later in other regions influenced mostly by a Portuguese-based culture.

Since Ur-Fascism includes the exaltation of communal purity, it is important in any consideration of Brazilian Fascism to recall Robert Paxton's refusal to treat Fascism as a single phenomenon.[30] The Fascist image of the body as constructed by many of those German–Brazilian communities, was formed by the convergence of the 'Blut und Boden' (blood and land) and ethnic traditionalism with the heroic rituals provided by sports. In retrospect, this syncretic and functional combination was particularly evident in the case of the *Turnen* (gymnastics) movement in the south of Brazil. Unlike the recreation and sports clubs of other immigrants, the *Turnen* associations were initially devoted to Friedrich Jahn's doctrine of *Deutschtum* (Germanism) a mixture of body discipline, group sociability and military preparation.[31] Jahn's combination of gymnastic method and nationalistic ideals originated in Germany at the beginning of the nineteenth century, and in Brazil the first *Turnplatz* appeared in 1867 in Porto Alegre, the capital of Rio Grande do Sul State.[32]

Lothar Wieser, a German historian, who in 1990 produced an extensive and detailed study of 57 *Turnen* clubs located in five Brazilian states, concluded that in contrast to the North American *Turnen* movement, southern Brazil's *Turngemeinde* (gymnastic community) became progressively more diversified in their sport activities, even introducing the Boy Scout movement into the country.[33] This less political and more cultural trend was confirmed by a 1932 survey in which only 17.8 per cent of the club members were active in gymnastics, with the major group dedicated to outdoor recreation.[34] For Aurelio da Silva Py, a chief police officer, who wrote a book in 1942 about Nazi activities in Rio Grande do Sul[35] these nature-oriented activities were often covert military training for the Deutsche Brasilianische Jugendring (German-Brazilian Youth Movement), an organization similar to the Hitler Youth (Figure 7.3). The iconographic archives of Nazi activities in Rio Grande do Sul kept by the Getulio Vargas Foundation, the main Brazilian centre for historical studies, offer evidence in support of Py. This source[36] also makes it quite clear that the Turnen Jugendring used similar uniforms to, as well as reproduced the rituals of, the Hitler Jugend in Germany (Figure 7.4).

FIGURE 7.3

GERMAN-BRAZILIAN YOUTH MOVEMENT ON PARADE IN PORTO ALEGRE CITY CENTRE, NOVEMBER 1937 (Cordeiro de Faria Collection)

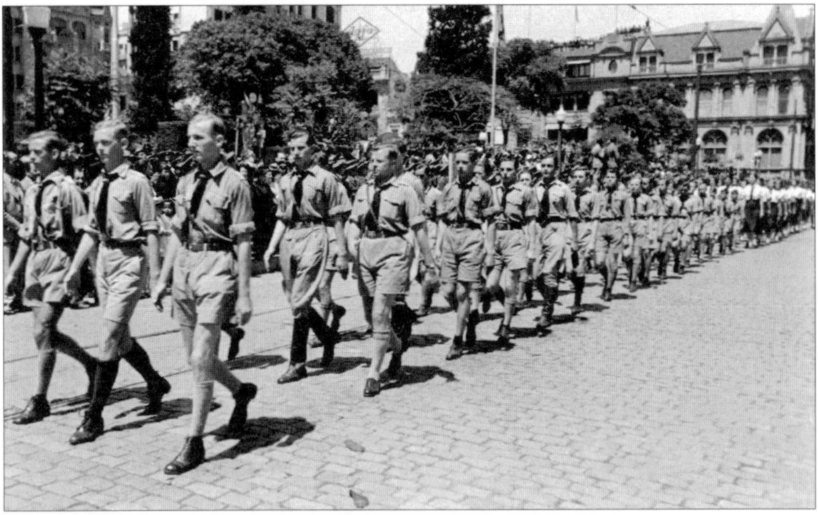

FIGURE 7.4

NAZI'S RITUAL IN RIO GRANDE DO SUL COUNTRYSIDE PROMOTED BY *TURNEN* MOVEMENT, MAY 1934 (Cordeiro de Farias Collection)

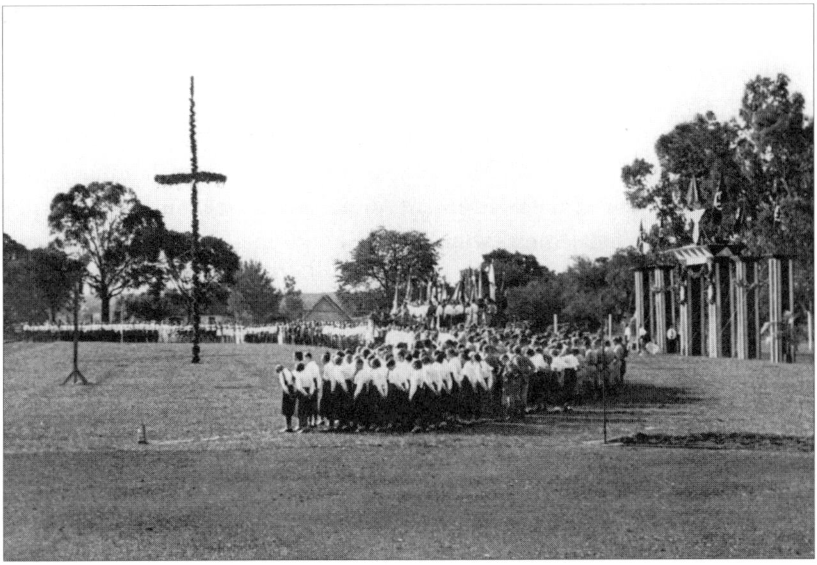

FIGURE 7.5

FRONT COVER OF THE OFFICIAL BOOK OF SÃO PAULO *TURNERSCHAFT* FEATURING JAHN IMAGE OF MUSCULAR YOUTH, PALM TREES AND OTHER LOCAL FEATURES (Clube Germania, São Paulo, 1920)

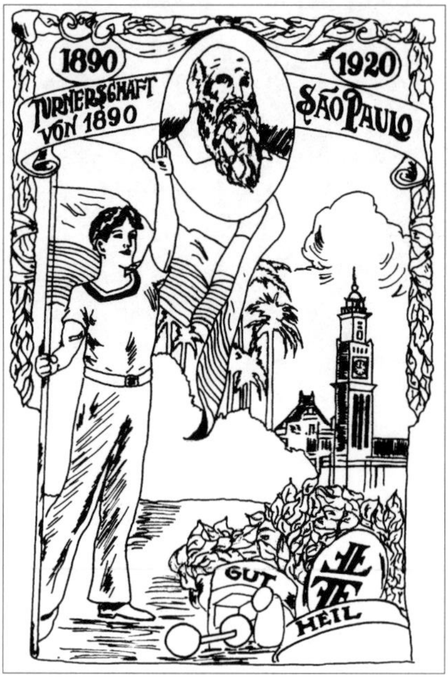

Certainly the emphasis on cultural values by Brazilian *Turnen* was a feature from the late nineteenth century onwards. In São Paulo city's *Turnerschaft*, the official history of the movement's history from 1890 to 1920,[37] the drawings and photos celebrate symbolically memories of the past as well as aspirations and adaptations in the new land – Jahn's image, the local natural environment, local 'muscular' youth and *Turnen* participation of local men, women and children (Figure 7.5). Leonar Tesche in 1996 concluded, regarding the *Turnen* association with the Nazi party during the 1930s, that the *Mitturners* (gymnastic companions) were not ideologically involved but only responded to a call to Germanic community spirit.[38]

A lack of ideological underpinning suggests that Brazilian *Turnen* is yet another manifestation of the beautification of Brazilian society, in which social and sports clubs and organizations gave scope and encouragement to reflect on the aesthetic and ethnic commonality of the community and to strengthen unifying traditions.

In reviewing the practice of sport by community clubs of Italian immigrants in Brazil more light can be shed on what has been referred to above as eugenic aesthetics. Images of this major ethnic group of Brazil (only surpassed by Portuguese and Mulatto populations) in sport are available in Regina De Rose's research which also covers the Rio Grande do Sul.[39] Italian immigrants arrived in this southern state after the Germans, but also in the late nineteenth century. They also sought to affirm their cultural identity by means of traditional games, other recreational activities, the churches and the schools.[40] In contrast to German practice, however, Italians created their first sport clubs as a branch of the existing Mutual Insurance Association from 1871 onwards.[41] Thus these clubs embraced competitive sport as well as remaining recreational clubs at grass roots level. During the 1930s the Brazilian-Italian sport clubs ranked among the best in many regions of Rio Grande do Sul. Even though the Vargas government in 1938 attempted to pressurize them into 'nationalization', what can only be interpreted as a reaction against the role of 'a foreign Fascist proselytizer' characterized many of these associations in various regions of the country. This is true, for example of São Paulo, a more northern state, where nearly 30 per cent of the total population were Italian or descendants. Being already the nation's industrial centre by the 1930s, São Paulo had an urbanized population with a high percentage of blue and white collar workers. In this context, Fascist activities inspired by Mussolini's *fasci de combattimento* (combative Fascism) rather than Vargus' Nationalism took place in many Italian associative groups and institutions, especially in sport clubs.

This preference, which can be detected also among German descendants, was confirmed by Plinio Labriola's survey of Vargas' DOPS (National Department of Political and Social Order) archives. Consequently the clubs were eventually forced by the Vargas regime to 'nationalize' their functions and boards after surveillance by the DOPS.[42] Ultimately, sport facilities and clubs, however, remained *genius loci*, that is attractive sanctuaries for the various Brazilian stems of Fascism.

The link between Fascism and sport was particularly strong in the case of the Integralista party. Acting more openly in comparison with German and Italian counterparts, the Brazilian Party had publicized its ideological credo by 1937. This included a programme of 'moral, civic and physical education'. According to guidelines, sport was associated with moral propaganda and a bastion of the fundamental principles of national unification: 'God, Fatherland and Family'.[43]

Sport, therefore, was an ideological plank in the Integralistas' (the Party's affiliates) political platform reproducing the body's affirmative values recommended by all types of Fascism and even becoming a means of specific identification.[44] With the sigma emblem (equivalent to the Nazi swastika), the greenshirts (equivalent to Mussolini's blackshirts) and the political parades, sport shared fully in the attempt to make Brazilian Fascism more distinct and more visible than any other political force in the country. This combined exhibitionist behaviour, sometimes melodramatic, ensured a unique style of Integralista action in their competition with other Fascist factions.

For instance, for the Integralistas communal spirit embraced the nation as a whole, with local mobilization in local indoctrination centres. In the 1930s, to ensure a common ideological message was widely diffused, there was a total of 150 weekly newspapers, eight daily newspapers, and two monthly magazines, besides several books.[45] Since the aim of the Party was to reach all regions of the country, nearly 4,000 centres were created by the end of the 1930s in which sport was part of a day-to-day programme involving education, health and professional courses.[46]

Thus, what distinguished the Integralistas most from German, Italian and Vargas adherents was the Party's machinery and the possibility of influencing the ethnic and cultural mosaic of the so called Brazilian Federation. While the Vargas government concentrated efforts in the biggest urban centres of Brazil, especially in Rio de Janeiro and São Paulo, the followers of Plinio Salgado, the Great Leader of the Greenshirts, operated at grass-roots level. It was for this reason that the party in 1936 had approximately one million active members, an outstanding enrolment when compared with the German Nazi party's membership of 1,400,000 by 1934.[47]

Another distinctive feature of the Integralistas was the systematic attack on the very influential Jewish minority in Brazil. The eugenic tradition played its part together with new doctrines emanating from Germany. The Vargas regime also repressed the Jews albeit discreetly.[48] But the belief in a racial conspiracy was not shared by German or Italian Brazilian Fascism, perhaps because of preoccupation with local concerns.

The deeper the study of Integralista history, the more different it appears from other forms of Brazilian Fascism, with the significant exception of the eugenic and aesthetic cult of the body. This assumption gains momentum when the party's unique adherence to the '*Führerprinzip*' (the principle of a supreme chief) is taken into account. For all its efforts, the Integralista movement eventually collapsed. The dramatic defeat of Salgado and the dissolution of his party occurred when he led an unsuccessful coup d'état in the late 1930s. Although Plinio Salgado, Vargas' chief rival, was intellectually sophisticated and more charismatic as a personality than Getulio Vargas, he was defeated by the Machiavellian leadership of the Dictator, usually presented as a pragmatic patriot or as a visionary despot.[49]

The hierarchical structure developed by the Integralistas could not match the linkages of free and local initiatives with central government as promoted by Vargas' authoritarian impetus. The apparent paradox of the Vargas era is now being called 'neo-corporatism', a doctrine that apparently characterized Brazilian sport institutions until the early 1990s.[50]

Many similarities and differences are found between the Brazilian Fascist versions and their European equivalents. Zeev Sternhell's theory regarding a diversified global Fascist movement, is relevant here. Fascism remained pure if it did not come to power.[51] In Italy, for example, the Duce violated his early principles as a consequence of the tactical needs of the moment. In France, there was only a 'first Fascism' largely because of the limited political space available to evolve a 'mature Fascism'. Sternhell postulates a culturally bound Fascism, initially committed to an ideology but eventually adjusting to the local requirements of mass politics.

This view is pertinent to Fascism's evolution in Brazil. The German and Italian initiatives certainly belong to a 'first Fascism' with the instincts of blood set above ideological influences. The Integralistas also fit this classification. They were distinctive in their proposed radical Utopia of an integrated and revolutionary nationalism. In contrast the Vargas regime practised a mature Fascism full of ambiguous relations, with many similarities to Mussolini's 'second Fascism' which began in 1921 with the expulsion of the early idealists (Marinetti included) and with Mussolini's association with conservative landowners from northern Italy.[52]

Nevertheless preoccupation with the body (and sport) in Brazil and Europe was, first and foremost, the common feature of all Fascisms. This sort of exaltation, furthermore, presupposes that emphasis on the aesthetic values of the body had the functional purpose of uniting individuals, elites and masses. Support for this statement is to be found in the concept of an 'aesthetic of the sublime', the attempt at creating a totalitarian society as a visual entity or in a grand narrative. Jeffrey T. Schnapp has referred most aptly to Mussolini's Fascism as a 'theater of masses for masses'.[53] Bodies and spectacle belong together in Fascism's theatricals and narratives.

Further analysis, however, is needed in order to escape from a possibly limiting all-embracing functionalist approach. The unintended consequences of 'a second Fascism' as in the case of the Vargas regime, are significant illustrations of the functional needs of Fascism becoming associated with unintended actions. Thus, the Fascist cult of the body constitutes a simplification if only concerned with spectacle and narrative. Recent studies of 'the instrumental aesthetic' practised in the 1936 Olympic Games in Berlin, allow an assessment of perceived functional needs and permit an examination of wider consequences.

Gunter Gebauer and Christoph Wulf, for instance, argue that totalitarian regimes in general use the 'mask of beauty' in mass events.[54] This was especially the case with the Berlin Olympics and its Stadium which portrayed through its shape and resources a spectacle of 'total art': a variety of performing arts in one single scenario, as earlier proposed by Wagner for his operas. The 1936 Olympics rehabilitated total art in the opening and closing ceremonies, juxtaposing thousands of performers in dancing, singing and gymnastic demonstrations synchronized with the athletes' parades, celebrations involving the symbolic Olympic torch and equally symbolic salutes from spectators and the Führer.

Such dynamic action contrasted effectively with the static role of nude statues in the Nazi's art style, also located in the Olympic arena. Note how the 'images of men show their strength and invulnerability', suggest Gebauer and Wulf, and they further suggest an inspirational impact on the spectators.[55] In *Körper, Kult und Politik* Thomas Alkemeyer concurs and adds in an analysis of the same setting, that the celebration of the heroically athletic body in which perfect physicality is praised, produces wishful and cohesive identification among the ritual's participants.[56]

Concurrent explanations of the phenomenon of Fascism by contemporary Brazilian scholars may bring further clarification of its instrumental purposes. Stimulated by an authoritarian mentality, still extant in the country, these scholars have been intrigued by the residual attraction of non-democratic rule: as late as 1996, 44 per cent of

Brazilians put trust in authoritarian government and displayed indifference to democratic rule.[57] For some commentators, the *Führerprinzip* is still widely embraced by most voters who recently backed a president with Hitler's style and an athletic body – Fernando Collor, elected in the early 1990s.[58] For others, Brazilian physical education, whilst militaristic in the past,[59] now overwhelmingly follows a politically neutral, international fashion for health, fitness and aerobics.[60]

The tradition of aesthetic eugenics in Brazil has now apparently combined with the imperial aesthetic tradition. Lucien Sfez, the French critic of the now worldwide 'great health' ideology, recently included Brazil among the countries which favour the modern so-called 'body Utopia'![61]

A thought provoking synthesis for the Brazilian academic world is the connection of Fascism with paganism.[62] The theatrical and aesthetic glorification of the human body is still found in Brazilian society and has elements of past Fascist spectacles. For Germany, paganism was clearly behind those Fascist glorification rituals despite Germany being a highly developed society by the mid-twentieth century. In the twentieth century, technology, it could be argued, has revealed itself as strongly associated with pagan ritual. Even religious leaders, eminent scientists and famous philosophers have submitted themselves to the pagan representation of an united ethnic community.

Descriptions of Fascist experiences in Brazil and Europe capture and confirm the essential pagan link in which the body has relevance to both collective ritualism and the celebration of beauty. In short, the body mediates the beautification of society by means of collective performance or individual image; by the multiplication of mass action or by selected representational models. Has this relationship relevance for the political practices of today? Are today's politics also a product of aesthetic experience? Is Fascism primordial?

These provocative and demanding questions have already been posed by 'innovative art'. In another celebrated film from the 1970s, *The Boys from Brazil*, the director Allen Shaffers describes a Nazi dream of conquering the world by means of a plot in which cloning was to be used to multiply Nazi leaders. Is that suggestion simply an appropriation from history involving a hidden sanctuary for Fascist experiments or is it another prospect from science fiction, now being turned into threatening reality?

NOTES

1. P. Cohen, *The Architecture of Doom*, cinema film produced by Swedish Film Institute, Stockholm, 1991. Hitler's statement was quoted from this documentary film.
2. R. Da Matta, 'For an Anthropology of the Brazilian Tradition', in D.J. Hess and R. Da Matta (eds.), *The Brazilian Puzzle* (New York, 1995), p.274.
3. For an interesting discussion of the replacement of social norms by an aesthetic view of the world in Brazil, see i.a. M. Vieira de Mello, *Desenvolvimento e Cultura – O Problema do Estetiso no Brasil* (Rio de Janeiro, 1970).
4. Quoted in P.M. Resenau, *Post-Modernism and the Social Sciences – Insights, Inroads and Intrusions* (Princeton, 1992), pp.141–2.
5. M. Maffesoli, *A Contemplacao do Mundo* (Rio de Janeiro, 1995), pp.11–12.
6. For a detailed description of the origins of social values in Brazil by means of geographic and nature's representations, see L.P. Da Costa, 'Valores e Moral Social do Brazil' (Ph.D. Dissertation, University Gama Filho, Rio de Janeiro, 1989).
7. The racial debate is scrutinized by L. Schwarcz, *O Espataculo das Racas* (São Paulo, 1993). For this study, the proportion of the black ethnic group in 1798 was 48.7% of the total population, whereas in 1872 it was reduced to 15.2% (p.13).
8. Ibid., pp.11–12.
9. Further comments on the influence of medical doctors on the eugenic trend of physical education in Brazil during the nineteenth century are found in L.P. Da Costa, 'The Medical Domination on Knowledge Construction of Physical Education in Brazil (1845–1995)' (unpublished paper, 1997).
10. See, for example, M.R. Cantarino, *Teses Brasileiras em Educacao Fisica* (Brasilia, 1986), pp.31–52.
11. Alberto Reppold, *The Emergence and Development of the Biological Model of Physical Education in Brazil*, Images of Sport in the World Congress, Cologne, Germany, 1–5 November 1995.
12. M. Chor Maio and R.V. Santos (orgs.), *Raca, Cienca e Sociedade*, Rio de Janeiro, 1996). The institution is the Oswaldo Cruz foundation based in Rio de Janeiro.
13. Ibid., pp.15–58.
14. From L.P. Da Costa, 'The State versus Free Enterprise in Sport Policy; The Case of Brazil', in L. Chalip, A. Johnson and L. Stachura (eds.), *National Sport Policies – an International Handbook* (Westport, CT, 1996), pp.23–8 (hereafter *Free Enterprise*). The apparent contradiction was argued by the following comment at page 25: 'An effort had also been made to adapt the existing private federations of sport discipline, professional soccer included, to Fascist ideology, dominant during the 1930s until 1942 when the dictatorial government joined the Allies in the Second World War. Contrary to later experiences in Eastern Europe and Cuba, the first sports policy in Brazil primarily mobilized and used the leadership and managerial levels of sports practice and competitions, allowing the clubs to maintain much of their freedom. This conception assumed the need to preserve local cultural tradition as was stated by João Lyra Filho, a lawyer dedicated to sport sociology and chief author of the final test of the 1941 Act.'
15. Quoted in G. Peixe, 'O Indio das Arabias', *Revista do Brasil*, 1 (1988), pp.41–4 (special edition dedicated to Villa-Lobos, the celebrated Brazilian composer, leader of Singing Movement during the Vargas regime).
16. Ibid., p.5; introduction of the special edition of *Revista do Brasil* under the title of 'Cronologia'. Villa-Lobos directed the Singing Movement from 1932 to 1943, when musical education became compulsory in Brazilian schools.
17. For the Latin American version of syncretism, see L.P. Da Costa, *Images of Sports in South America, Images of Sports in the World Congress* (Cologne, 1995).
18. The example was quoted in L. Cavalcante, *As Preocupacoes do Belo* (Rio de Janeiro, 1995), pp.53–131.
19. The combination of tradition and modernization gave grounds to the consensus, as revealed by E. Borghi Cabral, 'o Homem Novo no Estado Novo', in V.M. Oliveira (ed.), *Fundamentos Pedagogicos –Educaçao Fisica* (Rio de Janeiro, 1987), p.74 (hereafter *Educacao Fisica*).
20. Ibid., pp.75–80.

21. This effect is denominated 'corporeality' by P. Frankel, *Principles of Architectural History: The Phases of Style*, 1420–1900 (Cambridge, 1968), pp.1–3.
22. U. Eco, 'Ur-Fascism', *The New York Review of Books*, XLII, 11 (1995), 12–15.
23. See W. Martins, a *Literatura Brasileira – O Modernismo* (São Paulo, 1977), pp.109–26. The influence of the 'father' of Futurism on the Brazilian Modernism movement occurred only in its initial stages up to the First World War. Marinetti had even visited São Paulo and Rio de Janeiro by 1924, but he did not impress former adherents (hereafter *O Modernismo*).
24. As was fully argued by W. Chacon, *O Estado e o Povo no Brasil* (Rio de Janeiro, 1977).
25. For further details on the mobilization actions taken by Vargas' government using physical education, see A. Gomes de Faria Junior, 'Professor de Educacao Fisica, Licenciado Generalista', in *Educacao Fisica*, pp.15–33.
26. The theory of social development by means of sport is discussed by L. Chalip, D.R. Thomas and J. Voyle, 'Sport Recreation and Well-being', in D.R. Thomas and A. Veno (eds.), *Psychology of Social Change* (New Zealand, 1992), pp.132–56.
27. A. Guttmann, *A Whole New Ball Game: An Interpretation of American Sport* (London, 1988).
28. L.P. Da Costa, in *Free Enterprise*, pp.24–5.
29. Quoted in P.G. Oliveira, 'A Imigracao Alema e a Introducao do Punhobol no RGS' (unpublished Master dissertation, University of Santa Maria, 1987).
30. R. Paxton, 'Radicals', *New York Review of Books,* XLI, 12 (1994), 51 (hereafter 'Radicals').
31. Quoted in L. Tesche, *A Pratica do Turnen entre Imigrantes Alemaes no Rio Grande do Sul (*1867–1942) (Brazil, 1996), pp.11–15 (hereafter *Turnen*).
32. Ibid., pp.60–1.
33. L. Wieser, *Deutsches Turnen in Brasilien* (London, 1990), p.286.
34. Ibid., p.282
35. A. Silva Py, *A Quinta Coluna no Brasil* (Porto Alegre, Brasil, 1942).
36. Getulio Vargas Foundation – CPDOC Archives, Collection Cordeiro de Farias, Album Nazismo no Rio Grande do Sul, photos 32 and 170. The comparison with the Hitler Jugend activities was made in N. Müller (ed.), *Sportunterricht in der NS-Zeit*, Seminar WS 1991/92, Universität Mainz, 1992, pp. (XIV), 1–18.
37. Clube Germania, *Geschichte der Turnenschaft von 1890 in São Paulo zum 30 Jährigen Jubelfeste,* Typografia Henrique Scheliga & Cia, 1920.
38. L. Tesche, *Turnen*, pp.80–8.
39. R. De Rose, 'A Influencia da Imigracao Italiana no Desenvolvimento do Esporte no Rio Grande do Sul' (unpublished Masters dissertation, University of Rio Grande do Sul, 1996).
40. Ibid., pp.26–30.
41. Ibid., p.28.
42. P. Labriola, 'Arquivo do DOPS: os Clubes Esportivos Durante o Estado Novo' in *Coletanea do IV Encontro Nacional de Historia do Esporte* (Belo Horizonte, 1996), pp.486–93.
43. See Monitor Integralista – *Boletim da Acao Integralista Brasileira*, Rio de Janeiro, ano III, no. 11, 25 August 1935.
44. Ibid., item 'd' of the guidelines.
45. See in W. Martins, *Historia da Inteligencia Brasileira, 1933–1960* (São Paulo, 1996, 2nd edn), p.116. The data presented by this author were taken from primary sources.
46. Ibid., p.70.
47. Ibid.
48. See, for example, P. Labriola, 'Collective Body in Brazilian Fascism' (unpublished paper, 1997).
49. W. Martins, *O Modernismo*, pp.68–80.
50. See in L.P. Da Costa, *Free Enterprise*, pp.28–32.
51. Z. Sternhell, *The Birth of Fascist Ideology: from Cultural Rebellion to Political Revolution* (Princeton, 1994). This edition had as collaborators M. Sznajder and M. Asheri.
52. R. Paxton, *Radicals,* p.52.
53. J.T. Schnapp, *Staging Fascism* (Stanford, 1996).
54. G. Gebauer and C. Wulf, 'Les Jeux de la Violence', *Actes de la Recherche en Sciences Sociales*, 79 (Sept. 1989), 63–75.
55. Ibid., p.70.
56. T. Alkemeyer, *Körper, Kult und Politik* (Frankfurt, 1996), p.481.

57. See 'Two Cheers for Democracy', *Economist*, 341, no. 7989, 59.
58. See L.E. Soares, *Os Dois Corpos do Presidente* (Rio de Janeiro, 1993), pp.151–6.
59. See A.G.F. Junior, *Educacao Fisica*, pp.15–20.
60. See L.P. Da Costa, *Free Enterprise*, pp.25–30.
61. Lucien Sfez, *La Santé Parfaite – Critique d'une Nouvelle Utopie* (Paris, 1995). For Brazil, see Vinicius Freire, 'A Grande Saude', *Mais – Folha de São Paulo*, 7 April 1996, 4.
62. See Zeljko Loparic, *Heidgger Reu* (Campinas, 1990), pp.161–216.

Militarism, Sacrifice and Emperor Worship: The Expendable Male Body in Fascist Japanese Martial Culture

J.A. MANGAN and TAKESHI KOMAGOME

This letter was written to the youth of the homeland by a member of the Youth Volunteer Army for Pioneering Manchuria (north-east China), a volunteer agricultural force of pre-conscript male adolescents.

> We, as soldiers with ploughs, are pioneering uncultivated vast fields that were acquired at the expense of our heroes' blood. This is our honourable mission ... When the weather is bright, everyone works hard stripped to the waist so that we are as brown as south sea natives. Our pride as pioneering youths is heightened by the consciousness that we are physically tough and full of energy. Even if we have a severe winter, our well-disciplined bodies have nothing to fear.[1]

As 'a soldier of the plough', while the writer's main role was to cultivate the fields, he was also expected to act as an auxiliary to the frontier army units facing the Soviet Union and to the military police responsible for the suppression of the 'rebellious' Chinese who resisted the Japanese occupation of Manchuria.

The Youth Volunteer Army illustrates some fundamental aspects of Japanese Fascism. Firstly, the aggressive expansionism of the Fascist period occurred in part as a reaction to nationalist movements in the 1930s in China and Korea. Chinese nationalists took action against Japanese imperial interests in Manchuria; Koreans under Japanese colonial rule persisted in demanding independence. Furthermore, increasing Korean immigration to Japan caused political unease. Although, unlike in Germany and Italy, Communist-influenced labour unions were not powerful in Japan, nevertheless, the Japanese authorities were afraid that the Communists would collaborate with disaffected

Koreans and Chinese both outside and inside their empire. In 1931 one solution to these problems was another invasion of Manchuria, which it was claimed, also offered *Lebensraum* for Japan. In emulation of the Western powers, the 'Prussianization' of Japan in the hands of the old samurai class together with Japan's industrialization which demanded both raw materials and markets for goods were further factors in the rise of militant imperialism.[2]

Secondly, the development of Japanese capitalism had produced a huge disparity between the prosperity of the highly industrialized sectors and the non-industrialized farming areas. In response, an 'agriculture as the base' (*nohonshugi*) movement arose, which attacked modern capitalism, party politics and Western individualistic values. Then after the Great Depression in 1929, miserable conditions in the agricultural areas benefited the Fascist movement which was led by rightists and radical army officers. Since farming villages were recruiting grounds for the army, Japanese Fascism now gained new supporters: 'here was a vast reservoir of the attitudes and ways of the traditional authoritarian society'.[3] Furthermore, a high proportion of the officers themselves came from the farming districts and they had first-hand knowledge of the hardships afflicting the peasants, especially from 1930 onwards with the catastrophic collapse of the silk market. In 1934 there was actually widespread famine in north eastern Japan.[4] Their allegiance was strengthened in the second half of the 1930s when virtual total military rule was established in Japan and large scale agricultural emigration to Manchuria was encouraged by the army to alleviate Japanese peasant poverty. But more than this. The peasant had a special affinity with the military. Modern mass education, to be discussed below, had diffused the intense nationalism of the upper classes downwards to all the Japanese:

> more remarkably, it had soon convinced the descendants of peasants, who for almost three centuries had been denied swords and other arms and had been exploited by a military caste above them, that they too were members of a warrior race. Making up the great bulk of the conscripts, the peasants found their experience in army barracks as educational as the time spent in primary school. Both inculcated in them the glory of Japan's great military traditions and the ideal of death on the battlefield in the service of the emperor.[5]

Thirdly, 'The Meiji Restoration of 1868 separated two dramatically dissimilar epochs in Japanese history. Castles, samurai, a decentralized political system, and a policy of national isolation stood on one side of the event; heavy industry, citizen soldiers, a unitary regime headed by an authoritarian emperor, and an era of empire building stood on the other.'[6] By the twentieth century the Emperor had become a sacred, omnipotent figurehead. He was constitutional sovereign, commander-in-chief and head of the state or quasi-religion, *Shinto.* As emperor he was expected to define the uniqueness and superiority of the 'Japanese race'. To this end he was deified. The result was the Emperor Cult. As far as the cult was concerned there was remarkable continuity between the pre-Fascist and Fascist periods. This is reflected in the Oath of the Youth Volunteer Army. 'We swear to devote our lives to the sacred mission of establishing manchukuo [the Japanese puppet state in Manchuria] and thus to serve our Emperor's will.'

It is as well to be clear that for all its strong links with the Meiji past State Shinto was not a simple reflection of some pre-existing Asian willingness to submerge the individual in the collective whole. *Kokutai* may have been an ancient word, but the Kokutai cult arose only in the 1930s. The whole notion of the nation as a mystical 'body' or organism centred in the actual body of an individual leader was a phenomenon of the modern era – the era of mass armies.[7]

There is a clear similarity to the German and Italian Fascist ideal of the mystical 'body' of the people as a community unified by a mystical head: 'a significant uniformity among the fraternalist religions is that their cults of the sacred "chief" were in each case regarded as the most important element in their set of beliefs'.[8] Furthermore it has been said that it is easy to fall into the trap of believing that the Japanese endured sacrifices for emperor and nation due to some innate ethical imperative and even easier to overlook 'the great lengths to which the Imperial state had to go, legally and ideologically to create the idealized Tennosei [emperor system] in which the emperor functioned effectively as the supreme focus of patriotic loyalty'.[9] The reality, as in Fascist Germany, was that all the national agencies and agents of socialization, prior to and in the Fascist era, were bent to the purpose of ensuring recognition of the Emperor as the Supreme Racial Icon. Their success is both a lesson and a warning. The full extent of this success is clearly revealed in this memorial:

> I married very young and for a long time had no children. My wife finally bore a son and died. My son grew up fine and healthy. Then he joined the emperor's forces in the Seinan War and died a manly death in southern Kyushu in a great battle. I loved my son. When I heard that he had died for the emperor, I cried with joy, because for my warrior son there could be no finer death. My son was buried on a mountain top near Kumamoto. I went there to care for the grave. My son's name was carved on a war memorial for those from Izumo who had fallen for the emperor's sake. I felt glad when I saw my son's name there. I talked with him and felt that he was again walking by my side beneath a great pine tree.[10]

The officer class, as already mentioned, were acutely, concerned by the agricultural repression of the late twenties and its possible effect on the well-being of the peasantry from which it drew its soldiers: 'thus there was a genuine resonance in emotional attitudes between the military and rural Japan'.[11] This resonance vibrated all the more strongly since the 'militaristic and ultra-nationalist reaction that swept Japan in the thirties was atavistic in that it looked back to a simpler, more harmonious, more agrarian and more authoritarian past …'[12]

Unsurprisingly, therefore, the soldier of the plough, obedient, loyal, committed, muscular and disciplined epitomized the idealized masculinity of Japanese Fascism. This owed much to the education system before and during the Fascist period. As Carol Gluck remarks:

> Patriotism of the sort preferred by ideologies in the 1890s swept the schools during and after the Sino–Japanese War, although less as a result of the ideologues' efforts than as a consequence of the fervor of war among the teachers and the students. In September 1894 the Monbusho issued a directive in which it encouraged the singing of war songs to raise the proper spirit of vigor among the pupils. But the martial atmosphere soon grew so thick with mock military drill and enemy hostility that educators lamented what they called the schools' craze for 'shobu, shobu' (martial spirit, or militarism).[13]

By the 1930s schools for decades had played a fundamental part in the indoctrination of the young to an extent that 'Nazi and Fascist indoctrinators, as Saboro Ienaga has observed, could only dream about for their schools'.[14] In consequence, 'Inculcated with militarism through the school system, the Japanese people believed that dying for the nation on the battlefield was the supreme virtue.'[15] He added:

> After 1904, elementary school texts were compiled by the national government; all Japanese children were taught from books produced by the Ministry of Education. In premodern society, regardless of how powerful the rulers are and how weak vis à vis authority the people may be, it is virtually impossible for the ruling class to indoctrinate the entire populace. The requisite means of communication do not exist. A ruling élite needs a modern school system to get its message across.[16]

By 1900 it was in place and the standardized educational content stamped a uniform outlook on most Japanese minds. The diversity of ignorance was replaced by the conformity of state-approved knowledge. An impressionistic young child often retains his early education through adulthood despite later experiences. And in pre-war Japan, for most people formal education ended with elementary school.[17] Over time inculcation was thorough:

> By the time of the Second World War, Japan already boasted a 50 year tradition of secular nationalism, promulgated relentlessly through every institution of Japanese life. Public education, which reached 90 per cent of Japanese children by 1900, included military training for boys and the systemic inculcation of militarism and emperor worship for both sexes. Arithmetic classes did calculations based on battlefield situations; science class topics included 'general information about searchlights, wireless communication, land mines and torpedoes'.[18]

How then did the Fascist militarists penetrate the educational system? How were young men socialized into Fascist militarism? How were their minds and bodies shaped into Fascist ideological containers?

This essay will be devoted to a discussion of the ideological indoctrination into a Japanese Fascist militaristic manhood which sacrificed itself willingly for the emperor, to the successful introduction of associated military training into the education system from the pre-Fascist period of the mid-1920s onwards and to an analysis of the recruitment and training of the Youth Volunteer Army for Pioneering Manchuria in the latter half of the 1930s – a case-study of Fascist socialization.

SELF-SACRIFICE FOR THE EMPEROR

Prior to the Second World War Japan, unlike Germany, did not experience a major military defeat. The Sino-Japanese War (1894–95), the Russo-Japanese War (1904–5) and the First World War (1914–19) had all contributed to the establishment and expansion of the Japanese empire. These victorious wars made the Japanese self-confident, glorify war and embrace militarism. From the late nineteenth century myths of 'our military heroes' appeared in newspapers, stories for boys and school textbooks and were now handed down from generation to generation. In his *The Glorification of War in Japanese Education*, Saboro Ienaga has provided graphic examples:

> Ethics textbooks, even from the lowest grades, included militaristic content. A first-grade lesson cited an example from the battlefield. 'Kiguchi Kohei was hit by an enemy bullet and died, but the bugle was still at his lips.' Lesson 16 of the second-grade ethics text was entitled 'Loyalty'. 'Commander Hirose Takeo set out on a dark night to block the harbour entrance at Port Arthur with a steamship. Braving enemy fire, he … was about to leave the ship [when he discovered that] Chief Warrant Officer Sugino was missing. The commander searched all over the boat three times. [As he] finally … left the larger ship … he was hit by enemy fire and died a glorious hero's death.'[19]

Ienaga's conclusion would seem uncontentious. 'There is no doubt that the emphasis on militarism in the curriculum, combined with the media's glorification of war and the government's suppression of pacifist and liberal views, was a major factor in socializing the great majority of Japanese to support aggression enthusiastically.'[20]

The success of such militaristic indoctrination was recognized and admired in some Western circles as early as the turn of the century. Charles à Court Pepinton, the military correspondent for *The Times* wrote in his *The War in the Far East 1904–1905* of the moral strength and the sentiment of collective self-sacrifice which distinguished the warriors of Japan.[21] For other Europeans the Japanese army had become the embodiment of military virtue:

> The great bravery demonstrated by the Japanese in the Manchurian War grew out of a religious belief that no earthly reward was comparable to an opportunity to die for the fatherland:

> [death in battle] raised the soldier to the rank of a deified ancestor. It was this alone which made it possible for [Japanese commanders] to call for sacrifices which would have cost European generals their commands...When the commander of a Japanese battalion expressed doubts about the possibility of carrying out his mission, his superior officer replied: 'Then die!' These are heroic words from which we can learn.[22]

One of the most famous mythological heroes was General Nogi Maresuke (1842–1912) who won a narrow victory in a decisive battle against Russia, in which he lost his own sons. This poignant fact alone might have been enough to ensure his becoming a war hero. What made him a mystical martyr, however, was something else: on the eve of the Meiji emperor's funeral he committed ritual suicide, leaving a poem that said 'follow the lord to the grave'. Loyalty transcended death.

Reaction to his suicide was divided. Some frowned upon an anachronistic act unacceptable in a modern 'civilized country'. The famous poet, Sato Haruo, mockingly called him the great 'Japanese Don Quixote'.[23] Others admired his *bushido* (the way of the warrior) stance and *samurai* devotion to the emperor. The latter voices drowned out the former. In his lifetime stories of his eccentric character and incompetence as a commander were rife. All was forgiven and forgotten after his death.

The foreign press also contributed to the Nogi mythopoeia. *The Times*, for example, called his death 'a striking reminder of the persistence in Japan of the spirit to which our ally has owed her greatness'.[24] Stanley Washburn, an American war correspondent, wrote a biography of Nogi in which he paid him this elegiac tribute:

> He owed his allegiance to his imperial Master, and when that Master's death came there was no longer any obligation to live, and so, without a tremor, Nogi cut his throat and died. Perhaps deep in his heart, he felt that by his death he might kindle anew in Japan the idealism of the older days, sullied a little by contact with the Western civilizations ... who, in the last generations, can show a record of devotion, suppression of personality and an idealism that can equal that of the old Japanese Samurai?[25]

Ironically, the Japanese welcomed this encomium from the West. They were proud of their 'traditional culture' and desired its appreciation by the Westerner. Paradoxically the emperor system itself was invented in order to demonstrate the uniqueness and continuity of Japanese traditional culture and thus offset, and compensate for, the unrest and confusion caused by the emulation of Western ways. The death of the Meiji emperor might have stalled this recently invented system. Nogi tried to prevent this possibility by sacrificing himself for the emperor on the altar of the newly established nation state. In the words of Carol Gluck, Nogi became 'a symbol for loyalty and self-sacrificing service to the state'.[26]

The myth of General Nogi was disseminated across the nation through school textbooks published by the Ministry of Education. The surrender of the Russian General Stesel to Nogi was celebrated in ethics, history and music classes. Victory over Russia was commemorated as a splendid achievement that enabled Japan to be admitted into the select company of the world powers. Nogi was described as 'the God of War' replete with the soldierly virtues – loyalty, honesty and robustness. Reference to the manner of his death, however, was omitted, probably because the Ministry of Education was afraid that some parents would not welcome the adulation of suicide. However, in popular culture, especially in male adolescent literature, his heroic *samurai* suicide was celebrated.

Self-sacrifice as a solitary virtue, however, for all the acclamation it received, was not enough. The Manchurian Incident in 1931[27] and the subsequent military struggle that lasted until 1945 produced a different type of martial hero. The advent of total war, announced by the First World War, made élitist individualistic heroism, if not redundant, certainly insufficient: it demanded soldiers who willingly sacrificed themselves collectively on the orders of the commander. In a conformist culture with compliant members, the consequences of fanatical mass sacrificial ideologies were now realized. This is illustrated dramatically by the story of the 'three brave soldiers' of the Shanghai Incident. The *New York Times* reported under the banner headline, 'Japanese Give Lives to Open Barricade', that at Miaoshin Japanese troops had been halted by barbed wire entanglements 14 feet wide. 'Three soldiers volunteered to strap explosives around their chests and then made running jumps into the barbed wire. Their suicidal bombing opened the path for the Japanese charge, which routed the Chinese from a stoutly held position.'[28]

The Japanese army officially honoured their death and reported their courageous deed to the emperor. Plays and films dramatically portrayed the heroic act of the 'three brave soldiers'. The nobility of their self-sacrifice was extravagantly publicized, idealized and glorified. Such self-abnegatory acts could be the means of creating in the nation a sacred sense of duty. In reality, there was every possibility that the soldiers were forced to 'volunteer' in order to make up for deficiencies in the preparations for the operation. In no way was this allowed to interfere with their mythological usefulness: '... in the era of gun-based mass armies, *bushido* had to be democratized to include the masses, who were now free, as once only their superiors had been, to experience a "glorious death in war"'.[29]

Shortly after their death, the conservative magazine, *Nihon oyobi Nihonjin* (Japan and the Japanese), issued a special number devoted exclusively to the 'three brave soldiers'. It included 52 articles by military officers, philosophers and writers. All, with the single exception of an academic who questioned the vagueness of the military reasons for their death, admired their patriotic self-denial. One army officer wrote:

> The deeds of the three brave soldiers not only terrified the enemy and raised the morale of our Imperial Army, but also demonstrated the spirit of the Japanese race to the world ... The spirit of self-sacrifice for the sake of others, which embodies the highest ideal of the mankind, is the essence of what it means to be Japanese. In contrast, the Chinese race are so degenerate that they make profits at the expense of others and the Western races try to save others as long as they themselves are not exposed to danger ... As an Imperial edict for soldiers issued by the Meiji emperor states, 'righteousness is heavier than a mountain and death is lighter than feather'. The teaching of the emperor perfectly corresponds to the soul of our race and so it is easy for the Japanese to sacrifice themselves for the Emperor, a circumstance unique in the world.

In this passage self-sacrifice is glorified, patriotism is exalted, racial superiority is assumed.

As in the case of General Nogi, the tributes from foreign correspondents were valued and cited in the magazine. The carefully concealed inferiority complex towards Westerners and blatant contempt for the Chinese reflected the general Japanese concern with racial hierarchy. The Emperor cult supported and strengthened this obsession with the racial stratification of the world's nations. Giving one's life for the emperor both heightened the sense of Japanese racial superiority and the unique status of both emperor and nation. As the Western countries gradually came to be seen as enemies this defensive racial obsession grew more acute.

The carefully created legend of the 'three brave soldiers' symbolizes this obsession, but it represents more. First unlike Nogi, they were unknown soldiers. Since élitist individualistic heroism came to be regarded as an obstacle to efficient performance in modern total warfare, the fact that they were clearly insignificant privates was welcomed. Second, as a corollary they were representatives not of an élite but of the masses. In short, samurai élitist values were usefully diffused downwards in the interests of successful militarism. Most of the contributors to the *Nihon oyobi Nihonjin* recommended that the Ministry of Education should include the soldiers' story in school textbooks. And inevitably it was included. In 1941 a language textbook for third-grade students contained a song about the Miaoshin Three entitled 'Brave Soldiers'. Such songs incidentally, were commonplace in text books by this time. A fourth-grade song went:

> The cannons roar, the shells scream
> Standing on the deck awash with waves
> The commander's call pierces the darkness:
> 'Sugino, where are you? Are you there?'
> He searches every corner of the boat three times;
> He calls but gets no answer, looks but finds no trace;
> The boat gradually sinks beneath the waves;
> Enemy shells fly thick and fast
> The commander moves to the small boat
> A flying shell, he is dead.
> How tragic his death outside Port Arthur
> Heroic Hirose's fame lives on.[30]

The *National* [School] *Reader* also vividly and emotionally described the trio's sacrifice and claimed that they rushed eagerly to their glorious death shouting the words, 'Tonnoheika Banzai!' (Long Live the Emperor!). The moral message was unequivocal. Self-sacrifice for the Emperor was a sacred duty of the *whole* nation, but most especially, of men and boys.

After the outbreak of war with the United States and the United Kingdom in 1941, the radio frequently played the following martial elegy:

Across the sea, corpses soaking in the water
Across the mountains, corpses heaped upon the grass.
We shall die by the side of our Lord.
We shall never look back.

Although the original words were included in ancient anthologies, 'our Lord' clearly referred to the emperor. This requiem for dead Japanese soldiers encapsulates the death-wish atmosphere of the period. The male body had now become a symbol of self-denial, a self-abnegatory offering, a sacrifice to the living deity.

INTRODUCTION OF MILITARY TRAINING

The indoctrination of young men into devotional imperial militarism was attempted not only through the myths of 'our military heroes' but also through the military training of their minds and bodies. Military training was thought to be the pre-eminent method of inducing a martial mentality and as already noted, was well established in many schools by the mid-1920s. Captain M.D. Kennedy, a British officer sent to Japan as a Language Officer in 1917 to help cement the alliance between the two countries, wrote of the annual school sports of his local Middle School, that they were similar in many respects to that of the English public schools but that two events, connected with military training, were worth recording: a pitched battle between two sides in 'armour' with *gekken* (two handed bamboo training swords) and a fight combining wrestling and *jujitsu* between two sides for possession of the enemy's standard.[31]

The First World War in Europe made the Japanese realise the necessity of modernizing the army *and* training the young in preparation for any future total war. One officer, observing Britain, France and Germany during the Great War, maintained that victory in total war depended on the efficient mobilization of national human resources. It was necessary to inspire in the young generation, therefore, militarism, patriotism, self-discipline and self-sacrifice.[32] Guidelines published for training instructors now explained the patriotic importance of physical exercise. The West led the way before and after the First World War. Physical training had long been considered a means of instilling patriotism in young men and boys and preparing them for battle. The French ambassador to Germany, for example, said that even if German rearmament was restricted, Germany would remain dangerous unless associations for physical exercise were dissolved.[33] Compared to France, Germany, Britain and the United States, military physical training in Japan was behind the times. Sport was certainly becoming popular among school students, but it was not thought to produce the desired martial attitude.[34] It is important to appreciate that physical fitness for war was merely one element, albeit an important element, of a complete process of military education. This education was introduced into schools in two ways: through the introduction of courses for élite students and through the establishment of obligatory youth training institutions for the others.

Between the two world wars entry to secondary education was by selection. Only about a quarter of all boys could enter the élite five-year middle schools and about one half entered the upper elementary schools or supplementary vocational schools, both of which were usually attached to elementary schools. Graduates of middle schools, mostly of middle or upper-class origin, enjoyed the privilege of shortening their military service from two years to a year if they joined at their own expense. Moreover, they could be considered for commissions in the army; while the non-élite were almost all destined to be privates. Thus as elsewhere military status was linked to academic background. In 1925 all middle and higher schools were ordered to include military training in their curriculum. Prior to this, non-commissioned reserve officers instructed the pupils in elementary drill. After 1925, however, serving officers were assigned to schools as military training instructors. The training included battlefield command, shooting practice with live ammunition, lectures on modern weapons and military tactics. The Minister of the Army, possibly to assuage Western anxieties, speciously declared that the aim was not practical preparation for armed struggle, but rather to discipline the mind and body and to instil the virtues of obedience, *esprit de corps* and endurance![35] The Ministry of Education fully supported the Army's innovation and one of its bureaucrats justified the introduction of training into schools as a means of popularizing *bushido* which, in his estimation, was the equivalent of 'playing the game' in England.[36] Athleticism – with its concomitant of fair play – was often claimed as the ideal model for Japanese élite male education. In fact, this claim was utilized as a cover to mask the penetration of militarism into schools. The ideology of self-sacrifice was not overtly nor particularly emphasized in this period of international co-operation, but the 'popularization of *bushido*' inevitably resulted in the thorough inculcation of the sacred duty of self-sacrifice for the emperor in the 1930s and 1940s as it was clearly intended to do.

In the 1920s the aggressive promulgation of the emperor cult was one defensive and reactionary response to the pervasion of Marxist ideas. The political trend was towards democratization, and universal male suffrage was granted in the same year as the introduction of military training into the schools. Simultaneously, however, the Peace Preservation Law was introduced, which forbade any attempt to destroy the private ownership system or emperor worship. The main targets of this law were unpatriotic Communists, amongst whom there were not a few privileged students. Unlike Western élite schools in which a classical education was highly valued, the curriculum of Japanese middle and higher schools consisted mainly of contemporary Western culture so that students were vulnerable to newly imported Western ideas such as Marxism. Military training was intended to act as a bulwark against this infiltration. The link between training and ideological control was sometimes so obvious that it sometimes, if rarely, provoked hostility among the students.

In 1925, for example, at Otaru Commercial High School the following scenario was used for field manoeuvres. In the midst of the confusion caused by an earthquake and associated fires, refractory Korean immigrants led by anarchists attempted to destroy the cities, and the high school helped the Reservists to thwart them. This imaginary situation was to some extent based on fact. During the aftermath of the great Kanto earthquake of 1923 the Reservists slaughtered numerous Korean immigrants after a rumour that they were poisoning wells. Some students thought it blatantly inflammatory to virtually re-enact this situation and protested. They were suspended from school for an indefinite period. This action aroused some concern. One youth organization stated 'Field manoeuvres in Otaru clearly exposed the fact that the military exercises regarded the people as supposed enemies … If they demand our blood and lives, we must resist at the expense of our blood and lives. All the youth of Japan, stand up and stamp out this kind of military exercise'![37]

This statement was clearly influenced by Marxist idealism, which was capturing the imagination of some privileged young as an attractive, radical world view and a vehicle of social reform. Many 'social studies research groups' had been established in the higher schools. Their political influence, however, was limited, partly because the government suppressed them and partly because their privileged position cut them off from the people. Donald Roden in his *Schooldays in Imperial Japan* remarked on the commitment of these students.

> The Spartan standards of student leftists rivalled that of any athlete. 'Idleness is a sin; pleasure is selfish; decadence is cowardly!' These were the proud mottoes of Ichiko (the First Higher School) activists in 1925 as they committed themselves to a 'manly' life to 'total research in social studies'. In a recent article in the Ichiko alumni bulletin on 'Judo and the Communist Party', Suzuki Hajime argues that students in the martial arts were as likely to become socialists as right-wing defenders of the kokutai.[38]

Generally, however, the introduction of military training met with little opposition. Some students reluctantly participated but others admired and welcomed the strict discipline of the army. One student, who had experienced army life for only a few days, wrote that the army was a good place for self-development.[39] Moreover, the government promised that those who successfully finished their training would have their military service reduced by three months. Most students appreciated this arrangement.

After the Manchurian Incident, army officers assigned as training instructors came to play a more active role in schools. They opened the way for widespread military intervention in education. The main targets were private Christian schools and universities, which were influential and too often contained pacific students. A watershed event occurred in 1932 at the Jesuit Sophia University. Colonel Kitahara Kazushi, military training officer of the university, planned to take the students to the Yasukuni Shrine of the Japanese war dead. A few Catholic students, encouraged by Father Hoffman, president of the university, refused to go because they thought the visit was a breach of religious freedom. On receiving a complaint from Colonel Kitahara, the Deputy Minister of Education withdrew him and refused to assign a replacement on the grounds that the fundamental policy of Sophia University, namely Christianity, was contradictory to Japanese *kokutai* (emperor worship) and that the aims of military training could not be achieved in such a situation.

This action was effective. It became difficult for the university to attract new students. Without a military training officer students of the university could not enjoy the privilege of reduced military service.

After about a year of negotiations the president of the university proposed a radical set of changes. The university regularized compulsory shrine attendance for all staff and students, recruited right-wing scholars as professors of ethics and history, presented lectures on the fallacy of Marxism and taught the importance of the Japanese occupation of Manchuria.[40] A new army officer was assigned to the university; Christian education was virtually abandoned. Similar actions followed in other Christian educational institutions and the faith which had the potential to counter emperor worship was eradicated from education as the army intended.

In 1934 the Ministry of the Army published a pamphlet entitled *Principles for National Defence and its Reinforcement.* It began 'Fighting is the father of creation, mother of culture', and outlined the fundamental tenets of the Japanese Fascist regime. It laid down the following educational objectives:

1. To transmit clear concepts of the state and morality immune to any radical ideas infiltrating our Empire.
2. To hold as sacred the spirit of self-sacrifice for the state and discard internationalism, egoism and individualism which are against the interest of the state.
3. To train robust bodies and wipe out decadence.
4. To ensure recognition of the position of Japan in the world.
5. To enhance Japanese culture and avoid uncritical absorption of Western culture.[41]

Tosaka Jun (1900–1945), a brilliant Marxist philosopher, called this document nothing more than a blatant army manifesto on behalf of politicians, businessmen and landlords. Later he was arrested for violation of the Peace Preservation Law and died in prison. Most intellectuals and students now kept their own council. Unlike German students who played a crucial role in the establishment of the Nazi regime, many Japanese students did not support the Fascist regime. They withdrew into isolation surrounded by their Western books and remained relatively passive. They lacked the will and power to resist the regime which now went from strength to strength.

In 1935 youth training centres merged with vocational schools to form 'youth schools'. For the young male students military drill now took up a third, or sometimes even more, of their timetable. By 1941 the youth schools became compulsory for all of the young not at middle schools. Thus military training now existed at all levels of elementary and secondary education.

In 1937 the Ministry of Education published *Kokutai no Hongi* (Fundamentals of our National Polity). It was a political, ideological and ethical tract with the purpose of fully inculcating an intense nationalism. It included such statements as 'loyalty means to reverence the emperor ... and to follow him implicitly' and 'offering our lives for the sake of the emperor does not mean so-called self-sacrifice, but the casting aside of our little selves'.[42] The Fascist ideologue was in total control.

ORIGINS OF THE YOUTH VOLUNTEER ARMY FOR PIONEERING MANCHURIA

The Army unquestionably took the initiative in establishing the Japanese Fascist regime.[43] There was, however, also a grassroots Fascist movement in which the *nohonshugi* (agriculture as base) movement played a crucial role. It serves as case study of Fascist socialization. Kato Kanji (1884–1967) was a charismatic leader of this movement.

Kato was initially an élitist who came to deny élitism and intellectualism. After graduating from Tokyo Imperial University he became a civil servant. In 1913 he had a nervous breakdown. He resigned his position and became engaged in educating young farmers. In his youth he had converted to Christianity under the influence of the Russian novelist Tolstoy; now he renounced Christianity and converted to Shinto, the national Japanese religion. The cause of his neurosis was complicated. He suffered from a serious physical illness but also from an acute awareness of isolation from the masses. Both were contributory factors in his conversion and his breakdown. To cope with the second problem, he tried to overcome his identity crisis by returning to 'mother earth', hence his eagerness to educate the farmers in the countryside.

Kato came to have a close association with the army. The relationship between Kato and the army can be divided into two stages. The first is from 1931 to 1937 when they began to collaborate in encouraging emigration to Manchuria. The second was the establishment of the Youth Volunteer Army for Pioneering Manchuria in 1938 which made Kato an influential figure as head of the training institution for the army. During the first stage, both the army and Kato tried to engage the minds of rural youths in different ways. The army used the same methods as it used for élite students. At its behest in 1926 the government ordered local authorities to establish youth training institutions that would provide four years of part-time schooling. Each institution was usually attached to an elementary school and half of its training hours was spent in military training. Those reservists who belonged to local branches of the Imperial Military Reserve Association (Teikoku Zaigo Gunjinkai) became its instructors. The recruits to the institution were young workers between 16 and 20 years old, who had not entered secondary school. The institution was not compulsory, but as in the case of middle schools, those who successfully enrolled could enjoy a reduction of military service from two years to one and a half years. Employed youths had to weigh the advantage of a six-month reduction of service against the disadvantage of four years schooling in the evening and on holidays. As a result, some 70 to 90 per cent of those available registered, but attendance rates were usually very low which suggests that the youth training institution was not particularly popular.

In the same year as the introduction of the institutions, the members of the *nohonshugi* movement founded the Japanese National High School. the purpose of this private school was set out as follows:

> It is our belief that prosperity of the country relies on agriculture. The present situation, however, is deplorable because of the shortage of talented people for reconstruction of the impoverished rural areas. We need those who have the knowledge and skills for the innovation of agricultural management, who have the courage to improve defective rural lives, and who have deep faith in the sacred character of farming and will work with a sense of mission.[44]

Kato was appointed principal. In the Japanese National High School all the young men lived and worked together. They prepared their bodies, minds and emotions for service to the emperor. They performed Shinto rituals, sang the national anthem and martial songs and practised traditional martial arts of which Kato was a master. Kato attached the greatest importance to 'Japanese exercise' (*Yamato Bataraki*) as the expression of 'the faith and ideals of the Japanese race' through the body. Each movement had the same five spiritual functions:

> Strengthening a racial belief that Self is enlivened by the grace of Gods.
> Throwing away all the incompleteness of Self and Others to the eternal world.
> Rowing against the wild waves of reality toward the ideal world.
> Taking a deep breath at the gates of paradise.
> Glorifying the joyful world of the Japanese ancestral gods.[45]

The 'gods' were those of ancient mythology. The chief god was Amaterasu, the sun goddess from whom Jimmu Tenno, the first human emperor, was said to have descended. Ancestor worship and the emperor cult merged in him and he represented 'the uniqueness of Japanese traditional culture'.

Agriculture, of course, was at the core of the curriculum. The students were divided into two groups, eldest sons and others. Since in law the eldest son inherited the family property and became head of the family, others could have little hope of owning their own land. Even if second and later sons acquired the skills of agricultural management and wished to farm, they had no land to farm. After the Great Depression especially, many of them left their village to be workers in the cities. The only solution to their problem, in Kato's view, was agricultural emigration to the colonies, which was impossible without the support of the government and the army.

The second stage of the relationship between Kato and the army began with the Manchurian incident in 1931. The Kwantung army was deployed in the Japanese leased territories in south Manchuria. Without consulting the central government, it annexed all of Manchuria, using a minor clash with Chinese troops as a pretext. Its officers were keenly aware of Japan's continental interests. From their point of view, the establishment of 'a highly systematized state for national defence' in Manchuria was an urgent necessity in order to prepare for the coming of total war against the anticipated enemies, the Soviet Union but also possibly the United States and the United Kingdom. Thus Manchukuo was founded in 1932. Kato applauded the occupation of Manchuria and published an article to stimulate emigration. In his view the only problem was the danger to the Japanese in Manchuria from Chinese bandits. This danger could be overcome if armed emigrants worked with the Kwantung army as auxiliary forces. The army would welcome this arrangement. Who would deny those young country farmers this opportunity in a 'new world'?[46] Just before publishing this article, Kato met Captain Tomiya Tetsuo[47] of the Kwantung army who was an eager supporter of agricultural emigration. It was the start of a fruitful collaboration.

The Kwantung army did welcome the emigration plan, because it was necessary to increase the number of Japanese in the face of large numbers of Chinese. Furthermore, its officers shared Kato's sympathy for the suffering of the people in the agricultural areas of Japan. The farming villages had long been traditional recruiting grounds for the army and their economic predicament was deleterious to national defence. *The Principles for National Defence and its Reinforcement* emphasized the urgent need to assist impoverished farmers and condemned the unequal distribution of wealth in society. With the support of the Kwantung army, agricultural emigration began in 1932. The slogan of 'too narrow country, too poor natural resources, too dense population' was used together with an alluring image of 'vast fertile fields that are waiting for the Japanese to cultivate'. In 1936 the government sanctioned an even larger scheme to send a million households to Manchuria over 20 years. The following year the Kwantung army proposed the emigration of young men under the age of conscription because it would be easier and cheaper. Following the proposition members of the *nohonshugi* movement, including Kato, petitioned the government to establish 'The Youth Volunteer Army for Pioneering Manchuria'. They maintained that the concentration of young men in big cities was a cause of unemployment and the deterioration of the physical and mental health of the nation. If the government established the Youth Volunteer Army it would have the enthusiastic support of young men and their parents.[48] Kato's petition added to the original plan of the Kwantung army the attractive title of the 'Volunteer Army'. And so, the Youth Volunteer Army was established and the first group emigrated to Manchuria in 1938.

The recruitment and training of these emigrants was highly organized. The government required each prefecture to recruit a designated number of young men. Local public officers, military reservists and schoolteachers collaborated in the recruitment. Special training was given through quasi-military organizations, first for two months in Japan under the direction of Kato, then for three years in Manchuria. At the end of his training each young man had to move to a Japanese immigrant village and play a leading role there. In the course of their training the young men were systematically indoctrinated with a sacred sense of their mission to expand and protect Japanese *Lebensraum* in the service of the divine emperor. Boys between the ages of 16 and 19 who were physically strong, could apply to join the Youth Volunteer Army. The government and other recruitment agencies saw youths with an unpromising future, namely those who were neither middle school students nor eldest sons, as the main source of recruits. One brochure published in 1938 by the government said that application to the army would give youth opportunities for making full use of their latent energy and that the national policy of expansion on the Chinese mainland and their secure futures would be achieved simultaneously.[49]

Desirable imperialism, paternalism and masculinity were seductive elements in the government's presentation of emigration. One brochure described the significance of pioneering in Manchuria as follows:

> Many Western countries have their sights set on Manchuria. Japan has helped Manchukuo to be an independent country and has protected it. Through the diffusion of knowledge and technology and improvement transformation facilities, Japan has energetically developed Manchuria. The Chinese are wholeheartedly grateful to Japan. Since this vast uncultivated land has only a sparse population, the Chinese say, 'Please come and develop it'. The Japanese government has promised to send them excellent young men – the Youth Volunteer Army.[50]

This is typical of the Japanese view of the Chinese at the time. Only two types of Chinese existed: 'children' asking for Japanese protection, instruction and assistance or ungrateful 'bandits'. The support given by the ordinary Chinese to those 'bandits' was ignored, consciously or unconsciously. This atmosphere of imperialist paternalism reinforced a sense of mission among the young emigrants.

An idyll of a masculinity paradise was also projected. Letters from members of the Youth Volunteer Army already in Manchuria were published to encourage volunteers from home. The muscular Japanese male (*nippon danji*) was present in much of the correspondence. One youth, for example, wrote of the pleasure of washing his face in pure, cold water, hunting rabbits and deer and of walking around singing a 'Song for Colonization':

> Venerating the Emperor
> Whose Imperial line continues eternally,

> Planting the Japanese spirit [Yamato Damashii] in wide and wild fields,
> That is an honour of the Japanese male.[51]

By emphasizing their primitive life-style the 'soldiers' demonstrated Japanese masculine qualities. The government for its part filled brochures, newspapers and schools with appealing and attractive images of the army. This kind of propaganda was effective with schoolboys. However, parental consent was necessary before they could volunteer. Here schoolteachers had a crucial influence, as in the case of the boy who was persuaded to join the army by the eloquence of his schoolteacher. However, just before entering the training institution he changed his mind. His mother and brother had objected. His brother was critical of the war and his mother did not want to part from her son until he was of call-up age. In response his teacher made the boy stand alone on the platform at school assembly and branded him publicly as a 'non-Japanese', the most insulting term of wartime Japan.[52] Shaming strategies were not the only weapon teachers possessed. Teachers' methods of achieving the quota required of their localities could come dangerously close to coercion. In short, the recruiting process had two faces: the attractive smile offering hope and self-esteem to young men in hopeless circumstances and the ruthless scowl intimidating young men into compliance.

TABLE 8.1

A TYPICAL TIMETABLE AT THE UCHIHARA TRAINING INSTITUTE, JAPAN

6.00 a.m.	Reveille – Roll call — Morning service at the shrine – Japanese exercise
7.30 a.m.	Breakfast
9.00 a.m.	Subjects – Military Drill – Martial arts – Agricultural Practices
12.00 p.m.	Lunch
1.30 p.m.	Agricultural Practices – Military Drill – Subjects
5.30 p.m.	Supper
6.00 p.m.	Bathing – Study Time – Singing
8.00 p.m.	Evening service at the shrine – Bedtime[53]

As mentioned earlier those who volunteered for the army first received two months' training at the Uchihara Training Institute in Japan. Kato was head of the Institute, and graduates of the Japanese National High School formed his staff. The volunteers lived together in isolated camps. They were organized into battalions, companies, platoons and squads as in the regular army. The elements of the training were similar to those of the Japanese National High School, namely Shinto rituals, traditional martial arts, Japanese exercise and agricultural training. Morning and evening services at the shrine included singing the national anthem, hoisting the national flag and veneration of the emperor. Before supper the volunteers repeated the Volunteer Army oath: 'We swear to devote our lives to the sacred mission of establishing Manchukuo and thus to serve our emperor's will' (see Table 8.1). The academic subjects studied were ethics, basic Chinese, practical knowledge about Manchuria, agriculture and sanitation. Intellectualism was frowned upon. Military training had a central place in the curriculum. Both militarist and the *nohonshugi* movement were united regarding the practical aims and practices of the effective training of the Youth Volunteer Army. 'Soldiers of the plough' were made not born.

Most finished the training in good spirits. In memoirs written in the post-war period many recalled how inspiring and how affectionate Kato was. He always had kind words for his young men. In their memory, he was never a man of words without action: he licked human excrement to examine its suitability as fertilizer and he ploughed for hours to ensure his students ploughed for hours. They were not permitted to stop till he did. His Fascism had the attractive face of fraternalism.[54]

In Manchuria the volunteers came face to face with harsh reality. During their three-year training there most of them suffered from the poor accommodation, severe weather and deadly diseases like dysentery, and from homesickness. This reality never appeared in the letters published by the government. A novelist who visited the army in Manchuria, however, reported their anguish. One volunteer wrote of a keen sense of betrayal:

> When we left Japan, officials of the village saw us off as the bearers of significant national policy. When we arrived here, however, they did not care about us ... The most painful thing was to be forgotten. Many letters of encouragement and comfort came to the soldiers, but to us nothing, in spite of the fact that we were said to be the equivalent of soldiers.[55]

The volunteers reacted in two ways toward such neglect: one was mental depression, another was sadism. Fighting between units and arbitrary attacks on Chinese women and children gradually became widespread. These further realities may be seen as the logical outcome of the Japanese Fascist regime.

By 1945 the total number of youth emigrants was some 80,000, about a quarter of whom died in the fighting before and after the defeat of Japan.

In the history of global and Japanese Fascism the Volunteer Army is both a common and an uncommon army of exemplars. For a high percentage a self-sacrificial role was realized – not in honour but in humiliation. Nevertheless their bodies were iconic instruments of Fascist imperial intention; their muscles were symbols of Fascist chauvinistic ambition. They were not supermen in the Aryan sense but they were men of a 'super race.' And they were shaped through action and imagery to be effective members of this Oriental Super Race.

NOTES

1. Takumusho Takumukyoku (The Ministry of Colonization), *Manmo Kaitaku Seishonen Giyugun Genchi Tsushinshu* (Correspondence of the Youth Volunteer Army), Vol.1 (Tokyo, 1938), p.220.
2. G. Hurst, 'Death, honour and loyalty: The Bushido ideal' in *Philosophy East and West*, 1990, Vol.40 (Internet: http// www. Ac.uk/cgi-bin/set).
3. E.O. Reischauer, *Japan: The Story of a Nation*,(hereafter *Japan*) (New York, 1970), p.185.
4. R. Storry, 'Fascism in Japan: The Army Mutiny of February 1936', *History Today*, 718–19.
5. Reischauer, *Japan*, p.185.
6. C. Totman, 'Ethnicity in the Meiji Restoration: An Interpretive Essay', *Monumental Nipponica*, 37, 3 (1982), 269.
7. Barbara Ehrenreich, *Blood Rites* (New York, 1997), p.215.
8. Paul Brooker, *The Face of Fraternalism – Nazi Germany, Fascist Italy and Imperial Japan* (hereafter *Face of Fraternalism*) (Oxford and New York, 1991), p.255.
9. See Rudolph Hartmann, 'Zum historischen Bild des Militarismus in Japan. Ursachen und Erscheinungsformen', *Zeitschrift für Geschichtswissenschaft*, 39, 3 (1991), 309–21.
10. Quoted in H. Hardacre, *Shinto and the State 1868–1988* (Princeton, 1989), p.92.
11. Saburo Ienaga, *Japan's Last War: World War II and the Japanese1931–1945* (Oxford, 1978), p.20 (hereafter *Japan's Last War*).
12. Reischauer, *Japan*, p.186.
13. C. Gluck, *Japan's Modern Myths: Ideology in the Late Meiji Period* (Princeton, 1985), p.150 (hereafter *Japan's Modern Myths*).
14. Brooker, *Face of Fraternalism*, p.255.
15. Saburo Ienaga, 'The Glorification of War in Japanese Education', *International Security*, 18, 3 (Winter 1993–94), 115 (hereafter 'Glorification of War').
16. Ibid.
17. Ibid.
18. Quoted in Ehrenreich, *Blood Rites*, p.213.
19. Ienaga, *Japan's Last War*, p.119.
20. Ibid., p.117.
21. Quoted in Antulio J Eschevarria II, 'On the Brink of the Abyss: The Warrior Identity and German Military Thought before the Great War', *War and Society*, 13, 2 (October 1995), 32.
22. Ibid.
23. Ohamu Tetsuya, *Nogi Maresuke* (Tokyo, 1967), p.162.
24. *The Times*, 14 Sept. 1912.
25. Stanley Washburn, *Nogi* (New York, 1913), pp.132–3.
26. Gluck, *Japan's Modern Myths*, p.148.

27. 'The full turn of the tide came in 1931 in another case of 'direct action' by middle-grade officers in Manchuria, but on a larger scale than in 1928. On the night of September 18 they blew up a small section of the South Manchurian Railway that Japan owned, and claiming it had been done by the Chinese, used this as a pretext to overrun all of Manchuria in a series of rapid military pushes. Obviously they could not have done this without from the start tacit approval of elements of the high command in Tokyo, and the whole of the army closed ranks behind them. The emperor and the leaders of the civil government tried to keep the "incident" under control, but found themselves helpless ... The army started to form Manchuria into a separate puppet state, and in September 1932, Japan recognized this as the nation of Manchukuo, under a puppet, Pu-yi, who had abdicated the Manchu throne of China as an infant in 1912.' Reischauer, *Japan*, p.190.
28. *New York Times*, 24 Feb. 1932.
29. Ehrenreich, *Blood Rites*, p.216.
30. Ienaga, 'Glorification of War', p.120.
31. Captain M.D Kennedy, *The Military Side of Japanese Life* (London, 1924), pp.101–2.
32. Sato Tsunajiro, *Kokuboho no Shakaimondai* (Social Problems in National Defence) (Tokyo, 1921), p.109.
33. Rikugunsho, *Gakko Kyoren mnikansuru Sandoshiryo* (References for Military Drill in Schools) (Tokyo 1925), p.119.
34. Rikugunsho, *Gakko Kyoren Shinsa no Shishin* (Guidelines for Military Drill in Schools) (Tokyo, 1925), pp.37–8.
35. Ibid., p.81.
36. See J.A. Mangan, *Athleticism in the Victorian and Edwardian Public School* (Cambridge, 1981), *passim*.
37. Fujii Tadotoshi (ed.), 'Saigo Gunjinkai Shiron (History of the Reservist Association). *Kikan Gendaishi* (Journal of Modern History), 9 (Sept. 1978), 313–14.
38. Donald Roden, *Schooldays in Imperial Japan: a Study of the Culture of a Student Elite* (Berkeley, Los Angeles, London, 1980), pp.225–6.
39. Rikugunsho, 'Gakko Seito no Guntaikan' (Students' views of the Army', *Kaikoshakiji* (Bulletins of the Army), 629 (Feb, 1925).
40. Documents on Military Drill in the National Archives of Official Papers, Tokyo.
41. Rikugunsho Shimbunhan, *Kokubono Hongi to sono Kyoka no Teisho* (Principles for National Defence and its Reinforcement) (Tokyo, 1934), pp.34–5 (hereafter *Kokubono Hongi*).
42. See Catherine Blomberg, *The Heart of the Warrior: Origins and Religious Background of the Samurai System in Feudal Japan* (Folkstone, 1994), pp.191–2.
43. Shimbunhan, *Kokubono Hongi,* p.41.
44. Kyochokai (ed.), *Noson niokeru Tokushukuaru Kyoikukikan* (Educational Facilities Characteristic of Agricultural Areas' (Tokyo, 1933), p.24.
45. Kato Kanji Chosakushu Kamkokai, *Kato Kanji Chosakushu* (The Writings of Kato Kanji), Vol.1 (Ibaragi, 1979), p.147.
46. Kato Kanji – Manmo Shodumin Mondai (Colonization of Manchuria), *Seinen* (Youth), 17, 8 (Aug. 1932), 20.
47. Shiratori Michihiro (ed.), *Manmo Kaitaku Seishonen Giyugun Shiryoshu* (Documents relating to the Youth Volunteer Army), Vol.1 (Tokyo, 1993), pp. 1–13. With regard to the Youth Volunteer Army this paper owes much to Shiratori's numerous works published in Japanese.
48. Takumusho Takumukyoku, *Manshu Seinen Imin no Shiori* (Guide for Youth Emigrants to Manchuria' (Tokyo, 1938), p.3.
49. Takumusho Takyumykyoku, *Anata mo Guyugun ninaremasu* (You can be a Member of the Volunteer Army) (Tokyo, 1939), p.2.
50. Takumusho Takumukyoku, *Manmo Kaitaku Seishonen Giyugun Genchi Tsushinshu* (Correspondence of the Youth Volunteer Army', Vol.2 (Tokyo, 1939), p.335.
51. Ibid.
52. Tinno Morimasa, *Sensei Wasurenaide* (Teachers, Don't Forget) (Naskinonisha, 1988), pp.150–1.
53. Sakuramot Tomio, *Manmo Kaitaku Seishonen Giyugun* (The Youth Volunteer Army for Pioneering Manchuria) (Tokyo, 1987), pp.114–15.
54. Ibid., p.110.
55. Ibid., p.241.

Blue Shirts, Nationalists and Nationalism: Fascism in 1930s China

FAN HONG

In the 1930s two political movements occurred in China: the Blue Shirts (Lanyishe) and the New Life movement (Xinshenghuo yundong). The Blue Shirts movement was an imitation of the Fascist youth movements in Italy and Germany. The New Life movement was an attempted 'social regeneration of China' through the revival of the ancient moral principles of Confucianism.[1] However, it was not a simple neo-Confucian revival. It was a Fascist movement with a Chinese character. These two movements were integrated and interrelated. This essay will trace the origins of both movements, examine how the Fascist ideology with its emphasis on total control, military power and male supremacy was implemented in China, and how the Nationalists used militarized physical exercise to promote male bodies as political metaphors symbolizing and ensuring a strong state.

Fascism is one of the less precise terms in the social science lexicon. Since it first appeared in Italian in the 1910s the meaning and definition has changed over time.[2] In 1992 Stephen Turner declared: 'The puzzle of Fascism remains, half a century after the conclusion of the war against the Fascist regimes ... No sociology of the interior era grasped Fascism fully or produced an unambiguously 'correct' political receipt for dealing with it...The failure...indicates that the pretensions to political wisdom of social science are inappropriate...'[3] In this essay I follow Roger Griffin and Zeev Sternhell and define the political ideology of Fascism as 'a synthesis of organic nationalism and anti-Marxist socialism, a revolutionary movement based on rejection of liberalism and democracy...'[4] From this specific perspective, the subject under investigation here is the Fascist movement in China in the 1930s on two levels – political ideology and action. This will involve consideration of the creation of a single-party state, the founding of a mass youth movement and the training of male (and some female) bodies for 'national rebirth'. In Fascist studies the obsession with national rebirth and the need for a 'new man' has been frequently noted – in Europe. However, Fascism is not an exclusively European phenomenon. The Fascist movement in China in the 1930s illustrates the adaptability of Fascism to societies and cultures outside Europe as far distant as Asia.

The Nationalist party came to power in 1927. Led by Chiang Kai-shek, its Commander-in-Chief, the National Revolutionary Army drove the Communists from the cities into the countryside and attempted to unify China under one party rule. By 1928 the Nationalists had extended their territory north to the former capital of China – Beijing. From there their influence stretched on into Manchuria. The warlords in those areas were either destroyed or allied themselves with the Nationalists. In April 1927 Chiang and his supporters set up their own Nationalist Government in Nanjing. Chiang became President and remained the commander-in-chief of the Nationalist armed force. From 1928 to 1949, while challenging Western imperialist intrusion, facing up to Japanese aggression from the outside and waging war against the Communists from the inside, the Nationalists controlled about two-thirds of China's population and the greater part of China.

The Nationalists' ambition was to unite the whole country and create a new modern China. However, they were confronted with the challenge of reinvigorating a nation that had been declining at an accelerating pace for over a century, and with the further challenge of the Communists internally and Japanese imperialists externally. There was a brief period of optimism in the early years of the Nationalist government. Many thought that the new government would cope with the nation's problems, would restore political unity, economic prosperity, national pride and general security to the Chinese people. But the Nationalists failed. Its administration became increasingly ineffective and corrupt. The Nationalist Party was unable to impose any real unity upon the nation. It lost the popular support of some party members and most of the people.[5] Ludwig Rajehman reported in February 1930 that 'the Government ... soon began to lose its original driving force; eventually, after two years of office, little remained of the early schemes of reconstruction'.[6] The Nationalist Party's Manifesto of the Fourth National Congress in November 1931 admitted: 'China was plunged into the abysses of national crisis. Our only chance of surviving this catastrophe is to ... make the nation a genuine body of strength ... by sacrificing personal freedom and interests for national reconstruction.'[7] Chiang confessed in 1932 that 'The Chinese revolution has failed. My one desire today is to restore the revolutionary spirit that the Chinese Nationalist Party had in 1924.'[8]

As the consequence of the Nationalist Party's determination to hold on to power Chiang and some young loyal party members and military officers looked to Italy and Germany. They admired European Fascism with its emphases on faith in the leader, a sense of national superiority and the militarization of the nation for its survival. Chiang proclaimed: 'Fascism is … a stimulant for a declining, stagnant society. Can Fascism save China? We answer: Yes! Fascism is what China now most needs. At the present stage of China's critical situation, Fascism is a wonderful medicine exactly suited to China, and the only tonic that can save it.'[9] Fascism came to be seen in China as the most advanced and efficient political ideology and system. It was considered a progressive doctrine and practice that was suited to China's restoration.

Fascism was not a new phenomenon to the Nationalist Party, which had a long and close relationship with the Germans. After he turned on his Communist allies in 1927, Chiang had brought in the Germans as advisors when the Russians pulled out. The German military mission, led by Colonel Max Bauer, came to China in 1928.[10] Bauer had close ties with Hitler and the German Nazi movement. Many of his subordinates in the mission had been selected at least partially because they shared his political predilections. Bauer died in May 1929 and he was succeeded by an extraordinarily ardent Nazi, Lieutenant-Colonel Herman Kriebel. Kriebel had marched in the front rank with Hitler during the famed Beer Hall Putsch of 1923. During his subsequent imprisonment, he had shared Hitler's prison cell. Bauer, Kriebel and other Nazis in the advisory mission virtually dominated military education in the military academies. They had, therefore, unique opportunities to propagate their political views among the army élite.[11] Furthermore, in 1933, after the failure of the four years of his First, Second, Third and Fourth campaigns against the Communists, Chiang, with the support of Hitler, imported the German Fascist General Von Seecket and some 70 German military advisers to plan the Fifth campaign. Von Seecket led the Fascist trained Nationalist armies and employed the military tactics used by foreign imperialist powers in the conquest of Africa and India and destroyed the Communist resistance. The Communists lost their Red Area and had to start the famous Long March in search of a new base.[12] The victory brought Chiang closer to the Germans. Meanwhile, after 1928 a large number of Chinese officers were sent to study in European countries, most of them went to Italy and Germany.[13] The youthful 'new Italy' arising from the collapse of the played-out liberal order in the Giolittian era, Hitler's rise to power and the Nazis' cry of 'Germany awake', the British Union of Fascists' campaign for a 'Greater Britain' and the Romanian Iron Guard's call for the appearance of the New Fascist Man gave further impetus to the Chinese military. They believed that liberalism was not suitable to their changing world. Fascism with its cogent and lucid idealism, in their view, could overcome the nation's sickness, decline, disintegration and collapse. More than this, it could restore the nation's hope, pride and glory.

Inspired by the Italian and German Fascist movements, in 1931, a young progressive party member Liu Jianqiong wrote a proposal called 'Suggestions of Reforming the Nationalist Party'. He suggested that the party should be transformed. The new party should imitate the ideals and forms of the Hitler Youth in Germany and the Black Shirts in Italy. The new party should be called the Blue Shirts, for the members would wear blue shirts as their symbol.[14] Liu's proposal met with an enthusiastic response from Chiang and some young officers of Huangpu Military Academy – China's equivalent to West Point of the United States, Sandhurst of Britain and St. Cyr of France. The Academy was founded in 1924 and Chiang was its first principal. Chiang retained the post even after he became commander-in-chief of the army and the President. The aim of the Academy was to train future military *and* political leaders. The graduates of the Academy became known as the 'Huangpu group'. They dominated the important positions of the Nationalist Party and army. The ties between Chiang and many of the Huangpu graduates involved the deep personal commitment and mutual loyalty of a Chinese master and his disciples. For the Huangpu group Chiang was Principal not President!

Supported by Chiang, in Autumn 1931, 12 young officers from Huangpu Military Academy and Liu, the writer of the Proposal, formed the Fascist Blue Shirts.[15] It was an élite organization. Membership was very selective. The recommendation of two Blue Shirts members and a thorough background investigation were essential. Once approved for membership, the candidate would face a portrait of Chiang Kai-shek and vowed to obey the leader and preserve the secrets and discipline of the organization or suffer the penalty of death. Although the Blue Shirts

FIGURE 9.1
CHIANG KAI-SHEK

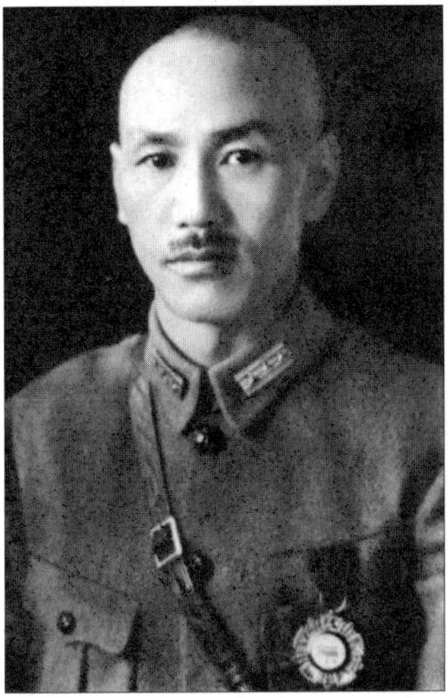

probably never exceeded 10,000 members, its power within the military and the party was pervasive.[16] It almost completely dominated the party's organization, political training in the army, government and schools. It also controlled the Nationalists' police force and public security organizations. The 13 founders were called 'the thirteen Taibao' (princes of the Nationalist élite). They were important figures in the Nationalist regime. For example, Dai Li and Zhen Jiemin became heads of the Chinese Special Service force (the Chinese SS). Dai's name became a symbol of terror and he was called 'China's Himmler'.[17]

The Blue Shirts claimed that their goal was national salvation through Fascism. They criticized the government as too soft, too liberal, too bureaucratic and too corrupt to continue the spirit of the reconstruction of China. They regarded Fascism as the only hope of saving China. They saw themselves not only as the embodiment of China's revolution, but indeed as its means of redemption.[18] An editorial article of *Shehui xinwen* (The Society Mercury), the Blue Shirts' mouthpiece, stated: 'Fascism is the only tool of self-salvation of nations on the brink of destruction. It saved Italy and Germany … Therefore, there is no other road than imitating the Fascist spirit of violent struggle as in Italy and Germany.'[19]

To imitate Italy and Germany was to assume total control. Obedience to a supreme leader was essential. Chiang stated:

> The most important point of Fascism is absolute trust in a sage, able leader … Now we in China do not have one leader. I believe that, unless everyone has absolute trust in one man, we cannot reconstruct the nation and we cannot complete the revolution … From the day we joined the revolutionary group, we completely entrusted our rights, life, liberty, and happiness to the group, and pledged them to the leader … Thus for the first time we can truly be called Fascists.[20]

The editorial of *Shehui xinwen* cried, 'We must not disguise that we demand a China Mussolini, demand China's Hitler.'[21] Chiang was regarded as the New Man for China. Therefore, faith in Chiang was the first principle of the Blue Shirts. 'Chiang Kai-shek is the only leader of the Nationalist Party and also the only great leader of China. Members, therefore, must absolutely support him, follow his order only, and make his will their own.'[22] Obedience to Chiang was unconditional. Members of the Blue Shirt were to live and die with him, sincerely and unwavering![23]

To the Blue Shirts, Western liberalism meant anarchy and individualism. This liberalism, in their view, had poisoned the Chinese since the May Fourth Movement (1915–19). It caused the people to yield to their personal whims and ignored the needs of society at large. Chiang stated: 'We have in vain become drunk with democracy and the advocacy of free thought. What has been the result? We have fallen into a chaotic and irretrievable situation.'[24] The Blue Shirts called for people to perform their duties not to speak of their rights. They should relinquish their freedom and even their lives for the nation. There was no room for individual freedom in the cause of national salvation.[25]

National salvation needed order and discipline. Paradoxically to achieve order and discipline violence was necessary. The Blue Shirts believed that the goal of restoration could only be achieved by 'fighting violence with violence'. An article in *Shehui xinwen* claimed: 'China today has no other road to restoration than to use an absolutely revolutionary body as a violent force that supports the principle of nation-first-ism.'[26] Chiang said in a speech to the Blue Shirts, 'all the comrades must unite their thoughts and beliefs. Party members … shall handle all matters in accordance with the principle of fighting violence with violence.'[27] The Blue Shirts directed this 'legitimate' violence not only against Communists, Japanese and political rivals, but also individual Blue Shirts who disobeyed orders. A *Shehui xinwen* editorial proclaimed: 'There must be a determination to shed blood – that is, there must be unprecedented violence to eliminate all enemies of the people.'[28] The Blue Shirts stated that all enemies must be punished and killed using extreme measures, so that the masses would be too frightened to disobey the laws.[29]

In summary, the Blue Shirts were a clear example of the Fascist movement in action in China. Its inspiration came directly from European Fascism. Liberalism in any form was equated with licence and personal indulgence. What was needed in China, they argued, was obedience to the leader, discipline and a new asceticism. Nationalism, exaltation of the state, glorification of the leader, subordination to the collective will and the glorification of violence and terror all had their place in this school of thought. Through the New Life Movement the credo of the Blue Shirts was widely spread across the whole country.

In February 1934 Chiang launched the New Life Movement from his Nanchang headquarters, Jiangxi province, where he served as commander-in-chief of the military operations for the suppression of Communism. As noted earlier, the leadership of the Nationalist Party held the view that the material and spiritual 'degeneration' of the people was responsible for China's continuing crisis. It was said when Chiang travelled through Nanchang city and saw a young boy in student's uniform with a cigarette in his mouth quarrelling and fighting in the street, he stopped to enquire why his family permitted such behaviour. He then found that such behaviour was common throughout the area. Chiang foresaw decline.[30] In his view the whole nation needed the spirit of the Blue Shirts. It was time to launch an indigenous moral crusade and restore social order in order to revitalize the country. Chiang intended to implant the Blue Shirts' spirit in the Chinese people and to turn the elite Blue Shirts movement into a national movement. Before the launch of the New Life Movement Chiang said to the Blue Shirts' conference of 1933: 'It is necessary to spread our revolutionary spirit to the masses of the entire nation, and to cause them to have faith in our group.'[31] A few months later, in February 1934, Chiang made a speech to a Nanchang mass meeting in which he called for 'a movement to achieve a new life'.[32] To the assembled citizens he cited the examples of Germany and Japan. He pointed out that such nations were strong because they had developed a proper way of life. What China needed in order to achieve strength was to *militarize* (my emphasis) the life of the people of the entire country.[33]

However, to make the Blue Shirts acceptable to the ordinary Chinese, Chiang attributed to them a moral code similar to that promulgated by Confucian thought. It was a Confucianism for the masses.[34] This is the reason that the essence of the Fascist movement has been overlooked by many scholars, who have viewed it simply as a neo-Confucian revival.[35]

The main purpose of the New Life Movement was to lead the Chinese people to a more rational life with three separate but interrelated aspects: the cultural, the productive, and the militarized modes of life. Through the cultural mode of life, it was hoped that rudeness and vulgarity could be eliminated. Through the productive mode of life, it was hoped that more people would contribute to the material welfare of the whole nation. Through the militarized mode of life, it was hoped that the people would become more disciplined and more able to defend the nation.[36] There were 96 specific rules issued to discipline the masses, including walk on the right side, stand straight, wash the face with cold water and drink water instead of tea or coffee.[37] Chiang believed that such strict rules would transform the 400 million 'scattered grains of sand' into disciplined citizens[38] guided by the four virtues *li*, *yi, lian, chi* (propriety, righteousness, integrity and a sense of shame), resulting ultimately in the creation of a new society and nation.[39] He stated that emphasis on the four virtues would make the people work harder, spend less, end corruption and make officials honest and patriotic – the secret of success of Italy and Germany.[40]

Chiang's call for a Chinese New Life, in February 1934, was followed by an immediate response by the population that exceeded his expectations. Following their disillusionment with democracy, partially because of China's recent experience with inefficient democratic institutions and partially because of political trends in the world at large, the Chinese became interested in dictatorship which they believed could effectively save the country from its deep crises. Since the military triumph of the democratic allies in the First World War, democracy as a system of government had everywhere come under attack for its seeming inability to cope with the mounting economic and political crises. In Italy, Mussolini's demand for a 'new Italy' had transformed a weak and humiliated nation into an international power. The achievements of Hitler left a deep impression on the Chinese people's political thinking.

The Chinese were well aware of ideological differences between Fascism and Confucianism, but they believed that both advocated the sacrifice of the individual to the state, both emphasized the stability of the society through the maintenance of the *status quo* and both praised the glory of the past. Fascism and Confucianism could deliver a future to the people. Therefore, with the endorsement of the government, within a matter of weeks, the movement had spread 'like wildfire' over most of China, encouraging some to believe that China's long-promised 'rebirth' was close at hand. Through March and April, New Life promotional associations were established in nine provinces as well as three municipal centres. By the first anniversary of the Movement in February 1935, 15 provinces, three municipalities and nine railway centres had New Life organizations. By the end of 1935, such organizations had spread to 19 provinces, five municipalities and 12 railway centres. At the lower administrative level, the organization had been extended to 1,132 counties by 1935.[41]

In May 1934 the Nationalist government sent a delegation of young officers to visit Italy and Germany to study Fascist military techniques. The correspondent in Berlin of the *New York Times* reported: 'Because of the revolutionary activities among the younger generation, the methods whereby the Chancellor Hitler has turned the revolutionary enemy in Germany to his own purpose are of particular interest to the Nanking authorities.'[42] The German Fascist techniques were applied to the New Life Movement. The movement transmitted German principles through simple Chinese expressions. People were taught to accept Chiang as the only true leader of the country because he was a man of the people, who could look deep into the soul of the people and thereby bring the movement closer and closer to Chinese tradition.[43] To achieve this the people themselves were to be disciplined by a social moral order and trained to be new citizens. To be new citizens meant to 'sacrifice personal freedom and enjoyment'.[44] Puritanism held sway, including sanctioned physical attacks on people attending cinemas or dance halls or engaging in other forms of liberalism. Puritan violence was sanctioned also by the police and the New Life promotion organizations. It was reported that in Shanghai a woman was arrested because she wore shorts on a hot summer day – immoral behaviour and that she had died in prison.[45] Women with short hair were regarded as Communists or radicals and were arrested. In Wuhan city, all cabarets were forced to close at midnight. People were not allowed to dance, and music was to be only classical in nature. Furthermore, the Ministry of Education resorted to extreme methods: centres of radicalism were closed down, radical teachers arrested and radical students expelled. Meanwhile, the government attempted to dissolve progressive workers' organizations and shut liberal schools.[46] The 'White Terror', as it was called by leftist critics and Communists, swept over China. In the dormitories of Beijing, to a lesser extent in other areas, 1934 and 1935 were years marked by pre-dawn police raids, surprise searches and sudden arrests carried out by the secret police aided by the Blue Shirts and their allies.[47] It has been estimated that 300 students, professors, and intellectuals were arrested in North China in 1934.[48] Two hundred and thirty Beijing and Tianjin intellectuals were taken into custody between November 1934 and March 1935.[49] George Shepherd, a Christian missionary, observed, 'Radicalism and communism are dead.'[50]

Political indoctrination and military training were two crucial aspects of the Blue Shirts and the New Life Movement. Political indoctrination 'informed' people's minds and military training strengthened men's bodies – both essential for preparation for war and national rebirth. The Blue Shirts saw militarization as central to China's education and future. The ultimate goal of education was training future soldiers for the nation.[51] School should be organized like military regiments, and teachers and school administrators should receive compulsory military training and live the frugal, disciplined life of the army.[52] Military education should begin in the kindergarten, because the children belonged to the nation not the family. The children should be given toy guns, and pictures of battle scenes should be displayed on the walls so that they would develop an interest in military equipment and battle situations.[53] Middle school pupils should be enrolled in the Tongzijun ('Boy's Army' in Chinese, 'Boy Scouts' in English), which, like the Hitler Youth, would have a strong military emphasis. In schools, heavy stress was to be placed on physical training and team sports, group activities, group co-operation, and group discussion.[54] In this way, students would learn to identify first and foremost with the social group and then with the nation. In this way, the bookish students of the past would be replaced by the strong scholar-warriors of the future. Boys in high school and college would receive formal military training. Girls would receive training as nurses. Academic courses would be oriented towards militarization. Physics, chemistry and engineering would be oriented towards their wartime applications. Classes in chemistry, for example, would stress the study of such matters as poison gases and explosives.[55]

In September 1933 Chiang had explained that the militarization of society was one of the three basic elements in Fascism (the other two were a sense of national superiority and faith in the leader).[56] Five months later the New Life Movement was launched. Chiang now declared that the militarization of society was the chief goal of the movement. He claimed,

> In Fascism, the organization, the spirit, and the activities must all be militarized ... In the home, the factory, and the government office, regardless of place, time, or situation, everyone's activities must be the same as in the army ... In other words, there must be obedience, sacrifice, strictness, cleanliness, accuracy, speed, diligence, secrecy ... and everyone together must firmly and bravely sacrifice everything for the group and for the nation.[57]

This vision of the whole of Chinese society performing with the discipline, obedience and efficiency of a military camp was essential to the New Life Movement. Chiang stated,

> What is the New Life Movement that I now propose? Stated simply, it is to thoroughly militarize the lives of the citizens of the entire nation so that they can cultivate courage and swiftness, the endurance of suffering and a tolerance of hard work, and especially the habit and ability of unified action, so that they will at any time sacrifice themselves for the nation.[58]

He pointed out that the best examples were Germany, Italy and Japan. Chiang's paramount aim was clear – the creation of a strong national state.

The goal of the Fascist militarization of the nation was to turn men into fighters. 'Train strong bodies for the nation' went the well-aired slogan. Strong bodies were not only the source of high morale but also the source of national salvation. Health, strength and nationhood were indivisible.

> In order to become a healthy modern citizen, it is necessary first to have a strong and robust body; having a strong body, one then has a strong spirit; having a strong spirit, one can then acquire all the abilities required to strengthen the nation, one can naturally

> defend the state and glorify the nation, help our state and country to forever accord with the world and never again suffer from the aggression and oppression of foreign countries or receive disdain and insults.[59]

The source of a healthy body, predictably and logically, was exercise. As Chen Lifu, the leader of the Nationalist Party, wrote in *Qinfen tiyu yuebao* (Qinfen Sports Monthly) in October 1934: 'Physical education is the only way to strengthen the body. With a healthy body one can achieve the intellectual and moral fulfilment.'[60] Simultaneously, Zhou Fuhai, the Director of Jiangsu Provincial Educational Council, wrote an article to explain the triangular relationship between exercise, the body and the New Life Movement: exercise was part of education. It promoted a healthy body as well as a healthy spirit. Both would lead to the fulfilment of the mission of the New Life Movement.[61]

On 2 March 1935 Chiang Kai-shek wrote an open letter to the nation entitled 'Promotion of Sport and Exercise' demanding the implementation of physical activity programmes:

> We must have a mass physical exercise campaign. From now on all the students and teachers of primary and middle schools, all staff of Party offices, social services and the army must participate in physical activity. They must choose one event as their regular exercise and without exception have their daily exercise time fixed between five and six o'clock every day. They are to be encouraged to do outdoor activities but they can do indoor exercise if the weather is not good. Physical exercise must be constant. The principals of schools, the heads of government offices and army officers must supervise and discipline their pupils and staff and report to their superior.[62]

On 19 April 1935 Chiang wrote a further letter to the public along the same lines to ensure the implementation of his demands.[63]

Chiang, head of state, made inspirational demands. Cheng Dengke, a professor at Nanjing University who studied physical education in Germany between 1929 to 1933,[64] made practical suggestions. He published an article in February 1935 in *Tiyu jikan* (Sports Quarterly) entitled 'Physical Education in Germany' advocating German militarized physical education.[65] In May, in 'On Militarized Sport and Exercise' published in *Qinfen tiyu yuebao*, he explained the difference between competitive sport and militarized physical exercise. He stated that competitive sport which came from the United States was not suitable for China. It advocated individualism and élitism. Militarized exercise was the best way to get the people to exercise their bodies *and* cultivated their patriotic spirit. It would teach them military discipline and Fascist obedience. It would produce fighters. What China needed was soldiers not players. Militarized physical education should be the backbone of Chinese physical training. He pointed out that the secret of success of Germany, Italy and Japan was military programmes and training systems.[66] Others had already taken up the same refrain. Dong Shaoyi, an influential physical educationalist and the Chinese IOC representative, had argued in an article in 1934, 'The Power of Promoting Sport', that 'Strong bodies were the foundation of reconstruction of our nation.' He continued, 'Look at Germany, since Hitler became the head of the government, nationalism is stimulated. Military training has become compulsory in schools. Germany, therefore, has become a strong nation.'[67] Cheng Dunzhen, another noted physical educationalist, claimed in his article 'On the Restoration of the Pride of the Nation', also published in 1934, that China should follow Germany's footsteps and train its people to be strong soldiers to defend the country so that the nation would restore its pride,[68] while in 1934, Zhejiang Province held a Pupils' Sports Essay Contest. Seven middle schools and 12 primary schools took part in the contest. The topic for the middle school was 'what kind of sport can save our country?' and the topic for the primary school was 'the relationship between sport and the restoration of the nation'. Most of the student essays argued that only militarized physical training could save China and restore the nation.[69] Cheng Dengke, mentioned above, the admirer of German militarized physical education, went further in the article 'How to use police and armed forces to promote sports among masses' published in April 1935. He set out a programme for militarizing people using the army and the police as instructors and monitors.[70] Shao Rugan, a physical educationalist and sports journalist, sang the same tune. In *Qinfen tiyu yuebao* in May 1935, in 'How to Promote a Mass Physical Exercise Campaign', he advocated the opening up of school playgrounds to ordinary people, the training of more physical educationalists and general participation in exercise, if necessary, enforced by police supervision![71] Military training was not a new phenomenon in modern China. At the beginning of the twentieth century it had dominated the physical education field. However, it was challenged in the May Fourth period when liberalism and individualism became favoured ideals and practices in the China of the 1920s. Military drill was attacked and eventually banned from the curriculum.[72] Games and modern sports were taught instead. During the 1930s, as stated above, when the country was in deep crisis, the ideal of the militarization of the nation again was reborn. Chiang's call for a mass exercise campaign and others advocacy of militarized physical training were the products of the time.

In November 1935 the Nationalists held their Fifth National Congress; its manifesto announced: 'Mass training should be promoted. An emphasis should be laid on military training in order to cultivate the habits of the collective life, provide educational programmes for social organizations and enhance the potential for national independence and freedom.'[73] Following the call of the party, the state machinery moved enthusiastically. The Nationalist Party established a Physical Education Department to promote military training among the masses. The Education Ministry gave orders to every provincial educational council to set up a Sports Council to promote the mass exercise campaign. By the end of July, 19 provinces and large cities had sports councils. A Physical Education and Sports Department was founded within the New Life Promotion Committee in 1935. The National Military Training Commission invited Cheng Dengke to be its head. In order to set up a network and make the state machine operate more effectively, in 1935, Chiang sent a telegram to the whole country suggesting the creation of a co-operation committee among the party, government, army and schools to promote military education and physical exercise at every level.[74]

A military education for the young was a crucial step in spreading Fascism. The Hitler Youth was a model for the Chinese. The Tongzijun became a popular youth organization in China. Originally the Tongzijun was an imitation of the British Boy Scouts. It was founded by educationalists in 1911 in Wuchang. It began as a small educational organization. Over the years it grew steadily in some cities and provinces. With a momentum imparted by enthusiastic Blue Shirts, the Tongzijun expanded dramatically during the 1930s. It appeared in almost every province and city. On 1 November 1934 Tongzijun's headquarters, the National Committee of Tongzijun, was established. Chiang was the Chairman. The committee set up a board, with the Minister of the Education as its head, in charge of all affairs of the Tongzijun in China. The Education Ministry issued a decree on the same day when the committee was established. It required all pupils of junior middle school to join the Tongzijun. It also stated that military training was compulsory for them. Pupils who joined the Tongzijun would vow to obey Chairman Chiang and the rules. Chiang himself approved the vow and the rules.[75] The responsibility of the Tongzijun was to educate boys to be patriots and to turn them into future soldiers through physical exercise and military training. In 1935 the publisher, Qinfen Books, published 151 books for the Tongzijun. Two thirds were on physical exercise and training.[76] The influential educationalist Liu Xuesong wrote an article in 1935 stressing the importance of moral and physical training for the young through the Tongzijun.[77] Now almost everywhere one looked, there were symptoms and symbols of a country in militarized transition. Boys wore uniforms, practised military drill and paraded through streets. Disciplined squads of these uniformed boys became icons of the new order. An American missionary in Huining recalled, 'At certain hours of the day – early in the morning, noon, and late afternoon – the streets were filled with lads in uniform … elementary school children … constructing tanks and warplanes and other war paraphernalia … '[78] A journalist reported in May 1934 that 'Mass meetings are frequently being held in public parks of Wuchang and Hanko. School children of all ages parade through the streets and are taught to march in very orderly fashion. Sometimes a lantern parade is organized.'[79] The government also held mass meeting to examine the results of the militarization of the young. When Zhejiang provincial government inspected the Tongzijun in April 1934, 1,000 boys took part the parade and 10,000 people watched.[80] A General Review of the Tongzijun took place in 1936 in Nanjing, the capital city, Chiang inspected 10,000 school children.[81] Photographs published in *Liangyou* (Good Friend) *Pictorial* in 1939 show that children between the ages of eight and twelve in Eastern Zhejiang were being organized and trained for the army. The magazine commented that their spirit, discipline and military skill could compete with the youth in Hitler's Germany and Mussolini's Italy.[82] John Israel in his book, *Student Nationalism in China, 1927–1937,* stated: 'The zeal of the Boy's Army in the urban middle schools of the lower Yangtze proved that military regimentation had considerable appeal for Chinese adolescents. Given time, Chiang might have developed a sizeable following of middle school youth.'[83]

At the same time the National Military Training Commission and the Ministry of Education in May 1934 issued the Regulation of

Military Training in All Schools. Military training became compulsory. Students in universities and senior middle schools were to have two years' military training.[84] The following year, in teachers training colleges, six hours per week were added for military training.[85] Special summer training camps were also established in major cities where students received an additional three weeks to a month of military training.[86] It was reported that 'A new military spirit was abroad in the country: during the summer of 1934 college students were required to take military training for the first time in history; indeed this "militarization of the mind of China" might well prove to be the decade's most significant development.'[87] In Shanghai, military display competitions among schools took place between 1934 and 1936. The best display received an award.[88] In Zhejiang province in 1935 and 1936 middle school students took part in military training during their summer holiday.[89] A Jiangsu party newspaper proclaimed the importance of summer training and declared the young should receive both military and political training. After their training, it argued, they should be sent to convert peasants, workers, merchants, women and primary school pupils to the Nationalist Party's cause.[90] Chiang Kai-shek also urged students to use their summer vacations for social service under the leadership of the New Life Movement headquarters. The National Military Training Commission recommended that college and middle school students indoctrinate the citizenry in obedience to the party leadership, and promote the New Life Movement.[91] The teachers had their military training too. The slogan was 'to be a teacher, first be a student'. An advanced military training of all middle school teachers in Hubei province took place during the summer vocation in 1936.[92] Furthermore, when the Olympic Games took place in Berlin in 1936 China sent not only athletes but also a delegation of 34 influential physical educationalists to observe and learn from the physical education and training programme and system in Germany and other European countries.[93]

To cultivate the young was not enough. The New Life movement committee and the National Military Training Commission aimed to militarize the Chinese population with the ancillary goal of creating a people's militia of 12 million men.[94] The Headquarters of the New Life Movement in 1934 issued a militarization scheme 'with Fascist ideals as the foundation'.[95] It stated that ordinary citizens between the ages of 14 and 60 should show respect for the party and its laws and attend simple military training, air-raid and first-aid training. Teachers and students, for their part, should be obedient, wear uniforms, receive military training and reject smoking, drinking and dancing. Civil servants for their part should respect the national and the Nationalist Party's flags, show obedience towards superiors and wear uniforms.[96]

Members of the Blue Shirts played a key role in the militarization of the nation. Six of the 13 executive directors of the New Life Movement Commission were Blue Shirts members and majority of the middle and lower-ranking cadre in the commission were members of the Blue Shirts.[97] They created training programmes and opened training centres for military instructors. George Shepherd, a Protestant missionary, who in 1935 became one of the 'directors' of the New Life Movement, complained in 1936 that military officers dominated the Movement.[98] Some secretaries of the YMCA were concerned that the movement was 'really a blue-shirt movement, looking forward to the regimentation of the country under a sort of Fascist regime'.[99] *China Weekly Review* commented in May 1934 that the New Life Movement was the masterpiece of the Blue Shirts.[100]

The New Life Movement went out of fashion in 1937. There were several reasons: first, an anti-military atmosphere was growing. Some radical students began to view military education as a farce. Those who had vehemently demanded training found that instead of the instruction in military science and the use of weapons they had expected, they drilled, saluted, and wasted time in seemingly useless martial ritual. Many students were in open revolt against military training and considered their drillmasters power-hungry, though somewhat inept, conspirators.[101] Second, the Blue Shirts' control of the movement was never complete and the YMCA and Christian churches became increasingly involved in the movement and changed its direction.[102] Third, the Japanese army's invasion of China in 1937 resulted in open war between China and Japan. This forced the whole of the nation to unite and the Nationalists and Communists soon established the United Front. To fight against the Japanese and win the war became the priority of the nation. The New Life Movement and associated Fascist ideals, ideas and actions gradually lost their importance in the face of this national emergency.[103]

The war also sounded the death knell of the Blue Shirts. The Organization and the Movement were disbanded in the spring of 1938. There were several reasons: first, for the sake of the United Front the

Nationalist Party and Chiang himself had to stop anti-Communist and anti-liberalist action and ban the terror organization – the Blue Shirts. Second, power struggles within the Nationalist Party weakened the strength of the Blue Shirts.[104] The Blue Shirts gradually fell out of favour with Chiang Kai-shek when the political situation changed and when he wanted to demonstrate to the West, especially his American friends, that he was a sound democrat and a true Christian. Third, the Blue Shirts were an élitist organization, which lacked the support of the public. It required the support of a strong political leader. Otherwise, it had no future. However, the spirit of the Blue Shirts was carried on by the new Nationalist youth organization, the Three People's Principles Youth League, founded in May 1938. Five founders of the Blue Shirts were in its executive committee.

In summary, the Nationalists in China in the 1930s embraced the international Fascist movement with enthusiasm. The Blue shirts and the New Life Movement were Fascist creations. They, like the Fascist movement in Italy and Germany, established a revolutionary new social and ethical order on the basis of indoctrinated youth and mass mobilization. They used mechanisms of intensive social engineering and repression to maintain a one-party rule. They stressed militarism as a bastion of Chinese security, pride and independence. However, they were not simple copies of the Fascist movement in Italy and Germany. On the contrary, they were a Fascist movement with Chinese elements and characters drawn from a Confucian past to create a Fascist future. This fact demonstrates the multifarious forms that Fascism assumed in different national settings. As James S. Barnes stated:

> Fascists in each country must make Fascism their own national movement, which conforms to the traditions, psychology and tastes of their own land. Do not seize on the accidentals of the movement or you will be in danger of missing the essentials. Remember that, though truth is universal, its acceptance need never make the world the same colour, for in its application to the individual case is born variety … One God in three persons.[105]

Nevertheless, in common with so many Fascist organizations across the world, the Blue Shirts considered male bodies as the property of the state, to be strengthened, disciplined and trained for martial expendability for the good of the state, with the result that sport of all kinds was assimilated into, and subordinated to, a militaristic cult in the interest of creating 'supermen' to bring about once again China's greatness.

NOTES

I wish to thank my parents for providing me with the information about the Blue Shirts. I am grateful for my Chinese colleagues, Professor Fan Wei and Professor Yan Shaolu, for providing some source material, and Yan Xuening for providing an invaluable photograph for this essay.

1. Chiang Kai-shek, 'The New Life', in T'ang Leang-li (ed.), *Reconstruction in China* (Shanghai, 1935), p.33.
2. R. Griffin (ed.), *Fascism* (Oxford, 1995), p.15.
3. S. Turner and D. Lasler (eds.), *Sociology Responds to Fascism* (London, 1992), pp.11–2.
4. Z. Sternhell, 'Fascism', in D. Miller (ed.), *The Blackwell Encyclopedia of Political Thought* (Blackwell, 1987), p.148.
5. L.E. Eastman, *The Abortive Revolution: China under Nationalist Rule, 1927–37* (Cambridge, MA, 1974), p.xiii and ch.1.
6. Ludwig Rajehman's report is in League of Nations Archives, 5 February 1930, Eastman, *The Abortive Revolution*, p.2.
7. M.J.T. Shieh (ed.), *The Kuomintang: Selected Historical Documents, 1894–1969* (Michigan, 1970), p.152.
8. Quoted in Yang Kongta, 'Faxisiti zi mi' (The Fascist riddle), in *Shidai gonglun*, 16 (1932), Eastman, *The Abortive Revolution*, p.1.
9. 'Ranisha no soshiki to hanman konichi katsudo no jitsurei' (The organization of the Blue Shirts and examples of anti-Manchukuo, anti-Japanese activities) (hereafter RNS), in Ranisha ni kansuru shiryo (Materials on the Blue Shirts) (a specially bound volume of materials in the Toyo Bunko), p.11, Iwai Eiichi, 'Ranisha ni kansuru chosa' (An investigation of the Blue Shirts) issued by the Research Division of the Foreign Ministry, p.6, Eastman, *The Abortive Revolution*, p.40.
10. H.E. Salisbury, *The Long March: The Untold Story* (London, 1985), p.16.
11. Jerry Bernard Seps, 'German Military Advisers and Chiang Kai-shek, 1927–38' (Ph.D. thesis, University of California, Berkeley, 1972), pp.10, 35, 82 and *passim*, Eastman, *The Abortive Revolution*, p.39.
12. A.L. Strong, *China's Millions: The Revolutionary Struggle from 1927 to 1935* (London, 1936), p.403, A. Smedley, *China's Red Army Marches* ((London, 1936), p.xvii, Salisbury, *Long March* p.16
13. Seps, p.10, 35, 83 and *passim*.
14. Jin Feng, *Juntong sijutou* (Biography of the Four Heads of the Chinese Special Service) (Beijing, 1995), pp.64–5 (hereafter *Juntong sijutou*), Liu, Huijun, *Chiang Kai-shek and Dai Li* (Nanjing, 1995), p.22 (hereafter *Chiang Kai-shek*).
15. There is debate and confusion about the name of the organization. Some have argued that there was a proposal but no such organization existed. See Liu, *Chiang Kai-shek* , pp.22–3. I found that the Blue Shirts as a terror Fascist organization existed during 1930s. The name might be different from one place to the other, for example, Lanyishe, Fuxingshe, Lixingshe, but they belonged to the same organization and had the same leaders: Chiang and Dai Li. My parents were radical students in 1930s and they remembered that Blue Shirts were a major Fascist organization. Members of the Blue Shirts were terrorists and counter-revolutionaries. After 1949 when the Communists took over China, one of the targets, according to some official documents, was to eliminate counter-revolutionaries, and members of the Blue Shirts were included. See also Li, Jixin, *Zhongguo tewu* (Chinese SS) (Nanzhou, 1996), pp.101–4, Gan, Guoxun, 'Si "Lanyishe" binhui Liu Jianqiong' (Explanation of the Blue Shirts and recollections of Liu Jianqiong), *Zhuji wenxue*, 21 (1972), 11–6, Jin Feng, *Juntong sijutou*, p.64.
16. Eastman, *The Abortive Revolution*, pp.55–6.
17. Dai Li was the Head of the Second Section of the Military Affairs Commission's Bureau of

Investigation and Statistics. He directed one of China's largest special service network. Zhen Jiemin was his assistant. Dai died in 1946 and Zhen became one of his succssors. See Jin Feng, *Juntong sijutou, passim.*

18. Eastman, pp.34–44, Jin Feng, *Juntong sijutou*, pp.66–7.
19. 'Guomindang yu faxishiti yundong' (The Nationalist Party and the Fascist movement), *shehui xinwen* (The Society Mercury), 4 (1933), 274.
20. Iwai Eiichi, 'Ranisha ni kansuru chosa', pp.38–9, Eastman, pp.43–4.
21. Editorial article, *Shehui xinwen*, 3 (1933), 147, Eastman, p.43.
22. Iwai, 'Ranisha ni kansuru chosa', p.188, Eastman, *The Abortive Revolution*, p.42.
23. Liu Chenchun, 'Yinho yiwang' (Memories at Yinho), *Chuanchi wenxue zoukan*, 6 (1966), 235.
24. 'RNS', p.5, Eastman, *The Abortive Revolution*, p.45.
25. Editorial article, 'Minquan yu zuyi' (People's sovereignty and freedom), *Shehui xinwen*, 3 (1933), 147, Chen Qiuyun, 'Faxisiti zhuyi yu Zhongguo' (Fascism and China), *Qiantu* (Future), 2 (1934), 3, Eastman, pp.42–3.
26. Lu Kejen, 'Shehui minzhu zhuyi shifou keyi jiu Zhongguo?'(Can social-democracy save China?), *Shehui xinwen*, 3 (1933), 435.
27. 'RNS', p.5, Eastman, p.46.
28. Editorial article, 'women xuyao zenyang de wenhua?' (What kind of culture do we need?), Shehui xinwen, 3 (1933), 354.
29. 'RNS', p.25, Eastman, p.47.
30. S.C.Chu, 'The New Life Movement 1934–1937', in J.E. Lane, *Research in the Social Sciences on China* (New York, 1957), p.4.
31. Iwai, pp.22, Eastman, p.67.
32. Chu, 'The New Life Movement 1934–1937', p.3.
33. Minguo ershisannian xinshenghuo yundong zongbaogao (Complete Report of the New Life Movement of 1934) (Nanchang, 1935), p.66.
34. W.H. Chen, 'The New Life Movement', *Information Bulletin*, 2 (1936), 189.
35. M.C. Wright, *The Last Stand of Chinese Conservatism* (Stanford, 1957), pp.300–12.
36. Chu, 'The New Life Movement 1934–1937', p.4.
37. See *Xinshenghuo yundong shouche* (New Life Movement Handbook) (Nanchang, 1935).
38. See Chiang's speech 'The New Life Movement', p.34.
39. Chiang's speeches were included in the Completed Report of the New Life Movement of 1934, op. cit., see also Chu, p.3 and Chen, pp.190–1.
40. Chinag Kai-shek, 'The New Life Movement', p.41 and Chu, pp.3–4.
41. Chen, pp.197–200 and Chu, pp.4–5.
42. *New York Times*, 22 May, 1934.
43. T.S. Young, 'The Chinese have found their Leader', *China Weekly Review*, 78 (1936), 452.
44. Chiang Kai-shek, 'The New Life Movement', pp. 33–5.
45. Lin Yutang, *My Country and My People* (London, 1936), p.89.
46. J. Israel, *Student Nationalism in China 1927–1937* (Stanford, 1966), p.90.
47. See Helen F. Snow, *Is Youth Crushed again in China?* (Peiping, 1935), Israel, p.98.
48. Helen F. Snow (under pseud. Nym Wales), *Notes on the Chinese Student Movement, 1935–1936* (Madison, CT, 1959), pp.9, 24.
49. Helen F. Snow, *Is Youth Crushed again in China?*, p.99, Israel, p.99.
50. G.W. Shepherd, 'The Chinese Communists', in *China Christian Year Book, 1934–1935* (Shanghai, 1935), p.96.
51. Yu Wenwei, 'Zhonghua minzu xianzai xuyao hezong jiaoyu?' (What kind of education does the nation need?), *Qian tu*, 1 (1933), 3–5, Qiu Chun, 'Jiaoyu yu Zhonghua minzu xing zi gai-cao' (Education and the rebuilding of China's national character), *Qiantu*, 1 (1933), 10, Eastman, p.49.
52. Lin Shicun, 'Guojia zongdongyuan' (On the mobilization of the whole nation), *Qiantu*, 2 (1934), 4, Eastman, p.49.
52. Yu Wenwei, pp.3–6, Eastman, p.50.
54. Qiu Chun, p.10, Yu Wenwei, pp.3–6, Eastman, p.49.
55. Ai Jen, 'Zhongguo geming jinchenzhong zi jiaoyu wenti' (Education issues in the Chinese revolution), *Qiantu*, 2 (1934), 3–7, Qiu Chun, pp.11–12, Yu Wenwei, pp.3–6, Eastman,

pp.49–50.
56. Iwai, pp.36–9, Eastman, p.68.
57. Iwai, pp.37–8, Eastman, p.68.
58. Chiang Kai-shek, 'Xinshenghuo yundong zi yaoyi', in Pei Qinghua (ed.), *Xinshenghuo luncong* (Selected works on the New Life Movement) (hereafter Selected works) (Shanghai, 1936), p.8.
59. Chiang Kai-shek, 'Lun xinshenghuo' (On the New Life Movement), in Pei Qinghua, *Selected works*, p.18.
60. In *Qin Fen tiyu yuebao* (Qin Fen Sports Monthly) (hereafter *Qin Fen*), 1 (1934), 10.
61. Zhou Fuhai, 'Zhongguo tiyu zi zhuixin shimin' (The New mission of Chinese physical education), *Qin Fen*, 1 (1934), 12.
62. Chiang, Kai-shek, 'Tichang tiyu tongdian' (On the promotion of physical exercise and sport), *Qin Fen*, 7 (1934), 1–2.
63. See the report in *Tiyu zhoubao* (Sports Weekly), 25 (1933), 51.
64. See Cheng Denke and Chen Weilin, 'Che Denke huiyi lu' (Cheng Denke's Biography), *Tiyu shiliao*, 14 (1989), 55–68.
65. Chinese Society for History of Physical Education and Sport (hereafter CSHPES) (ed.), *Zhongguo tiyu jindaishi* (Modern Chinese History of Physical Education and Sport) (Beijing, 1989), p.320.
66. Cheng Dengke, 'Du Fang Wanbang wen' (My view on Fang Wanbang's article), *Tiyu jikan* (Sports Quarterly), 3 (1935), 353–361.
67. Dong Shouyi, 'Tichang tiyu de yuandongli' (The original motivation of physical exercise), *Qin Fen*, 1 (1934), 26–7.
68. Cheng Dengzhen, 'Fuxin minzhu yu tichang guoshu zi yiyi' (On the restoration of the nation and the promotion of physical exercise), *Guosu zhoukan* (National Sports Weekly), 127 (1934).
69. Zhao Lin, 'Zhejiang jindai tiyu xiaoshiliao'(Modern exercise in Zhejiang), in *Zhejiang tiyu shiliao* (Archives of Zhejiang Physical Activities), 5 (1984) 32.
70. Cheng Dengke, 'Zheyang liyong junjin quanli fuzu minzong tiyu shi quanmin tiyuhua' (How to use police and armed forces to promote sports among masses), *Tiyu jikan*, 2 (1935), 179–187.
71. Shao Rugan, 'Ruhe tichang quanmin tiyu' (How to promote a mass physical exercise campaign), *Qin Fen*, 8 (1935), 53.
72. CSHPES, pp.104–5.
73. Shieh, p.160.
74. CSHPES, p.306.
75. Education Ministry, Taiwan, *Zhonghua minguo jiaoyu nianjian* (Educational Yearbook of the Republic of China), 5th edition (Taibei, 1984), pp.1785, 1790, 1791, 1908.
76. See *Qin Fen* 6 (1935).
77. Liu Xuesong, 'Kefou jiang tiyu Tongjun guosu dachen yipian' (Can we combine sport, Boy's Army and the Chinese Wusu together?), *Tiyu jikan* (Sport Quarterly), 1 (1935), 7–10
78. Dwight W. Edwards, '1934–35 Annual Report' (Peiping, 1935), in Historical Library of the Young Men's Christian Association, New York, N.Y.; Israel, p.99.
79. Unsigned, 'Chiang Kai-shek developing a Fascism à la Chine', *China Weekly Review*, 68 (1934), 387.
80. Seem *Zhejiang tiyu wenshi* (Archives of Zhejiang Sports History), 4 (1984), 34.
81. See *Liangyou* (Good Friend Pictorial), 121 (1936).
82. See *Liangyou*, 139 (1939).
83. Israel, p.191.
84. Chengdu Research Institute of Sports History (hereafter CRISH) (ed.), *Zhongguo jindai tiyusi ziliao* (Historical Material of Sports History in Modern China) (Chengdu, 1988), pp.190–1.
85. See *Qin Fen*, 1 (1935), 93.
86. 'Chiang Kaishek developing a Fascism à la Chine', p.387.
87. Quoted in James C. Thomson, *While China Faced West* (Cambridge, MA, 1969), p.168.
88. See *Lianyou*, 90 (1934).
89. See *Zhejiang tiyu wenshi* (Archives of Zhejiang Sports History), 4 (1984), 34.
90. See *Zhongyang ribao* (National News), 12 June 1934.
91. *Shishi xinbao* (China Times), 2 June 1936, *Zhongyang dangwu yuekan* (Central Party Affairs Monthly), 95 (1936), 558–9.

92. See Liangyou, 120 (1936).
93. 'Jiaobu juiding fude kaoca tuanyuan' (The Education Ministry decided the members of the Delegation for the Research of German Physical Education), *Qin Fen*, 9 (1936), 864.
94. Iwai, p.156, Eastman, p.65.
95. 'Chiang Kai-shek developing a Fascism à la Chine', p.387.
96. Chu, p.8.
97. Iwai, p.157–8, Eastman, pp.68–9.
98. Thomson, p.177.
99. Ibid., p.183.
100. 'Chiang Kai-shek developing a Fascism à la Chine', p.387.
101. *Da gong bao*, 4, 6, 11 December 1934.
102. See Thomson, ch.7 and 8.
103. Chu, pp.1–3, Arif Dirlik, 'The Ideological Foundations of the New Life Movement: A Study in Counter-revolution', *Journal of Asian Studies*, XXXIV (1975), 945–8.
104. Jin Feng, *passim*, Eastman, pp.77–9.
105. James S. Barnes, *The Universal Aspects of Fascism* (London, 1928), p.241.

EPILOGUE

Prometheus: Past, Present, Future

J.A. MANGAN

Arguably, no greater contrast can be found than between the European Renaissance and later European Fascism. The Renaissance is renowned for the emergence of confident individualism and Fascism for the infamous implementation of brutal conformity. But there are striking similarities, especially regarding war and warfare, which throw a light on Fascism as an historical adaptation rather than an aberration.

For Fascist man war was the reward for virtue; for Renaissance man, initially war was the punishment for sin.[1] In time, however, the Renaissance theological view of war was replaced by a sociological view: 'The sixteenth century learned to associate personal aggressiveness with war, partly through the image of the mercenary, a sexual swashbuckler, killing for cash and indifferent to the justice of any cause, an image created by artist-mercenaries like Urs Graf and Nicolas Manuel and given wide currency in woodcuts, stained glass, literature and song.'[2] The chisel of Arno Breker, the lens of Leni Riefenstahl, the brush of Walter Hoeck and the pen of Gerhard Schumann provided artistic images of the Fascist warrior as the epitome of martial aggression in the twentieth century. Renaissance man and Fascist man have their similarities.

Differences, of course, remain. The concern of Fascist propagandists was to promote an understanding of the moral value of war; the concern of early Renaissance philosophers was to ensure an awareness of the moral danger of war. Both Fascist man and Renaissance man believed that continuous violence produced a habituation to violence.[3] The Renaissance Italian writer Giovanni Botera argued that 'men who constantly see wounds, blood and death in their diversions will necessarily become fierce, cruel and sanguinary'.[4] The words of a soldier of the Renaissance, François de la Noue, serve to speak for the warrior of both epochs:

La guerre est ma patrie,
Mon harnois ma maison;
Et ma toute saison,
Combattre, c'est ma vie.[5]

However, for Fascist man this was laudable; for early Renaissance man it was regrettable.

Late Renaissance attitudes were to change. Eventually war was not seen wholly in a critical light. A naïve romanticism characterized both late Renaissance man and Fascist man. In late Renaissance Europe, 'the virtuous savage was held up as a reproach to the vices of civilized man'.[6] His wars 'were fought either in self-defence or to exercise and prove the valour of the individual'.[7] Montaigne asserted that such wars had 'as much excuse and beauty as this human infirmity can admit'.[8] Faced with overwhelming evidence of the violent nature of mankind, Renaissance romantics clung to the optimistic view that the savage could 'at least restrict the violent potential in human nature to tests of virility with limited repercussions on society at large'.[9] Fascist man for his part looked back to an agrarian golden age peopled by Aryan 'noble savages' and he certainly subscribed to war as a test of virility. This test of virility demanded of the Fascist 'Superman' across the globe was expected, however, to have considerable repercussions 'on society at large'. Societies were to be revolutionized.

While late Renaissance man and Fascist man shared a mutual admiration for the iconic 'noble savage' in martial mood, at yet another level, the patriotic duty of the citizen-warrior, late Renaissance and Fascist man shared similar views. Bartolomeo Cavalcanti, in an exhortatory harangue to the Florentine Militia, 'charged his Florentine Militia to compensate for generations of debilitating refinement by reacquiring a military frame of mind'.[10] Adolf Hitler's statement that he required from his martial Volk, men as lean as greyhounds and as hard as Krupp steel is well known.

In the late Renaissance period, suggests J.R. Hale, 'War may have receded from the public's imagination to the extent to which its sombre association had dimmed, but this retreat was more than compensated for by the advance made in its heroic and decorative aspect.'[11] This too was true, of international Fascism. Symptomatic of this Renaissance advance were changes to the image of Mars, God of War. In Medieval Europe, Mars was viewed as 'a bloodthirsty warrior, tinged with the demoniacal'.[12] He represented war at its most brutal; his appearance was uncouth and threatening. His *planeten kinder* were murderers, rapists and thieves. His progress through the heavens inspired terror and dismay.[13] In Renaissance Europe his image changed: he still ruled the sky over battlefields, but 'as the perfect knight looking down approvingly on an ordered combat in which no blood was seen to flow'[14] in anticipation of Arno Breker's calm, unmutilated, muscle-armoured, Fascist Superman.

The custom of the *Cinquecento* was to present Mars as 'a personification of the glorious, triumphant heroic side of war'. War was now to be admired, not despised: 'as war became more depraved, the god of war became more respectable'.[15] In late Renaissance Europe, as in the later world of Global Fascism, the arts played their part in familiarizing, ennobling and disguising the nature of war: 'with their power to prettify and dignify, they prevented the more appalling aspects from leading either to a conspiracy of silence or to a sense of dread. Whenever the glare of battle became too great for the eye to bear, the arts interposed a gauze which softened its intensity.'[16]

English Renaissance Protestantism, in the form of its literature of war, reveals a further point of contact with twentieth-century Fascism. Writers such as John Norden, Edward Cooke, William Barriffe and Matthew Sutcliffe took their theologically inspired, militaristic stance from the confident assertions of earlier writers of the Reformation such as Martin Luther, who argued that war was as necessary as eating, drinking or any other business, and that in righteous conflicts 'the hand that bears the sword is as such no longer man's but God's, and not man it is but God who hangs, breaks on the wheel, beheads, strangles',[17] while Calvin claimed that in war 'no consideration could be paid to humanity when the honour of God was at stake'.[18] Action was to be 'unadulterated by 'the decadent' spirit of compassion'.[19] Himmler, it will be recalled, once remarked of the Jews: 'We had the moral right, we had the duty to our own people, to destroy this people which wanted to destroy us.'[20]

There was a wave of English militaristic, spiritual propaganda in the period which deluged the common people, with the pulpit as a main source of the flood: 'of the minimum of 450,000 sermons delivered, a significant number, a *really* significant number, echoed the endorsement of military violence'.[21] The church itself was a centre of military activity. It housed armour, powder and shot. The churchyard was the location of musters. The pulpit was the place from which numbers were announced.

And from it, too, clerics urged financial support for military needs. Furthermore, it was the primary responsibility of the church to 'identify the enemies of England with the enemies of the Lord'.[22] The clergyman 'was needed... to goad men to take arms and to combat pacifism'.[23] And in a final and telling contribution to an active militarism, 'the divines sought, in the words of one of them, "to prove that war was a blessing". War, in the first place, could be a social good, a moral cleanser, God's scourge for vice. Peace led to laxity, to foul or at best indolent behaviour. War purified, energized. Peace corrupted, war restored.'[24] There emerged, states Hale, 'a mental frontier between man of peace and of war ... [and] moralists helped shape it.'[25] Similar beliefs, inspired by moralists of like mind, of course, were aired and accepted in late nineteenth century England.[26]

Of this incitement to violence from the lips and pens of sixteenth- and seventeenth-century English clerics and others, Hale remarks, 'if it was uncharacteristic that a generation of Englishmen fell to settling their differences by violence, a study of the theme of war in the age's only mass medium goes some way to reducing the element of surprise in the greatest anomaly in English history'.[27] It can, also, together with other aspects of the Renaissance, mentioned above, also throw light on the twentieth century. If the English Protestant Church establishment of the late Renaissance is replaced by the global Fascist leadership of a later period, if the pulpit is replaced by radio, film and newspaper, if Fascist militaristic romanticism is substituted for its Renaissance equivalent, and the European Renaissance Mars is replaced by the Global Fascist Superman, then the point that Fascism was an adaptation, not an aberration gains force. The significance of this remark about similarities between Renaissance man and Fascist man in their attitudes to war lies in the fact that in the Prologue attention was drawn to the comment of Roger Griffin that Fascism in many regards was hardly a historical aberration, but part of the continuing condition of mankind adapted to a particular moment in time and a particular set of circumstances – and, it should be added, carried ideologically, politically, culturally and technologically, well beyond Europe.

In *Shaping the Superman*, the emphasis in the Epilogue was on the remoulding of the Fascist malign Superman into a Democratic benign Superman and Superwoman in the face of the steady and inexorable shifts in the modern technological democratic world to a post-millennium, androgynous culture.[28] In this Epilogue an illustration of a new 'Fascist' iconography of the millennium will be briefly considered and its depiction of the male body as an iconic representation of desirable muscularity and militarism, explored.

While 'Fascism failed to achieve world significance as a driving force of the twentieth century',[29] it was not for want of trying. After the Second World War, enormous cultural and political changes ensured that past forms of Fascism 'could not be effectively revived'.[30] Nevertheless, 'though fascism had disappeared as a force, fascists in greatly diminished numbers remained'.[31] These numbers are now growing. Certainly historical Fascism can have no second coming. Nevertheless, European neo-fascism is a reality:

> In France, Russia, Italy and Austria, the parties of the extreme right are among the strongest. By adopting certain aspects of contemporary youth cultures (such as the shorn heads), neo-fascist groups have been able to gain a foothold in most European countries and beyond ... the presence of millions of foreign workers (and foreign unemployed) and the resulting tensions have become a major political issue, and this xenophobia has become a breeding ground of neo-fascism.[32]

Of course, definitions of neo-fascism pose the same problems as definitions of Fascism. Nevertheless, as in the case of Fascism, 'a single word is needed rather than several paragraphs'[33] and furthermore, as Laqueur remarks, there is a common misconception that study of a subject cannot begin 'without an exact definition and a good theory'.[34] In reality, however, the real world is complicated and usually research must proceed without precise definitions and apposite theories. They come at the end, not the beginning.[35]

In the real world an ideal generic definition covering every aspect of any phenomenon simply is not available, nor will it be – the phenomenon is too complex:

> The quandary facing students of history and politics is similar to that of physicians having to deal with a disease about which they have insufficient knowledge. Each case may be a little different; none corresponds entirely to the textbooks; and its similarities to other diseases may create confusion. But all this does not exempt the doctor from making a diagnosis, even if imperfect ... those not preoccupied with taxonomy – that is, the great majority – watch

> with fascination the emergence of a new species of fascism outside [and it may be added, inside] Europe.[36]

Neo-fascism, it has been claimed, while characterized by 'organizational complexity and ideological heterogeneity',[37] has certain basic features: 'rabid nationalism, a belief in the power of the state and the purity of the people, a hatred of the liberal-parliamentary order, and an opposition to Communism, on the one hand, and to capitalism, on the other'.[38] Fascism has left a permanent cultural residue.[39]

Within this residue the male body, whatever the political potential of neo-fascism, in at least one instance, remains a pre-eminent symbol of invulnerability, aggression and power. By way of example, as neo-fascism[40] grows in popularity in modern Russia, its images, from the brushes and palettes of the neo-academists, a school of painters based in St. Petersburg, as James Meek reports, in part, looks to the art of Nazi Germany for inspiration. The painting of Oleg Maslov and Victor Kuznetsov, 'Dream', with its depiction of a muscular semi-naked male seated on a mountaintop staring trance-like to the heavens, in Meek's words 'appears as an embryonic superman, an image with echoes of Nazi art as propaganda'.[41]

A spokesman for the Neo-academic movement, Timor Novikov, claims it 'is in touch with a Europe-wide thirst for beauty and physical perfection which the Western artistic elite has abandoned'.[42] Such images as those in 'Dream', he asserts, 'provide humanity with what it needs, beauty and form in proportion to the extent to which it has disappeared from painting and sculpture'.[43] This beauty harks back, states Novikov, to the Greeks who 'made beautiful sculptures only of those who were victorious in the Olympic Games when their bodies were considered to be at the maximum of perfection'.[44] The Neo-academic movement, in short, represents a Renaissance of Classical European Culture, of the Sculpted Body as an Icon of Mastery, of a terrestrial Mars as a symbol of superiority.

The similarity of this view to Nazi fascist aesthetics is made abundantly clear in this statement by Stanley G. Payne on the 'politics of beauty:

> More than any other new force of the early twentieth century, fascism responded to the contemporary era as above all a 'visual age' to be dominated by a visual culture. This relied on stereotypes of form and beauty drawn from neoclassical concepts as well as key

> modern images of the nineteenth and early twentieth centuries … as the epitome of the real and the natural, almost always in poses that emphasized the dynamic and muscular, even though normally balanced by a posture of discipline and self-control …

Payne has drawn attention to another aspect of the 'politics of beauty': 'extreme insistence on what is now termed male chauvinism and the tendency to exaggerate the masculine principle in almost every aspect of activity … fascists, … made a perpetual fetish of the virility of their movement and its program and style, stemming no doubt from the fascist militarization of politics and need for constant struggle.'[45]

Aggression, competition, muscularity, power and conquest are celebrated in the Neo-academic images. It is not a long step to explicit images of desirable militarism, and indeed, a painting by a Neo-academist based in Moscow, Ivan Dmitriyev, had pride of place in a 1997 exhibition at the New Neo-academist Academy of Fine Arts. The exhibition space was dominated by Dmitriyev's gigantic male portrait of a New Russian businessman with his outer garment parted to reveal the chain mail of an ancient Russian knight.[46]

The Neo-academist school rejects claims that it is Fascist in nature, but does not deny an admiration for some Fascist art which, it claims, depicts a pure European artistic tradition going back to Classical Greece and serves as an antidote to recent African influence in European art. This is a recurring theme among Neo-academists and their admirers. One organiser of a 1995 German exhibition of new St. Petersburg art in which Neo-academist paintings were prominent, Kathrin Becker, claimed at the time that, despite Nietschzean overtones and a Stalinist-era influence, the movement represented a new Russian expression of pure Western art,[47] while another Neo-academist, Bella Matveycva, has said that the movement is preserving the kernel of the classical foundation of Western art.[48]

Certainly, too much should not be made of past Renaissance and present Russian apparent similarities with Fascism, but never should it be overlooked that there are similarities. Fascism and the Fascist representation of the human body as an iconic symbol of militaristic romanticism had, and have, parallels in other cultures. This fact should engender a sensitivity to past, present and undoubtedly future use of the body in and beyond new 'fascisms', as a political icon, illustrating a perennial search for human invulnerability, safety and security. The imagery of the muscular male body is everywhere. Even the once gentle Ladybird book series for children now has its stories of the *Master of the Universe* replete with explosive semi-naked muscular male images!

Despite the fact that Fascism as a potent ideology appears dead, 'it could have a second coming in different forms. If the history of art is the history of revivals, so *mutatis mutandis*, is political history'.[49] The spectre of historical Fascism, states Laqueur, should no longer haunt humanity but other forms may come to take its place. Payne is of much the same opinion: 'specific historic fascism can never be recreated, but the end of the twentieth century may witness the rise of both new and partially related forms of authoritarian nationalism, particularly in eastern Europe, Africa and Asia'.[50] While Roger Eatwell has observed as recently as 1996 that there are 'growing signs that within the next twenty years significant aspects of fascism will be viewed in a more favourable light'.[51] Central tenets, he remarks, including the search for community, the desire to rediscover natural identity, and the conviction that a new socio-economic order is necessary, appear to be re-emerging.[52] So too are images of Prometheus Unbound; iconic fantasies of control. 'Never', Eatwell concludes, 'has the study of fascism – through all its history – been so *timely*' (emphasis added).[53] And in a striking statement, that may come to haunt the world, he remarks: 'neo-fascism has been the province of nostalgics'.[54] Prometheus may yet prove immortal.

NOTES

1. J.R. Hale, *Renaissance War Studies* (London, 1983), p.340.
2. Ibid., pp.341–2.
3. A paraphrase of the remark of an ambassador of Henry IV of France, who argued that 'the inhumanity and cruelty which often was of so long duration, have passed into custom and become a habit', quoted by Hale, *Renaissance War Studies*, p.342.
4. Quoted in Hale, *Renaissance War Studies*, p.351.
5. Ibid., p.342.
6. Ibid., p.357.
7. Ibid.
8. Ibid.
9. Ibid.
10. Ibid., p.365.
11. Ibid., p.370.
12. Ibid.
13. Ibid.
14. Ibid., p.371.
15. Ibid., p.372.
16. Ibid., p.373.
17. Quoted in Hale, *Renaissance War Studies*, p.373.
18. Ibid., p.488.

19. Ibid.
20. Quoted in Roger Griffin, *The Nature of Fascism* (Routledge, 1996 edition), p.235.
21. Hale, *Renaissance War Studies*, p.490.
22. Ibid., p.491.
23. Ibid.
24. Ibid., pp.493–4.
25. J.R. Hale, *War and Society in Renaissance Europe* (Leicester, 1985), p.129.
26. See J.A. Mangan, 'Duty unto Death: English Muscularity and Militarism in the Age of the New Imperialism', in J.A. Mangan (ed.), *Tribal Identities: Nationalism, Europe, Sport* (London and Portland, OR, 1996), pp.10–35.
27. Hale, *Renaissance War Studies*, p.511.
28. J.A. Mangan (ed.), *Shaping the Superman: Fascist Body as Political Icon – Aryan Fascism* (London and Portland, OR, 1999).
29. S.G. Payne, *A History of Fascism, 1914–45* (London, 1997), p.496.
30. Ibid.
31. Ibid.
32. W. Laqueur, *Fascism: Past, Present, Future* (Oxford, 1996), p.5.
33. Ibid., p.7.
34. Ibid., p.6.
35. Ibid.
36. Ibid., pp.9–10.
37. Griffin, *Nature of Fascism*, p.170, quoted in Payne, p.498.
38. Lacqueur, *Fascism …*, p.93.
39. Payne, *A History of Fascism*, p.496.
40. For specific reference to this growth in Russia, see Payne, *A History of Fascism*, p.519.
41. James Meek, 'Art goes back to the body beautiful', *Observer*, 19 January 1997, 14.
42. Ibid.
43. Ibid.
44. Ibid.
45. Payne, *A History of Fascism*, p.13.
46. Meek, 'Art goes back', p.14.
47. Ibid.
48. Ibid. See also Geoffrey Harris, *The Dark Side of Europe* (London, 1997).
49. Laqueur, *Fascism*, p.3.
50. Payne, *A History of Fascism*, p.520.
51. Roger Eatwell, *Fascism: A History* (London, 1996), p.279.
52. Ibid.
53. Ibid., p.287.
54. Ibid., p.284.

Select Bibliography

Prologue: Global Fascism and the Male Body: Ambitions, Similarities and Dissimilarities
J.A. MANGAN

R. Griffin, *The Nature of Fascism* (London, 1994)

I. Kershaw, *The Nazi Dictatorship: Problems and Perspectives of Interpretation* (London, 1993)

W. Laqueur, *Fascism: A Reader's Guide* (London, 1976)

W. Laqueur, *Fascism: Past, Present, Future* (Oxford, 1996)

G.L. Mosse, *The Crisis of German Ideology: Intellectual Origins of the Third Reich* (London, 1966)

S.G. Payne, *A History of Fascism, 1914-45* (London, 1997)

Model of Masculinity: Mussolini, the 'New Italian' of the Fascist Era
GIGLIOLA GORI

M. Biondi and A. Borsotti (eds.), *Culture and Fascism: Literature, Arts, Performance in the Two Decades* (Florence, 1996)

R. De Felice (ed.), *Futurism, Culture and Politics* (Turin, 1988)

A. Del Boca, M. Legnani, M.G. Rossi (eds.), *The Fascist Regime: History and Historiography* (Rome–Bari, 1995)

L. De Maria (ed.), *F.T. Marinetti: Theory and Futurist Invention* (Milan, 1990)

P. Ferrara, *Italy in Gym: History, Documents, Images of Gymnastics from 1833 to 1973* (Rome, 1992)

E. Gentile, *The Cult of the Littorio: The Sacralization of the Politics in Fascist Italy* (Rome-Bari, 1993)

G.B. Guerri, *Fascists: The Italians of Mussolini, the Regime of the Italians* (Milan, 1995)

L. Malvano, *Fascism and Politics of the Image* (Turin, 1988)
G.L. Mosse, *The Image of Man: The Creation of Modern Masculinity* (New York, 1996)
L. Passerini, *Imaginary Mussolini: The History of a Biography 1915–1939* (Bari, 1991)

Muscular *Anschluss*: German Bodies and Austrian Imitators
WOLFGANG WEBER and PAULA BLACK

P. Bourdieu, 'Sport and Social Class', *Social Science Information*, 17 (1978)
R. Connell, *Masculinities* (Cambridge, 1995)
C. Eisenberg, 'Charismatic Nationalist Leader: Turnvater Jahn', *International Journal of the History of Sport*, 13 (1996)
M. Featherstone, 'The Body in Consumer Culture', *Theory, Culture and Society*, 1, 2 (1982)
A. Parker, 'Sporting Masculinities: Gender Relations and the Body' in M. MacAn Ghaill (ed.), *Understanding Masculinities: Social Relations and Cultural Arenas* (Buckingham, 1996)
C. Shilling, *The Body and Social Theory* (London, 1994)
W. Weber, *Von Jahn zu Hitler: Politik- und Organisationsgeschichte des Deutschen Turnens in Vorarlberg 1847 bis 1938* (Constance, 1995)
D. Wildmann, *Begehrte Körper. Konstruktion und Inszenierung des "arischen" Männerjörpers im "Dritten Reich"* (Würzburg, 1998)

Fascist Political Athletes and the Body Politic: Bulgaria Reborn
VASSIL GIRGINOV and PETER BANKOV

R. Bardareva, *Sportat v Balgaria– Pojava i Razvitie* (Sport in Bulgaria – Emergence and Development) (Sofia, 1991)
R. Bardareva, *Organizatziite za Fizicheska Kultura v Balgarija 1878–1944* (Organizations for Physical Culture in Bulgaria 1878–1944) (Sofia, 1995)
R. Crampton, *A Short History of Modern Bulgaria* (Cambridge University Press, Cambridge, 1997)
J. Hargreaves, *The Body, Sport and Power Relations, in Sport, Leisure and Social Relations* (London, 1987)

S. Kretchmar, *Practical Philosophy of Sport* (Champaign, IL, 1994)
L. Mitev, *Savremeni Problemi na Zakonodatelstvoto v Oblastta na Telesnoto Vazpitanie* (Topical Problems of the Legislation in Corporal Education) (Sofia, 1995)
Z. Natan, 'Harakter, Sashtnost i Glavni Etapi v Razvitieto na Balgarskija Fashism' (Character, Essence and Main Stages in the Development of Bulgarian Fascism), *Historical Review*, 6 (1966)
S. Nojkov and V. Radev, *Tsar Boris v Sekretnite Documenti na Tretija Raih 1939–1943* (Tsar Boris III in the Secret Files of the Third Reich) (Sofia, 1995)
R. Overy, *The Penguin Historical Atlas of the Third Reich* (London, 1996)
N. Todorov, *A Short History of Bulgaria* (Sofia, 1975)
Z. Zhelev, *Fashizmat* (Fascism) (Sofia, 1995)

The Iconic Symbolism of Neils Bukh: Aryan Body Culture Danish Gymnastics and Nordic Tradition

HANS BONDE

H. Bonde, 'Farmers Gymnastics in Denmark in the Late Nineteenth and Early Twentieth Centuries: A Semiotic Analysis of Exercise in Moral Action', *International Journal of the History of Sport*, 10, 2 (1993)
H. Bonde, 'National Identity and the Body, The Nordic Olympiad in Denmark in 1935, *Scandinavian Journal of History*, 20 (1995)
H. Bonde, *The Nordic Body, The Vision of an Aryan-Germanic Body Culture, Sozial- ind Zeitgeschichte des Sports* (1999)
M. Goksøyr *et al.*, *Winter Games, Warm Traditions* (Oslo, 1996)
O. Korsgaard, *Kampen om kroppen* (Copenhagen, 1982)
J.A. Mangan (ed.), *Tribal Identities: Nationalism, Europe, Sport* (London, 1995)
G. Redmond, *Sport and Politics* (Champaign, IL, 1984)
D. Steinhöfer, *Hans von Tschammer und Osten* (Berlin, 1973)
E. Trangbæk, *Mellem leg og disciplin* (Åbybro, 1987)

Fascists *and* Christians! In the Spanish Martial Tradition of the Soldier-Monk

TERESA GONZALEZ AJA

E. Giménez Caballero, *Hércules Jugando a los Dados* (Madrid, 1928)
J.C. Mainer, *Falange y Literatura* (Barcelona, 1971)
S.G. Payne, *Historia del Fascismo* (Barcelona, 1995)
S.G. Payne, *Falange, Historia del Fascismo Español* (Paris, 1965)
S.G. Payne, *El régimen de Franco 1936–1975* (Madrid, 1988)
V. Peña Sánchez, *Intelectuales y Fascismo* (Granada, 1995)
P. Preston, *Las Derechas Españolas en el Siglo XX: Autoritarismo, Fascismo y Golpismo* (Madrid, 1986),
D. Shaw, *Fútbol y Franquismo* (Madrid, 1987)

Return to Manhood: The Cult of Masculinity and the British Union of Fascists

TONY COLLINS

M. Durham, *Women and Fascism* (London, 1998)
G.L. Mosse, *Nationalism and Sexuality* (London, 1985)
C. Kooonz, *Mothers in the Fatherland: Women, the Family and Nazi Politics* (London, 1987)
D.S. Lewis, *Illusions of Grandeur* (Manchester, 1987)
T.P. Linehan, *East End for Mosley* (London, 1996)
R. Thurlow, *Fascism in Britain: a History, 1918–1985* (Oxford, 1987)
K. Lunn and R. Thurlow (eds.), *British Fascism* (London, 1980)

Bodies from Brazil: Fascist Aesthetics in a South American Setting

LAMARTINE P. DA COSTA and PLINIO LABRIOLA

L.P. Da Costa, *Images of Sports in South America, Images of Sports in the World Congress* (Cologne, 1995)
L.P. Da Costa, 'The State versus Free Enterprise in Sport Policy; The Case of Brazil', in L. Chalip, A. Johnson and L. Stachura (eds.), *National Sport Policies – an International Handbook* (Westport, CT, 1996)

L.P. Da Costa, 'Valores e Moral Social do Brazil' (Ph.D. Dissertation, University Gama Filho, Rio de Janeiro, 1989)

R. Da Matta, 'For an Anthropology of the Brazilian Tradition', in D.J. Hess and R. Da Matta (eds.), *The Brazilian Puzzle* (New York, 1995)

U. Eco, 'Ur-Fascism', *The New York Review of Books*, XLII, 11 (1995)

M. Maffesoli, *A Contemplacao do Mundo* (Rio de Janeiro, 1995)

P.M. Resenau, *Post-Modernism and the Social Sciences – Insights, Inroads and Intrusions* (Princeton, 1992)

L. Schwarcz, *O Espataculo das Racas* (São Paulo, 1993)

M. Vieira de Mello, *Desenvolvimento e Cultura – O Problema do Estetiso no Brasil* (Rio de Janeiro, 1970)

Militarism, Sacrifice and Emperor Worship: the Expendable Male Body in Fascist Japanese Martial Culture
J.A. MANGAN and TAKESHI KOMAGOME

C. Blomberg, *The Heart of the Warrior: Origin and Religious Background of the Samurai System in Feudal Japan* (Folkestone, 1994)

P. Brooker, *The Face of Fraternalism - Nazi Germany, Fascist Italy and Imperial Japan* (Oxford and New York, 1991)

C. Gluck, *Japan's Modern Myths: Ideology in the Late Merji Period* (Princeton, 1985)

H. Hardacre, *Shinto and the State 1868-1988* (Princeton, 1989)

S. Jenaga, 'The Glorification of War in Japanese Education', *International Security*, 18, 3 (Winter 1993–94)

S. Jenaga, *Japan's Last War: World War 11 and the Japanese 1931-1945* (Oxford, 1978)

E.O. Reischauer, *Japan: The Story of a Nation* (New York, 1970)

D. Roden, *Schooldays in Imperial Japan: A Study of the Culture of a Student Elite* (London, 1980)

Blue Shirts, Nationalists and Nationalism: Fascism in 1930s China
FAN HONG

A. Dirlik, 'The Ideological Foundations of the New Life Movement: A Study in Counter-revolution', *Journal of Asian Studies*, XXXIV (1975)

L.E. Eastman, *The Abortive Revolution: China under Nationalist Rule, 1927–37* (Cambridge, MA, 1974)
R. Griffin (ed.), *Fascism* (Oxford, 1995)
J. Israel, *Student Nationalism in China 1927–1937* (Stanford, 1966)
J.E. Lane, *Research in the Social Sciences on China* (New York, 1957)
M.J.T. Shieh (ed.), *The Kuomintang: Selected Historical Documents, 1894–1969* (Michigan, 1970)
A.L. Strong, *China's Millions: The Revolutionary Struggle from 1927 to 1935* (London, 1936)
T'ang Leang-li (ed.), *Reconstruction in China* (Shanghai, 1935)
J.C. Thomson, *While China Faced West* (Cambridge, MA, 1969)
Unsigned, 'Chiang Kai-shek developing a Fascism à la Chine', *China Weekly Review*, 68 (1934)

Epilogue: Prometheus: Past, Present and Future

J.A. MANGAN

R. Eatwell, *Fascism: A History* (London, 1996)
R. Griffin, *The Nature of Fascism* (Routledge, 1996 edition)
J.R. Hale, *Renaissance War Studies* (London, 1983)
J.R. Hale, *War and Society in Renaissance Europe* (Leicester, 1985)
G. Harris, *The Dark Side of Europe* (London, 1997)
W. Laqueur, *Fascism: Past, Present, Future* (Oxford, 1996)
J.A. Mangan, 'Duty unto Death: English Masculinity and Militarism in the Age of the New Imperialism', in J.A. Mangan (ed.), *Tribal Identities: Nationalism, Europe, Sport* (London and Portland, OR, 1996)
J.A. Mangan (ed.), *Shaping the Superman: Fascist Body as a Political Icon - Aryan Fascism* (London and Portland, OR, 1999)
S.G. Payne, *A History of Fascism, 1914-45* (London, 1997)

Notes on Contributors

Teresa Gonzáles Aja is in the Institute of Physical Education at the Polytechnic University of Madrid.

Peter Bankov is Associate Professor in Sport Management at the National Sports Academy, Sofia, Bulgaria. He served as Head of the Sport for All Department of the Bulgarian Sports Union during the 1980s; worked for five years as an adviser to the State Secretariat of Sport of Mozambique, and Pro-Dean of the Higher Pedagogical Institute in Maputo; and was a board member of CIEPS Sport and Leisure Committee (1985–91). His research interests and publications, including six books, are mainly in social and managerial aspects of Sport for All.

Hans Bonde is Associate Professor at the University of Southern Denmark. In recent years he has researched the relationship between politics and sport, especially during the inter-war period and Germany's occupation of Denmark. He is currently writing a biography of the internationally renowned Danish youth leader Niels Bukh.

Tony Collins is a Research Fellow at De Montfort University, Leicester. His book *Rugby's Great Split: Class, Culture and the Birth of Rugby League Football* won the Aberdare Literary Prize for the best sports history book of 1998.

Lamartine Da Costa is Senior Professor in the Master and Doctorate Programme on Physical Education at the University Gama Filho, Rio de Janeiro. During the 1990s he was guest professor at the University of Porto-Portugal and supervising professor at the International Olympic Academy in Greece. He is also a former consultant in sport, education, and health projects located in Kuwait, Tanzania, the United States and Peru. As author or co-author he has written more than 100 articles and 36 books, most of them in Portuguese and on sport issues.

Gigliola Gori teaches the History of Physical Education and Sport at the Higher Institute of Physical Education at the University of Urbino.

Her main field of interest is the development of physical education in Italy, with special emphasis on Futurism, Fascism and women. She is the author of *Physical Education, Sport and Journalism in Italy* and *The Athlete and the Nation: Essays on Sport History*.

Vassil Girginov is Senior Lecturer in Leisure and Sport Studies at Luton Business School, University of Luton. He holds Masters degrees in Sport Management (National Sports Academy, Sofia), and in European Leisure Studies from the Universities of Loughborough, Tilburg, Brussels, Bilbao. His research interests and publications (including three books) are in the field of the Olympic movement, sport management and policy analysis, and Eastern European sport.

Fan Hong received her BA and MA in China and her doctorate in Great Britain. She was editor of the *Journal of Sports History and Culture* and Executive Secretary to the Chinese Society for the History of Physical Education and sport in the Ministry of Sport in Beijing in the late 1980s. She is now a senior lecturer at De Montfort University in Bedford. She has written books and journal articles on the body, gender, politics and economic reform related to sport in China. She is the author of *Footbinding, Feminism and Freedom: The Liberation of Women's Bodies in Modern China* (1997).

Takeshi Komagome is Professor of Education at Ochanomizu University, Japan. He has a special interest in Japanese militarism and education prior to and during the Second World War.

J.A. Mangan is Director of the International Research Centre for Sport, Socialization and Society at Strathclyde University, author and editor of numerous books and articles on sport, culture and society and founder of the Frank Cass journals *International Journal of the History of Sport* and *Culture, Sport, Society*, as well as the book series Sport in the Global Society.

Wolfgang Weber is Senior Archivist and contemporary history at the Vorarlberg Provincial Archives, Austria, and Visiting Lecturer in History at Innsbruck University. He has written monographs and articles dealing with oral history, communist working-class history and sports history. He is currently working on a monograph exploring the biographical dimension of Nazism in Austria.

Abstracts

Prologue: Global Fascism and the Male Body: Ambitions, Similarities and Dissimilarities

by J.A. Mangan

The title of this second volume dealing with the male body in the iconography of Fascism reflects, of course, an ambition rather than an achievement. The supremacy of the Global Fascist Superman never became a reality but was certainly an intention. *Superman Supreme* explores the use of the image of the male body for this purpose in European, American and Asian Fascism of varying degrees and various interpretations, and the differences and similarities involved. Among the similarities is the fact that sport in all the cases in this volume was at the centre of the induction of the male body (and mind) into martial self-sacrifice. Sport was an important part of Fascist socialization. The reasons are not hard to find. Sport develops muscle and muscle is equated with power – literally and metaphorically. War, the essence of Fascism, demands physical fitness and sport helps promote this fitness. Competitive sport can help develop attitudes of aggression and aggression is essential in war.

Model of Masculinity: Mussolini, the 'New Italian' of the Fascist Era

by Gigliola Gori

At the start of the century, the predominant ideologies in Italy were represented by the Nationalists, Futurists and the followers of D'Annunzio. Nationalization, regeneration and modernization of the country and defence of the race came together in the Fascist revolution headed by Benito Mussolini after the Great War. Fascism very soon became a political 'religion' in which subscription to myths, rites and symbols were linked to faith in Mussolini, the 'envoy of destiny'. A Superman was proposed and promulgated. This new Italian, virile, dynamic, bellicose, was embodied by Mussolini who, through both his personal charisma and insistent propaganda, created a myth of himself, by successfully adapting the image of the Nietzschean Superman to the Superman of the Italian *forma mentis* (Italian mentality).

Muscular *Anschluss*: German Bodies and Austrian Imitators
by Wolfgang Weber and Paula Black

Contemporary Austrian gymnasts still believe in the possibility of pure body culture, existing in a vacuum, far removed from the influences of day-to-day politics. In order to decode the metaphor of non-political body culture inherent in Austrian gymnastics it is necessary to consider the historical and ideological roots of the German gymnastics movement in Austria and investigate its collaboration with the Nazi movement in inter-war Austria. This was carried out in the name of the welfare of the greater German nation through the politicization of exercise in order to strengthen the male body in readiness for war. This essay investigates this ideology in its historical context and shows how it reflected gender and class characteristics and drew on Darwinian theory.

Fascist Political Athletes and the Body Politic: Bulgaria Reborn
by Vassil Girginov and Peter Bankov

The study of Fascism in Bulgaria between 1920s and 1944 is given to different ideological interpretations. This essay explores the notion of the Superman as a dual metaphor for the *Political* athlete, and for the body as a *Politicum* in the form of three interrelated arguments. These concern the ideological preoccupation of Bulgaria's Fascist sport, its subjugation to and departures from German Fascist sports doctrine, and the socio-anthropological premises for the emergence of the Superman. It is argued that the ideology and practice of the Bulgarian vaariant of the Superman were inconsistent, and in the main replicated 'mainstream Fascism'. However, Bulgaria's Fascist sports ideology and practice clearly embraced nationalism, chauvinism and violence in pursuit of policies and anti-Communism, and the state introduced patterns of development which continued into the Communist period after 1945.

The Iconic Symbolism of Niels Bukh: Aryan Body Culture Danish Gymnastics and Nordic Tradition
by Hans Bonde

A founder of gymnastics schools, Niels Bukh became one of the great sons of the Danish nation but was later branded as 'un-Danish'. This essay focuses on Bukh's political development in the year of the Nazi's seizure of power in Germany in 1933. The story of Niels Bukh became the story of the struggle waged over the symbolic meaning of his gymnastics. The lack of a fixed link between gymnastics as expression and the interpretations to which it gave rise meant that on the one hand Bukh's team gymnastics could embody the democratic spirit of rural culture, and on the other could exemplify the unity of the Germanic tribe – a symbol of the 'aryan race'.

Fascists *and* Christians!: In the Spanish Martial Tradition of the Soldier-Monk
by Teresa González Aja

Fascism in Spain presents particular characteristics which clearly separate it from the Fascism which appeared in other countries. Spain is a country where Fascist politics took a long time to develop. Although they lasted longer than in any other country, they were consistent with weak Fascism and were marked by a strong Catholicism. Religion has always played an important role in Spanish culture and tradition. This essay reviews the political phases of Fascism in terms of its ideology and the images which writers, philosophers and artists used to transmit it.

Return to Manhood: The Cult of Masculinity and the British Union of Fascists
by Tony Collins

This essay explores the importance of the concept of masculinity to the British Union of Fascists in the 1930s, arguing that it was central to both the philosophy and political activities of British Fascism. Although this was partly the result of the influence of German and Italian Fascism on the movement, the essay argues that the origins of British Fascist ideas about masculinity, the body and sport can be traced to the ideal of imperial manhood of late Victorian and Edwardian Britain.

Bodies from Brazil: Fascist Aesthetics in a South American Setting
by Lamartine P. Da Costa and Plinio Labriola

Brazilian Fascism reveals a preoccupation with the aesthetic rather than militaristic. Fascism in Brazil was uniquely Brazilian – a mixture of modern European influences and local and cultural traditions. Nevertheless, the male physique was central to this Fascism, too. The various Fascist festivals were 'testimonials to the body's imperative in political life'. This essay shows that although a preoccupation with sport was common to all Brazilian Fascist groups, it was less an ideological preoccupation than an aesthetic enterprise reinforcing unity through the theatrical. Body and spectacle combined to fuse élite and mass into a totalitarian community.

Militarism, Sacrifice and Emperor Worship: The Expendable Male Body in Fascist Japanese Martial Culture
by J.A. Mangan and Takeshi Komagome

By the twentieth century the Emperor had become a sacred, omnipotent figurehead. As emperor he was expected to define the uniqueness and superiority of the 'Japanese race' – to this end he was deified. The result was the Emperor Cult. This essay is devoted to a discussion of the ideological indoctrination into a Japanese Fascist militaristic manhood which sacrificed itself willingly for the Emperor, to the successful introduction of associated military training into the education system from the pre-Fascist period of the mid-1920s onwards and to an analysis of the recruitment and training of the Youth Volunteer Army for Pioneering Manchuria in the latter half of the 1930s – a case-study of Fascist socialization.

Blue Shirts, Nationalists and Nationalism: Fascism in 1930s China
by Fan Hong

In the 1930s two political movements emerged in China: the Blue Shirts (Lanyishe) and the New Life Movement (Xinshenghuo yundong). The Blue Shirts Movement imitated the Fascist youth movement in Italy and Germany. The New Life Movement attempted 'social regeneration of China' through the revival of the ancient moral principles of Confucianism. However, it was not a simple neo-Confucian revival. It was a Fascist movement with a Chinese character. These two movements were integrated and interrelated. This study traces the origins of both movements, examines how Fascist ideology with its emphasis on total control, military power and male supremacy was implemented in China, and how the Nationalists used militarized physical exercise to promote male bodies as political metaphors symbolizing and ensuring a strong state.

Epilogue: Prometheus: Past, Present and Future
J.A. Mangan

Fascism and the Fascist representation of the human body as an iconic symbol of militaristic romanticism had, and has, parallels in other cultures. This fact should engender a sensitivity to past, present and undoubtedly future use of the body in and beyond new 'fascisms', as a political icon, illustrating a perennial search for human invulnerability, safety and security. The imagery of the muscular male body is everywhere. Despite the fact that Fascism as a potent ideology appears dead, 'it could have a second coming in different forms'. As Roger Eatwell has observed, 'neo-fascism has been the province of nostalgics'. Prometheus may yet prove immortal.

Index